PRAIRIE LION

THE LIFE & TIMES
OF TED BYFIELD

BY JONATHON VAN MAREN

Prairie Lion: The Life & Times of Ted Byfield

Authored by: Jonathon Van Maren

Edited by: Charmaine Van Maren

Contributing Editors: Caroline Heikoop and Justina Van Manen

Cover Artwork and Book Design by: Dean Pickup

Proofed and Indexed by: Louise Fairley

Published by: Christian Heritage Press

Website: www.christianheritagepress.com

ISBN 978-1-7781072-4-5

CONTENTS

Dedicated to my grandparents,
who believed in Ted Byfield's Canada:

Joe and Pia den Bok
&
Arie Jan and Christina Van Maren

FOREWORD

Ted Byfield is well deserving of this excellent biography by Jonathon Van Maren, which describes Ted's life from its humble beginnings in a broken home, the profound impact of the Depression and the Second World War on his formative years, his first exposure to journalism, and his at-first haphazard encounters with the Christian faith.

The story then continues to describe Ted's adventures in Christian education through the founding and operation of the St John's Boys' Schools, his robust application of Christian values to life and the controversial moral issues of the day, his adventures in journalistic entrepreneurship through publications such as the *Alberta* and *Western Reports*, his vigorous championing of the political interests of western Canada, and finally his completion of two monumental history projects – the 12 volume journalistic history entitled *Alberta in the 20th Century*, and the 12 volume history of Christianity simple entitled *The Christians*.

What a story! What a man! What a life!

Ted himself loved stories – the funnier and more likely to disturb the status quo the better – and was a great storyteller himself. So what better way to pay tribute to him and introduce this story of his life than by telling a couple of stories – one looking backward and drawn from my personal association with him, and one looking forward and still unfolding.

As Jonathon explains in his chapter on Ted as a champion of the West, Ted was instrumental in the formation of the western-based

Reform Party of Canada. It began at a conference in Vancouver in 1987 at which the challenge was to decide what was the best way to advance the West's current and future interests, including the option of creating a new political party after the West's third-party tradition.

The main vehicle for advertising this conference was Ted's *Alberta Report* and I joined him at its offices to put together a two-page centrefold to do so. As was usually the case with Ted, this was a frantic exercise with the centrefold needing to be completed by midnight. But there was a last-minute problem. It was supposed to include pictures of the conference's organizing committee which included Bob Muir, legal counsel for Dome Petroleum and one of the committee's most prominent members. But no picture of Bob could be found. What to do?

Ted has an answer. He said he had an "obituary desk" at the back of the office into which he threw any and every picture of anybody he came across since inevitably it would be needed upon their demise. He disappeared into the back and soon came back with the "negative" of what he claimed was a picture of Bob. "That's Bob isn't it?" he asked me. I really couldn't say just by looking at the negative, so I murmured, "Maybe, but I can't say for certain." "Sure it's Bob", replied Ted with convincing certainty, so into the centrefold went the picture of Bob Muir as one of the founders of what turned out to be the Reform Party of Canada. It was only weeks later that we discovered that it wasn't Bob's picture after all but that of a federal deputy minister in Ottawa – perhaps one of the last people in the country who would want to be identified as a western Reformer.

For weeks Ted was on pins and needles waiting for the possible notice that *Alberta Report* was being sued for misrepresentation and defamation. But fortunately, the notice never came—apparently the Ottawa deputy didn't read the *Alberta Report*.

One last story, but this one looking ahead and still ongoing. The greatest passion of Ted's life was no doubt his commitment to the fundamental tenets of the Christian faith. Perhaps for some, the current decline in public understanding and commitments to those tenets is disheartening, but not so for Ted. One of those fundamental tenets of the Christian faith is that there is such a thing as "resurrection" – of life after death. And in the long history of the Christian faith with which Ted was very familiar, its opponents have often pronounced it "dead and buried" only to later find the tomb empty and "resurrection" to be a spiritual reality.

And so Jonathon's story of Ted Byfield, the Prairie Lion, may appear to end with the description of his death and burial at the Holy Cross Cemetery in Edmonton, Alberta. But for those of us who share his faith in the fundamentals of the Christian faith, that is only the apparent end of a story that really has no ending.

Preston Manning
May 2022

Preston Manning [standing right] applauding Virginia and Ted Byfield [seated] at a 25th anniversary dinner in 2011 for the Reform Party of Canada in Edmonton.

PREFACE

Hudson Bay. The city of Vancouver. The Mackenzie River.
Canada has never been bashful about honoring its great pioneers
and explorers, but where oh where will we find a mountain or
river big enough to merit the name of Byfield?

—David Frum, Foreword to *The Book of Ted:*
Epistles of an Unrepentant Redneck

T
ed Byfield was a consummate storyteller and would, of course, have been uniquely qualified to produce his own autobiography. He was too busy telling other stories, including the story of Christendom itself. In some ways this book is an authorized account, as much of it is based on many hours of interviews with Ted, who reviewed most of the first draft several months before he passed away. Creating a readable biography out of mountains of material and oral history was a difficult task considering that entire books could be written about each period of Ted's life and career.

I interviewed many people and I could have spoken to hundreds of others. It sometimes seems as if there isn't a single veteran of the Canadian conservative movement or in the media world who doesn't have some epic Ted story or hilarious anecdote about him, usually embellished by years of retelling.

I embarked on this project because Ted Byfield was, without question, a consequential Canadian and one of this country's most notable public Christians. When he died in 2021, he had lived through all but 61 of Canada's then-154 years. Ted was an award-winning journalist, launched an unprecedented educational venture in three provinces, ran a string of influential magazines, pioneered massive popular histories of Alberta and Christianity, and became a key voice of both Christian values and Western Canada. The only reason Ted never received the Order of Canada is the fact that his steadfast efforts to save Canada were consistently thwarted by those in power busily destroying this nation in the name of "progress."

To the Canadian elites, Ted Byfield was on the wrong side of the cultural revolution that utterly transformed Canada during the decades between the two Trudeaus. He watched, decried, and spilled gallons of ink chronicling and protesting Canada's metamorphosis from a nation rooted in Christianity into a bastion of secular progressivism where sexual liberation and abortion are not only considered to be fundamental freedoms, but key aspects of the Canadian identity both at home and abroad. Scarcely 10% of Canadians now attend any form of regular worship—this in a nation where the Scripture "Where there is no vision, the people perish" is carved over the West Window of Parliament's Peace Tower.

Ted Byfield was born in a nation founded on Christian principles, and he departed a post-Christian country where those who shared his beliefs increasingly feel like strangers in a strange land. Canadian history has been colonized by progressives who seek to paint a portrait of a Canada moving inexorably away from the alleged bigotry of the Christian past into a future of tolerance and rainbow diversity. When Christians are discussed in the media, it is usually because progressive heresy hunters have decided to target another Christian institution for stubbornly refusing to change with the times.

Christians have been cut off from Canada's past. In the progressive narrative arc of the nation, they are reactionaries who need to be defeated for Canada to become truly herself. In such a world, men like Ted Byfield who resist the revolution are deemed to be the villains, while his ideological opponents—the likes of Henry Morgentaler and Pierre Trudeau—are the heroes of Canadian history books. Ted will likely never get the sort of academic biography his life and accomplishments deserve. With the exception of a handful of obscure personal memoirs, the story of the moral revolution that transformed Canada has largely been told from the perspective of the revolutionaries, not the resistors.

To the end, Ted remained a patriot, utterly loyal not to the Canada that is, but to the Canada that was. He described that country in a beautiful 1986 essay that proved he had no illusions about the heritage he spent his life defending, but that he believed it was worth the fight nonetheless:

> For what, when you get right down to it, *is* the national heritage? How did we get here? Are we not a people who crossed the seas, pushed back the forests, charted the rivers and lakes, rammed the railways through the mountains, broke the prairies, and tamed the barrens of the Arctic? Are we not a people who found gold in the Pre-Cambrian, oil in the Beaufort, and grew food for the world where men could hitherto scarcely find food enough for themselves?
>
> Are we French? Are we English? We are both, and German, Polish, Ukrainian, Dutch, Chinese and who knows what else. Why did we come here? For most, there was a single answer: land. For land, the Carignan-Salières Regiment established the first substantial settlement in Quebec. For land, the Loyalists came. For land, the eastern Europeans peopled the western prairie. For land, the Chinese built with their blood the railways,

the Japanese opened the fisheries, and the Jews of Russia created Winnipeg's north end and the thousand cultural endeavours that have flowed from it. What all these people wanted, in other words, was private property, safe from expropriation, safe from tax collectors, safe from thief and marauder. Property, that is, meant freedom, and freedom was worth life itself.

What did we believe? We believed in God. Religion was either the chief motive for, or indispensable companion of, almost every settlement. It was both puritanical and authoritarian, be it the authority of the Bible or the authority of the church. It was narrow, intolerant of non-conformity, and quick to condemn what it viewed as corruptive. But it was not anti-intellectual. Religion, in fact, established our school system. And a tough system it was, sparing neither rod nor child. It knew its goals, and against them it examined pupil and teacher remorselessly, overworking both. Indeed, work was a thing it revelled in, lots of it, with back and brain, dawn till long past darkness, men, women and children included. If a man would work, he should live. If he would not work, he should starve. If he *could* not work, it was up to the community to care for him, generously and positively and with the hope that he would one day care for himself.

With the faith came the family. In families we arrived. In families we divided the land. In families we saw our children grow and prosper. In families we found companionship, purpose, comfort, warmth, guidance and an occasional clout on the ear. Was the mother of this family exploited and oppressed? She certainly was. Being exploited and oppressed was at once her burden, her privilege, and her delight. That's what motherhood was about. In fact, in a sense, that's what the whole family was about. Either you believed in it, or you didn't.

We believed in it so much we quite readily fought for it, whether in the schoolyard or in the trenches. For we are indeed a fighting nation. Scarcely had the first shots been fired when we plunged into two world wars, years before the Americans, and those years we spent berating them for their backsliding cowardice. We left our blood and bones on the slopes of Vimy Ridge until we had hacked our way to the top of it, something the army of no other nation had been able to do. We were tied to posts and bayoneted in Hong Kong. We tore through the skies in the Battle of Britain, and we littered Germany with the corpses of our bomber crews. But these were wars of justice and we won them. We do not apologize for this.[1]

In 1980, Ted mourned the dismantling of this nation: "The land of my birth has, in a sense, vanished. The Canada I grew up in and was expected, should the occasion arise, to fight and die for, has changed so much that it has effectually ceased to exist. I think of it as Old Canada, a country pulled together in the latter 19th century by Sir John A. MacDonald and endowed with a constitution. New Canada on the other hand has been fashioned in the latter 20th century by Mr. Trudeau."[2]

Canada, as Ted Byfield knew it, is now gone. My family, too, crossed the ocean from the Netherlands to that Old Canada: my paternal grandparents for a farm and my maternal grandparents for a bakery. They saw Canada the way Ted Byfield saw it, and they settled down to raise large families. (Ted once called the post-War arrival of thousands of Dutch people "one of the most successful immigrations we ever had.") My maternal grandparents buried two of their children in British Columbia's beautiful Fraser Valley; the first land they owned in their new country was a little grave for an infant daughter. All worked tirelessly to set up Christian schools and churches and build communities. The Canadians had liberated them from the Nazi Occupation. Now they were Canadians too.

It was from my maternal grandfather, Joe den Bok, that I first heard of Ted Byfield. He saw what was happening to Canada, and like thousands of other Christians across the West, he relied on Ted Byfield's magazines to keep informed of what was going on. The *BC Report* could be found next to his chair, on the kitchen table, and piled in boxes in the basement. A cousin lent me a collection of his columns, *The Book of Ted: Epistles of an Unrepentant Redneck*. One of our boy scout leaders raved about Ted's history series, defiantly titled *The Christians: Their First Thousand Years*. Christians in Canada had very few voices willing to defend them and trusted very few people to speak for them, and they treasured Ted Byfield for that very reason.

I first interviewed Ted in university for the campus newspaper and met him in person after moving to Alberta to work for a pro-life organization, where he was the keynote speaker at the Edmonton March for Life, despite being over eighty years old. Eventually, like so many other young conservatives, I had the privilege of becoming friends with him. He even did me the honour of writing the foreword to my 2016 book, *The Culture War*.

As the West enters the post-Christian night and those with living memories of the Canada Ted Byfield grew up in take their place in the cemeteries of a country they scarcely recognize, I think it essential that we remember those who fought back against the tide of secularization and the anti-Christian sexual revolution. There has been much discussion in Christian communities about how we should respond to these times, and I believe the lives of men like Ted Byfield and other counterrevolutionaries provide us with some answers. He lived joyfully but defiantly; he hated sin but never the sinner; he loved deeply and always refused to compromise on what he believed to be true.

Those who made up the backlash to the moral revolution that swept the West have not been good at telling their own stories, and thus their lives and their battles have either been relegated to the footnotes of history books dedicated to praising those who championed the great changes, or cast in the role of bitter reactionaries swept away by the forces of progress. I believe it important for us to tell our own stories and the stories of our heroes—as flawed and imperfect as they are. The stories of their lives are a reminder of what was—and is—worth fighting for.

Ted spent his life telling such stories with piercing insight and was determined to die continuing his work rather than writing an autobiography. I thought it worthwhile to tell his story and I make no pretensions as to having written a definitive, academic work. My biases are obvious, and I have made no attempt to hide them. I have tried to write this book just as Ted would: "As if Christianity was true." I suspect that many Canadian Christians feel, as I do, that any loyalty they have to this country is to a nation that *was* rather than the one that *is*. Increasingly, for those of us who are young, it is to a nation that does not exist outside the few Christian communities that preserved something of the old ways.

Perhaps Ted Byfield's story can remind us once again that not all bowed the knee to Baal, not all remained silent while the revolution raged, and not all agreed with the destruction of our collective heritage. The history of those who did not stand down or stand by is *our* history, too—a piece of the Canadian story that nobody will tell if we do not. Ted never claimed to be an intellectual or to have championed any new or unique ideas. Like a conservative, he championed the old ways because he believed they were tried, true, and worth defending. As a Christian, he believed that truth was eternal and did not change with the passage of time.

As his self-authored biography on the back of his first book defending Christianity observed: "[Ted Byfield] offers no radical new plan for the salvation of the Church in the Twentieth Century—only the same old plan that's been offered for the other 19 centuries. He thinks, however, that this plan is worth a second look."

So do I.

CHAPTER ONE

THE WAR, THE DEPRESSION, AND CHILDHOOD

*I was not in the War,
but I was of the War.*

—Ted Byfield

The Canadian Broadcasting Corporation would call him "Terrible Ted." *Jacobin Magazine* would describe him as a "reactionary militant." Canadian union activist and journalist David Climenhaga would dub him a "latter-day Jeremiah" and didn't mean it as a compliment. Perhaps *Calgary Herald* publisher Catherine Ford summarized the views of Canada's establishment best when she referred to Ted Byfield's pioneering magazine—and the man himself—as a fundamental offence: "I think I stand for everything he objects to. Anybody who thinks *Alberta Report* is fair and accurate needs to have a lobotomy."[1]

In many ways, Ted's very existence was an unlikely event. His parents, the fierce Caroline Gillett and the dashing but boozy Vernon Byfield, had a stormy relationship right from the beginning. The blonde and beautiful twenty-year-old Caroline, working as

1

a clerk in Toronto, was from small-town Ontario, the daughter of an English painter (she had five siblings). Vernon was from a prestigious family that included the mayor of Toronto but was himself an alcoholic journalist.

"Though courted by many, she fixed her sights on the dubious Vernon Byfield, a news reporter," Ted wrote later. "Their relationship was explosive from the start. He said she talked too much; she said he drank too much; they were both right. After one terrible fight, apparently to spite him, she left town and married an automobile worker in Toledo. Following her, he persuaded her she'd made a serious mistake. So she divorced the automobile worker, returned to Toronto, and married him. Their first child was born a year later, namely me."

Edward "Ted" Bartlett Byfield was born in Toronto, Canada on Tuesday, July 10, 1928. The prime minister was William Lyon Mackenzie King, the king was George V, and the Canadian Supreme Court had just ruled that women were not persons who could hold office according to the British North America Act. Born that same year were hockey player Gordie Howe, Alberta Premier Peter Lougheed, artist Andy Warhol, revolutionary Che Guevara, and Nobel Prize recipient and Holocaust survivor Eli Wiesel.

Whenever Ted peered back into the mists of childhood memory, it was always streetcars that emerged first. Nearly everyone used streetcars in those days, both before and during the Second World War (which everyone referred to then, and for decades after, as "the War"), and when a new style of streetcar arrived it was a cause for civic celebration. Everyone knew them inside and out: the system, the transfers, and which ones ran where. Each streetcar was run by two men: the motorman, who drove, and the conductor, who sat at a desk in the middle of the car and collected the fares.

For a time, the Byfields lived in a house on Fallingbrook Drive, across from the Toronto Hunt Club. It was an enormous house for just the three of them, and Ted suspected his father had gotten a deal on the rent. The streetcars arrived in the area in 1843, and the great Canadian railway tycoon Sir Donald Mann had built his enormous estate between Fallingbrook and the Hunt Club (the mansion would later burn down in 1930 in a raging fire that lasted for eleven hours). Once, when Ted was a small boy, he was sitting on the streetcar with his grandmother when she leaned down and whispered in his ear: "See that man?" Ted did see him, an elderly, bearded, dignified fellow. "Well, that's *Sir Donald Mann.*"

Years later, Ted would write an entire chapter on Sir Donald Mann and his Canadian Northern Railway in one of his many

Edward "Ted" Bartlett Byfield, age one. Despite a Dirty-Thirties Depression upbringing, young Teddy's infectious enthusiasm would go on to inspire thousands of western Canadians.

3

history books, and he always wished he'd gone over and sat next to the great man on the streetcar and asked him to tell the story of one of Canada's greatest railways. Perhaps Mann would have regaled him with memories of his partnership with William Mackenzie or the tale of the Russian count who challenged him to a duel while on a business trip in China. (The count decided to withdraw his challenge when Mann informed him that his choice of weapon would be the broad-axe, which he claimed was Canada's national weapon.)

It was on the streetcar, too, that young Ted tried to puzzle through the facts of life. Across the road from the family's Fallingbrook home lived the Pattison family and their three boys: Bill, Buddy, and Freddy, ("the runt kid"). Ted was forbidden to play with the Pattison boys, and the reason he was given by his mother was that "they were *bad, that's* why." It was Bill Pattison who told Ted, at the age of ten, about sex. Back then, parents didn't talk to their children about such things, and boys, at least, were expected to learn it on "the street." The street, for Ted, was Bill, who possessed "a vast fund of misinformation" and an enthusiasm for sharing it.

The streetcar was a good place to think about things, and so after these revelations Ted sat on the jerking and rocking car, eyes wide and thoughts racing. He had no way of knowing if Pattison was telling the truth, as he had no sisters and girls were thus a mystery to him. He had one close girl cousin named Florence, but their childhood baths together had abruptly ended when Teddy began to exhibit too great an interest in her anatomy.

He scanned the car, examining his fellow passengers in the light of what Pattison had told him. Would *she* do *that?* he thought. *No. Impossible.* Another fellow climbed on the streetcar, and Ted suppressed his mirth. Just imagine a guy like *that* doing *that!* Ted switched his attention to the big black conductor seated at the middle of the car. There was certainly no chance that someone so enormous could conceivably participate in such activities. After a time observing people, Ted made up his mind: Pattison could not possibly be correct. He had obviously been deceived.

When he came to realize that Pattison had not been entirely wrong about all this later on, he was delighted. "It came, I remember, as a sort of rewarding discovery," he wrote in a column. "All along, you had these strange and exotic feelings. And now, why by heaven, there was something you could do about them, something you had already half suspected. It was simply marvellous."[2]

Teddy in 1933 with cousin Florence in front of grandpa Edward Byfield's home on 55 Courcelette Road, Toronto.

Despite his mother's wishes, Ted and Bill became friends. In those days, boys roved about in gangs. Pattison was a natural leader, mostly because he could thrash anyone their age at school. "Among the fist fighters of Courcelette Road [School]," Ted recalled, "Bill Pattison was…a perpetually undefeated champion. He simply never lost a fight…he was accepted as unbeatable and rarely had to prove it."[3]

Brawling was a key part of boyhood. Ted, unfortunately, was "a tall, skinny, gawky person, singularly inept at the thing that mattered most…which was, of course, the ability to fist fight. We called it that. Actually, it consisted of grabbing, kicking, clutching, tearing of garments, rolling in dirt, twisting of arms, all performed to the cheers of a highly appreciative audience which was, it seems, partisan to whoever was winning. In my case, this was always the other guy."[4] Despite these early experiences, Ted's enthusiasm for unwinnable fights in which he was obviously outmatched would last a lifetime.

As misfortune would have it, Pattison's skill and Ted's lack thereof did collide on one occasion. "Now it happened," Ted recalled, "that Bill Pattison and I joined the Boy Scouts at the same time, and shortly after our initiation the scoutmaster announced we were going to have a 'boxing night.' All 20 or so of us in the troop were forthwith weighed and measured in various ways—height, length of arm, etc.—and on the basis of such relevant statistics we were matched. 'You,' the scoutmaster told me, 'are No. 7 on the list. You are going to fight No. 8. Now, you have a considerable advantage over him in both weight and height, so I want you to take it easy.'"

"Who is No. 8?" Ted asked warily. "Bill Pattison," the scoutmaster replied. The match lasted just long enough for Pattison to exit his corner, stroll over to Ted, knock him down, and head back. The scoutmaster was disgusted by both the duration and efficiency of the fight, grumbling that someone of Ted's height, weight, and arm length should have put up a far more impressive performance.

For all that, Pattison was not a bully. He had his gang of five boys, and together they spent much of their time building forts, which could be constructed on empty properties in the area so long as the owners of these properties remained unaware of the ongoing colonization. Pattison was always building something, and as a result "he had a great need for wood." This suited Ted perfectly, because although he was inept at construction, he was excellent at stealing lumber.

Pattison would give Ted a list detailing the two-by-fours and two-by-eights and other scraps necessary for the fort-building. Ted would take the list and head to one of the cottages that was under construction in the area surrounding the Toronto Hunt Club. It was a tricky business, because one had to steal the wood after the construction crews left, but before dark so it was still possible to see what there was to pilfer. Because Ted successfully stole everything on Pattison's lists, he soon achieved a sort of executive position within the gang. He gained the reputation of someone who had the wherewithal to make things happen. Things like building forts.

The Pattison forts became increasingly sophisticated as Bill's architectural ambitions and Ted's aptitude for small-scale robbery grew. Finally, it was decided that something unprecedented would be attempted: An *underground* fort. There was an empty lot near the Hunt Club where the boys could dig a hole "deep enough to drop a pickup truck into," and a roof would be erected over this huge hole at ground level. This bunker would require two-by-twelves. Ted informed Pattison that planks of that sort would be too hard to acquire. Pattison informed Ted that if he thought hard enough, he'd be sure to come up with something.

The problem of the planks remained unsolved until a few days later, when Ted was wandering one of the paths near the Hunt Club and came upon a little bridge over a stream. The bridge was constructed out of two-by-twelves of precisely the length Pattison required. He scurried off to inform the gang, and the heist was planned for a Saturday, when carpenters were gone and cops were lazy. It took three boys, one wagon, and six trips to strip the bridge and cart the planks over to the empty lot, where they were carefully laid across the gaping hole. The planks were covered with sand, soil and plants, and the bunker was perfectly camouflaged. (The Hunt Club didn't kick up much of a fuss, because it turned out that they were already planning to replace the bridge.)

The grounds of the Toronto Hunt Club became a frequent crime scene for the gang, who were often plotting things Ted later described as "simply awful." One scheme involved an elaborate booby-trap on a winding path that had been dubbed "Lover's Lane" (or something of that nature). To adolescent boys, the necking young couples were nauseating, and it was decided that it would be great fun to disturb proceedings. The boys dug a hole in the middle of the path and carefully covered it with little sticks, mudding them over until there was no sign of the pit. Then, they laid a careful ambush.

When an amorous couple came promenading down the lane, the Pattison gang flew into action. Several rocks were tossed. Some, Ted later admitted, may even have been flung. Enraged at this painful and unprovoked interruption of a romantic date, the male suitor gave chase, thundering after the boys as they fled down the path. Behind them, they heard a great crash and loud cursing as he tromped across the pit and the flimsy camouflage cover gave way, abruptly ending his pursuit. "I don't think he was hurt, but he easily could have been," Ted remembered ruefully. "We didn't even think of that. Kids just don't. We could have broken the guy's neck."

Pattison, as it happened, was not the only important Bill in Teddy's life. Throughout his childhood years, a handsome and incorrigible Doberman Pinscher was nearly omnipresent. Vernon was an avid dog-lover and as the secretary of the Toronto Kennel Club, he managed to secure a great deal on a fine dog named Duke Claws van der Spree—otherwise known as Bill. This fine purebred, Vernon was sure, would earn him a small fortune in stud fees. This was after he married Caroline but before Ted arrived on the scene, and the new Mrs. Byfield was enormously displeased when her husband appeared at the door with the huge canine.

"What's that?" she demanded.

"Our dog," her unflappable husband replied.

"Our dog!" she exclaimed. "The thing is going to occupy half of our apartment, look at the size of it!"

Young Teddy with the infamous family dog Bill. Unwelcome at first by Caroline, Bill later earned her instant loyalty one day by instinctively yanking toddler Ted back from a busy street.

"Yes," Vernon agreed serenely. "He's a wonderful dog."

Ted's mother carefully considered her options, and then came up with a proposal: "Either that dog goes, or I go." Vernon had obviously anticipated this response. "Goodbye," he responded calmly.

Within a week, Bill no longer belonged to Vernon and had pledged his undying loyalty to the lovely woman who fed him. When little Teddy arrived, that loyalty promptly encompassed the fresh family member, as well.

Bill's loyalty could manifest itself in inconvenient ways. On one lazy summer day, while the family was relaxing on the porch at Vernon's parental home, Teddy was in the baby carriage on the lawn with Bill standing guard. With the abundance of family members and the absence of strangers, Bill decided that his small human was probably safe, and he could take a break to go around the house for a drink of water. At that moment, a door-to-door salesman began to traipse across the enormous lawn and, seeing the baby carriage, spotted a good opportunity to suck up to his prospective customers. He stopped in front of the carriage, peered in, and began to comment on the superiority of the child within.

Bill, meanwhile, wandered back around the house after satiating his thirst and saw, to his horror, that a stranger was bent over the carriage containing his baby. He streaked across the lawn and, as the story went, "tore the salesman right out of his pants." Grandma Byfield's ensuing purchase constituted a new pair of trousers for the traumatized salesman.

Bill generally didn't bite people—he bit felines. Ted "spent much of [his] childhood apologizing as Bill methodically killed most of the neighbourhood cats."[5] He was rarely caught in the act of dispatching one, but cat people despised him, and as a result, Ted recalled, "owning Bill was a burden." His mother, Bill's original sceptic, firmly disagreed: "They attack him first," Mother insisted. "She always defended him, however overwhelming the evidence. Anything that was hers was right."[6]

Despite all that, Bill was a beloved member of the family. "We had Bill for about twelve years," Ted recalled. "The old man started taking him to work when he was covering the legislature. One day he didn't bring Bill because Bill had died. Other reporters told Mother that the old man had sat at his typewriter, crying nearly the entire morning."

For eight years, the Byfield family was a foursome: Father, Mother, Teddy, and Bill. Then John arrived on the scene. Ted regarded the newcomer as a complete nuisance—the four of them had been doing just fine without a little brother. "I was the show for eight years, and all of a sudden there's another show, and I wasn't very acquiescent in this at all," Ted remembered ruefully decades later. "'He stood in awe of you,' said my mother, 'and you regarded him as nothing more than a nuisance.' She was right, I'm afraid. But it was not for many years, when I saw the genuine affection and responsibility which many older brothers hold for younger, that I realized how wholly self-absorbed I had been. Lord, have mercy."*

When his family fell apart, the trauma Ted experienced would be fundamental in forming many of his later views on divorce and the essential nature of both mothers and fathers.

• • •

It is difficult to know whether the uncertainty of the family financial situation during Ted's childhood was due to the Great Depression or the great quantity of alcohol Vernon Byfield drank. "He was an extraordinarily accomplished journalist," Ted remembered, "but an even more accomplished alcoholic. He found job after job in the Dirty Thirties because of his astonishing ability to figure out what was going on behind the scenes, both politically and in the business world, but always wound up fired for undependability." He was a talented enough writer to get a job,

---

* This feeling of shame increased even further decades later, when Ted received the opportunity to purchase *The Alberta Report* from the Hardiman Group for $125,000. He called his brother, who handed him the cash—no questions, no contract. "Just pay me back if you're able to," he told Ted.

and a prodigious enough drinker to promptly lose it. One of Ted's earliest memories was of his father's typewriter clacking through the night—but "if his paycheque survived the pubs, it had to get past the races."[7]

Many people were struggling to find work. "Of all the young guys that I knew—of course I was just a kid—the question that was asked first when they met was: *Are ya working?*" Ted recalled. "That was common to everybody. Finding a way to earn a living was an uppermost consideration even for kids in elementary school. They didn't know if they'd go through high school and even if they did, they didn't know if they could get a job so 'getting a job' became a preoccupation after you were about seven or eight years old." Economic uncertainty loomed large in Ted's consciousness for the decade prior to the start of the Second World War in 1939, with sporadic reprieves when the family lived with his father's parents in Toronto in their enormous, 4,000 square foot home.

Ted always called it "Grandma's house," although, he noted, "it was in fact Grandpa's, and Grandpa himself had built most of it, along with much of the beautiful furniture inside. However, Grandma [Christine] was the more self-evident presence there. Grandpa [Edward] largely lived on his own in his bedroom, which, with an adjoining storeroom, constituted the third floor of the building. Grandma slept in a second storey of the tower that graced the southwest corner of the building. This sleeping arrangement—separate bedrooms for husband and wife—was frequent for Victorian households. And my father's parents were eminently Victorian."

His paternal grandparents provided the only stability Ted experienced in childhood. His grandfather, who lived on the pension he received from a career as a retired school principal, was "a very sensible person" and as a result "there was utter security there," especially as he still served as the chairman of the Scarborough school board in retirement. Instability would re-enter their lives the moment Vernon got together just enough cash to pay one month's rent, drag the furniture back out of storage, and proudly set the family up in another house. In two or three months the booze would take over again, Vernon would stop paying the rent, and a couple of months later they'd get tossed out. "In the first eight years of my life, we lived in seven houses, all in the area known as the 'Beach' on what was then the eastern flank of Toronto," he wrote. "We were evicted from all seven for non-payment of rent."

And thus it would be back to the Byfields for Ted and his transient parents once again.

The Byfields were of English stock and came over to Canada to the Toronto area in the 1830s. Ted's grandfather was born near London, Ontario, at St. Mary's, and he and three brothers had tried their luck in the United States towards the close of the American Civil War. Edward decided to return, go to school, become a school principal, and marry Christine Church, one of the teachers. (He remained a cabinetmaker by trade.) They had two children, Vernon and a daughter named Gwen.

The Church family had come from Ireland, and Christine's brother Tommy became something of a political celebrity. He ran the city as Mayor of Toronto from 1915 to 1921 for an unprecedented seven consecutive one-year terms and was then elected to the House of Commons from the riding of Toronto North. He lost his seat in the 1930 election in Toronto West Centre, but promptly returned to Parliament after securing the seat for Toronto East in a 1934 by-election.

Church was a brilliant and cunning politician, winning the mayor's office in part by personally calling over 1,000 voters who just happened to owe him favours prior to election day. By the time of his death in 1950, the *Telegram* observed that he could scarcely walk a block without stopping to greet someone he knew. He was a populist to the core, opposing the fledgling United Nations as a "modern tower of Babel" and frequently responding to arguments he wished to ignore by claiming that, due to his partial deafness, he could not hear them. He was much beloved for visiting Canadian troops shipping out during the First World War at Union Station, where he saw them off personally. Ambitious to a fault, at one point he attempted to hold a parliamentary seat and the mayor's office concurrently.

His tenure as mayor earned him the support of the *Toronto Telegram*, but he was roundly mocked in the *Toronto Weekly Star*—sometimes by none other than Ernest Hemingway. In a piece published on March 13, 1920, titled "Sporting Mayor at Boxing Bouts," Hemingway satirized Church's famous political persona:

Mayor Church is a keen lover of all sporting contests. He is an enthusiast over boxing, hockey and all the manly sports. Any sporting event that attracts voters as spectators numbers His Worship as one of the patrons. If marbles, leapfrog, and tit-tat-toe contests were viewed by citizens of voting age, the mayor would be enthusiastically present. Due to the youth of the competitors the mayor reluctantly refrains from attending all of the above sports.

The other night the mayor and I attended the boxing bouts at Massey Hall. No; we didn't go together, but we were both there.

The mayor's entrance was impressive. He remained standing for some time bowing to his friends and people who knew him.

"Who is that?" asked the man next to me.

"That's the mayor," I replied.

"Down in front!" called out the man next to me.

The mayor enjoyed the first bout hugely. During it he shook hands with everyone around him. He did not seem to know when the bout stopped, as he was still shaking hands when the bell rang for the end of the last round.

Between the rounds, the mayor stood up and looked over the crowd.

"What is he doing—counting the house?" asked the man next to me.

"No. He is letting the sport-loving people look at their sport-loving mayor," I said.

"Down in front!" shouted the man next to me in a rude voice.

During the next two bouts the mayor recognized a number of acquaintances in the crowd. He waved to all of them. He also shook hands with all the soldiers in uniform present, shaking hands with some of them two or three times to make sure.

Scotty Lisner was taking a bad beating in the next bout. The mayor's eyes never strayed to the ring, but he applauded vociferously—whenever the crowd did.

He turned to his right-hand neighbor.

"Lisner is beating him, isn't he?" said the mayor.

His neighbor looked at him piteously.

"I thought Lisner was the better fighter," said the mayor, satisfied, looking eagerly around for someone to shake hands with.

At the end of the fight the referee consulted with the three judges and hoisted a hand of Lisner's opponent as a sign of victory. The mayor stood up.

"I'm glad Lisner won!" he remarked enthusiastically.

"Is that really the mayor?" asked the man next to me.

"That is His Worship, the Sporting Mayor," I replied.

"Down in front!" yelled the man next to me, in a rough voice.

It looked as though the mayor enjoyed the last bout best of all. Of course, he didn't see it, but he discovered several people he had not shaken hands with, and also there was a great deal of booing and cheering. Sometimes the mayor would absent-mindedly boo when the crowd cheered but he always righted himself instinctively at once. He seemed able to shift a boo into a cheer with the same ease and grace of shoving a Ford into low gear.

At the close of the fights the Mayor absent-mindedly said, "Meeting's dismissed," and dashed for his motorcar, thinking he was at a City Council meeting.

The mayor is just as interested in hockey as he is in boxing. If cootie fighting or Swedish pinochle or Australian boomerang hurling are ever taken up by the voters, count on the mayor to be there in a ringside seat. For the mayor loves all sport.[8]

For years after his great-uncle's death in 1950, Ted Byfield would meet men and women who had known and loved him. During the Great Depression when they couldn't afford to buy coal, they said, Church would personally pay to have a coal truck deliver some to them. They were never *told* that it was Tommy Church, but they *knew* who had done it. Family lore had it that he would never forget a name or a face, and that the soldiers he had seen off from Union Station during the Great War would some-times return two or three years later only to be greeted by Church, who would call them out by name. Nobody could confirm whether that story was actually true, Ted would say decades later—but it certainly seemed as if it could be. That was the sort of man Tommy Church was.

Ted also experienced that generosity. "Going to Uncle Tommy's was an ordeal," Ted recalled. "He'd order everyone around. He'd say, *now you sit in that chair there, and you talk to so and so here, and you sit on the couch, and you can talk to such and such.* This was his hospitality. But I don't think anyone ever asked him for money who didn't get it, including me when I was a reporter in Ottawa and was broke half the time. He'd give me ten bucks, right away, no questions. Not a loan, just *here's the money*—and he did this with a great many people. A bossy guy, but almost limitlessly charitable and kind to people."

Despite Church's insistence that he was eternally 57 years old (much to the mirth of his colleagues), the indignities of age eventually caught up with him and his sharply honed political

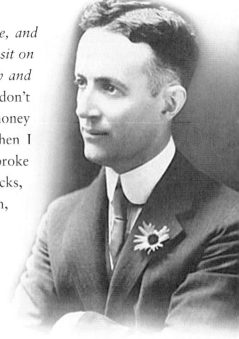

Ted's great-uncle Thomas Langton "Tommy" Church, was elected mayor of Toronto seven consecutive years from 1915 through 1921.

skills were sometimes humorously transformed by his growing senility. "There was a joke told about him," Ted remembered. "He'd meet a guy at a picnic or something and say, *Roger, Roger, how's Louise and the children?* Well, I'm sorry to have to tell you this, but Louise died several years ago. *Oh, I'm sorry to hear that, isn't that awful, I didn't know!* And then he'd meet the same guy, at the same picnic, having met forty people in between, and go, *Oh, Roger, how are ya, how's Louise?* The guy said: She's still dead."

Tommy Church was just one of the many uncles and aunts who seemed to materialize out of nowhere at the Byfield residence. The grand old three-story house had no driveway, an enormous front lawn where the large family could play croquet, and a prize garden. One great-aunt, Rebecca M. Church, was a fastidiously proper woman who served as president of the Imperial Order Daughters of the Empire, and once wrote letters to complain to the editor about an "offensive" song that was being passed off as the national anthem: "O Canada."

• • •

The Toronto of Ted's childhood was an Anglo-Saxon town, and he recalled that "we were almost expected to dislike those coming in who were not British." This expectation was ignored by Ted and most other children "because boys are boys and those things aren't important," but it was still clear that Toronto was a city of the British Empire. Children sang "God Save the King" at the beginning of each school day along with a recitation of the Lord's Prayer. To get anywhere, you drove on the King's Highway, and if you received a letter, it was carried to your doorstep by the Royal Mail (not Canada Post.) "The monarchy was a fact of life, not a peripheral thing," Ted recalled eighty years later. "Over my lifetime, that has disappeared from most of society."

Queen Victoria's birthday was a school holiday, and children sang a little ditty that ran: "The 24th of May is the Queen's birthday. If we don't get a holiday, we'll all run away." Most of the children weren't totally clear on who Queen Victoria was, except that she had been very important back when their grandparents were young. "If anyone along Courcelette Road did not have flags or something on Victoria Day, honouring that day, it would have been scandalous," Ted said. "Everybody had to do firecrackers. Once when we were living in Birchcliff, my old man bought a rocket—a big bloody thing. He put it in a milk bottle on the table and lit it. But it fell over after the fuse was lit, and so instead of rocketing into the air, it went scurrying over the backyards of at least fifteen houses."

When Victoria's grandson King George V died on January 20, 1936, eight-year-old Ted wept bitterly in his bedroom, convinced that the country itself died. His parents had to console him, assuring him that the country would simply carry on with the next king. This, of course, seemed somewhat in doubt later that year, when King Edward VIII announced that he would be abdicating the throne to marry American divorcee Wallis Simpson ("the woman I love"), a decision that rocked the Empire. It was nearly unthinkable, and Ted remembered that everyone was simply "stunned that the monarchy could possibly get involved in a dirty thing like divorce." This was the world of Ted's youth.

In 1939, Edward's brother and successor, King George VI, and Queen Elizabeth arrived in Canada for a royal tour, a colossal cross-country extravaganza that attracted massive crowds across the nation. It was the first time a reigning Canadian monarch had visited, and the trip—which included a four-day visit to America—was viewed as crucial to Anglo-North American relations as conflict with Hitler loomed. It was a resounding success, with the crowning moment being the dedication of the National War Memorial in Ottawa on May 21, after which the King and Queen mingled with the crowd of nearly 25,000 First World War veterans instead of promptly heading back to their motorcade.

It was an extraordinary moment, as the royals were then generally distant and dignified figureheads. CBC's breathless live coverage highlighted just how unusual the moment was and noted the bond King George and Queen Elizabeth seemed to share with their subjects: "One of these old veterans is patting the King most affectionately on the shoulder...Her Majesty is chattering with one of the veterans of the amputations association...The Queen is speaking to a blind veteran now...The King is shaking hands..."[9]

A day earlier, on May 20, King George VI had visited the House of Commons to grant Royal Assent to nine bills in person. Vernon Byfield was working as a parliamentary reporter for the *Toronto Telegram* at the time, and to his family's shock, he managed to secure seats in the press gallery for his wife and son. "I was ten feet away from the King, because at the time the press gallery was right over the Speaker's Chair," Ted remembered. "You can't begin to understand the mysticism involved in the King and Queen. The idea of being ten feet away from them was an electrifying experience."

The experience gave him spectacular bragging rights, but his pals were incredulous when he told them. "The kids said: You were *not* that close. I said: I was *definitely* that close."

• • •

The arrival of the Second World War was marked by a conscious and palpable shift in people's attitudes. Throughout the Great Depression, it was *I gotta find work*. After September 10, 1939, it was *We gotta win this war*. The economic uncertainty that had defined Ted's childhood up until that point vanished as Canada geared up to join the Empire in the fight against fascism, and the War would become a defining event in the shaping of Ted Byfield's worldview. He was not *in* the War, as he put it, but he was *of* the War, and he and his peers went from asking each other about jobs to inquiring as to which branch of the military they planned to join. Ted wanted to join the Royal Navy. Most kids wanted to join the Navy or the Air Force. The Army was always their third choice.

In long conversations decades later, he would return, time and again, to the marked contrast in his mind between the young people of the sixties generation and those of the Greatest Generation. The children of the sixties with their laziness and long hair and "all this stuff," he would say with obvious contempt, could not have been more different from the young Canadians who headed overseas during the War. "If anybody between 1939 and 1945 had talked negatively about young people, their lives would have been in danger," Ted recalled. "These young people were preventing *us* from being invaded by the Germans and the Japanese. We were so proud of these guys. It was an age in which youth was idolized, because everybody was so conscious of what they were doing. It was the opposite of the sixties, when everyone was *appalled* at what the young were doing."

In hindsight, it might seem strange that Canadians genuinely feared an invasion, but at the time there was a very real sense that the Germans, as they hammered through Europe, could cross the Atlantic and reach Toronto, too. The War was the chief topic of conversation everywhere and for all ages—especially during the first two years, when the Empire seemed to be hanging on by a thread. In fact, the first event that Ted became vividly aware of was the Battle of the River Plate, the inaugural naval battle of the Second World War—a fight that happened not in European waters, but in the South Atlantic. The situation unfolded on a non-stop radio broadcast for nearly 72 hours, and 11-year-old Ted hunched by the radio, refusing to sleep. "I remember sitting up for two nights, waiting to see what was going to happen." Nearly eighty years later, he still vividly remembered every detail.

The Battle of the River Plate ended with a victory for the Allies, albeit an anticlimactic one. The German heavy cruiser *Admiral Graf Spee* began raiding British commerce in September of 1939, successfully sinking nine merchant ships and detaining ships' officers as prisoners. In response, the British Admiralty ordered the Royal Navy to send out hunting groups in pursuit, and on December 13, 1939, one group located their quarry. The HMS *Exeter*, *Ajax*, and *Achilles* engaged the *Admiral Graf Spee* near the estuary of the River Plate off the coast of Uruguay, with the *Exeter* sustaining

21

heavy damage and pulling back. The *Ajax* and the *Achilles*, though damaged, were able to pursue, and the mildly damaged German cruiser limped into the port of Montevideo, Uruguay's capital.

The *Admiral Graf Spee's* fueling system needed urgent repairs, but Captain Hans Langsdorff was soon informed by Uruguayan authorities that they would not permit a stay longer than 72 hours. In the meantime, the Royal Navy had successfully given Langsdorff the impression that an enormous force awaited him outside the harbour, and he decided to scuttle his own ship to spare his crew further casualties and to avoid capture by the British. Three days later, he shot himself with a pistol in the Naval Hotel in Buenos Aires while lying on the *Admiral Graf Spee's* battle ensign. The entire affair was considered a resounding victory for the British and worked to greatly enhance the reputation of the then-First Lord of the Admiralty, Winston Churchill.

Churchill, of course, loomed large. Like everyone else, Ted listened to Prime Minister Winston Churchill's speeches throughout the War, and vividly remembered Churchill's address to the Canadian Parliament on December 30, 1941, when the old bulldog growled: "When I warned [the French] that Britain would fight on alone whatever they did, their generals told their Prime Minister and his divided Cabinet, 'In three weeks England will have her neck wrung like a chicken.' *Some chicken. Some neck.*"

"I heard the speech on the radio," Ted recalled. "The House went wild. We needed someone like that. It is impossible to describe that period adequately to someone who didn't live then. The War was uppermost in everyone's mind, because if we lost it, we were going to be slaves." Kids knew a lot more geography because they were all breathlessly tracking the War's progress around the world. There were many Brits in Toronto, and they were profoundly affected by the Blitz. Everything on the radio was patriotic. Everyone had at least one or two relatives in uniform, and as a result, "the idea of sacrifice was part of everybody's life." It was visible, too: "The railway stations were crowded with people because everybody was on the move. More and more women were in uniform, too, because of the Women's Auxiliary."

Every kid Ted's age knew that the moment they turned eighteen, they would join the service to fight the Nazis. Kids knew terms like "conscription," and despised the French-Canadians for forcing William Lyon Mackenzie King into the compromise that permitted them to enlist in the army but not fight overseas. "We called them 'zombies,' and most of them were from Quebec," Ted said. "People were furious at them: *My brother just died fighting for you, you son-of-a-bitch.*" Back then, Ted wrote later, "quite ordinary people had been routinely prevailed upon to put their very lives at risk by doing 'the right thing' and 'fulfilling their duty.'" Back then, according to Ted, people actually knew what that meant.

"Doing the right thing" had a real cost that people were very aware of. It wasn't just that food was rationed, including jam, sugar, butter, and meat, or that you needed books of ration cards to purchase groceries. When Ted was at school in Lakefield, every month or so "there were commemorations or memorials for this or that kid who had recently graduated, and then had been killed in Europe. Many others were wounded." That brought things home: Just a short time ago, these boys had been just like Ted, but they were a little older, and had gone to war just a little sooner. Now they were dead. Some new classmates were refugees from England and France. It was all, quite literally, close to home. One moment in April of 1945 stood out starkly in his memory over seventy years later:

I was 16 years old, and every morning for the entire month I remember looking at a little box that appeared daily on the front page of the *Globe and Mail* newspaper. It gave the number of Canadians reported killed in action in the prior 24 hours. I don't remember the specifics, but from memory the daily toll often exceeded 200. Almost all the victims were young men, some barely beyond boyhood.

Yes, there was certainly sorrow, particularly for the mothers and fathers who had lost sons, the children who had lost fathers, the wives who had lost husbands. Families watched in terror for the appearance of the telegraph boy, bearing the dreaded news. I became part of this once. Housing was so short in wartime cities that homeowners were enjoined to rent out any empty rooms. We had a widow living in my grandmother's house whose son was training as an American fighter pilot.

When a telegraph boy brought a message to the door, I brought it up to her room. She opened it anxiously, read it, groaned in agony, and collapsed on the bed, sobbing. The telegram lay open on the bed beside her. To this day, I remember its six-word message: "Barry killed. Canal Zone. Letter follows." The telegram was from her daughter-in-law. I didn't know what to do, and I still don't in such circumstances. I patted her on the shoulder and ran to get my recently widowed grandmother…It is part of the human lot to receive such things.[10]

As men headed overseas and women followed them into uniform, jobs suddenly became abundant—and the boys like Ted who were left behind leapt at the chance to be useful and above all, to work. The Great Depression, he said later, had entrenched in the minds of his generation the simple fact that working was a privilege. And Ted first began to develop skills he would use all his life on the "enchanting place" he would forever after call "the Island."

"The Island" referred to Toronto's Centre Island, and Ted later said that those sun-drenched days on the beach were "one of the great glories of my life." The Island was a place where people went to picnic in the summer, and it was always thrilling because ferry-boats (with wonderful names like the *Mayflower* and the *Primrose*) had to be taken to get there. People usually just holidayed on the Island, but when Vernon Byfield realized in the late '30s that you could rent the summer cottages there for cheap, he jumped at the chance. Ted was beside himself with excitement when he was told that they would be living on the Island. "It was like being told you could live at Disneyland. I absolutely fell in love with the place."

"There is one island that runs from the eastern gap to the western gap," he recalled. "It doesn't have a name. It forms a sort of crescent, facing the Lake on one side and sheltering Toronto Bay on the other. Big ships came in through the eastern gap and you could watch them very closely as they came in. You could see the crews on them as they were getting ready to dock. I fell in love with the whole business of islands and the parks, and there were three or four islands that had not yet been developed. The Lake was a mystical thing. They never called it Lake Ontario, they called it 'the Lake.' It dominates the culture in a way, because that harbour with the Toronto Islands shouldering was a natural harbour which created the Port of Toronto—which created Toronto." It was watching the ships come and go that made up Ted's mind: When it was his turn to fight, he would join the Navy.

Ted would never forget his days on the Toronto Islands, and his memories seem snatched from a Norman Rockwell painting of a snaggle-toothed gang of raggedy boys, traipsing about the islands, building forts and browning in the sun. "It was marvellous, and it lasted three or four summers before the War kind of put an end to it," ninety-year-old Ted said with wistful laugh. There were houses on Centre Island, Ward's Island, and Hanlan's Point, although most of them were pulled down after the War due to rat infestation and bad upkeep. (As Ted remembered it: "Nothing that wasn't war-related got built during the War.") Ted begged to stay on the Island over the winter, but the adults decided that it was too cold and he was sent back to the city to live with Grandma until spring and warmth returned.

It was in July of 1938 on the "tree-bowered Toronto Islands" that Ted first worked, albeit in a very junior role, in the newspaper business. Ted's mother had been constantly reminding him that one day soon, he was going to have to earn a living, strongly implying each time that today would be a great day to start. He'd just turned ten years old, and he decided to be one of the many sales-boys peddling copies of the *Saturday Evening Post*, which you could sell for a nickel—netting a commission of a cent and a half per copy. He figured that if he could sell even five or six copies a day to the picnickers enjoying a hot afternoon on the Island, he could net a cool thirty to thirty-five cents a week. This was a small fortune--hamburgers, soft drinks, and chocolate bars all cost a nickel. Ted described how his first venture selling newspapers unfolded:

> I had headed for the park, armed with my first copies and my canvas bag, approached several hundred people, was turned down by them all, and come home in despair to face something much worse: my mother. As I expected, she marched me back to the park, lecturing me on the disgrace of being "a quitter," on how you have to smile to sell, on how you have to "speak up" if you expect to persuade anybody to do anything, and how success would depend not on what the prospect did but on what I did. With me endlessly repeating my sales pitch, we arrived back at the scene of my earlier defeat.[*]

---

[*] As Ted remembered it later, his sales pitch was: "I see you're enjoying the sun, but you could be enjoying a *Saturday Evening Post* at the same time!"

Surveying the park with the practised eye of the professional huckster, she spotted a solitary figure leaning aimlessly against a tree. "Go sell a magazine to that man over there." I approached, fixed my smile in position, and launched loudly into my pitch. To my utter astonishment, he bought the magazine. "Now go sell that one," said Mother and, incredibly, he bought too. In the next hour I sold about seven magazines and returned home triumphant, step firm, head high, ruler of the world. Before long I set up a makeshift stand on the island's crowded boardwalk and was selling a hundred or so magazines a week. Which mattered. My father wasn't working and we needed the cash.[11]

From selling the *Saturday Evening Post* (he added *Liberty Magazine* to his stock later that summer), Ted would move into selling newspapers once the War started, and "there you made real money—you could make three dollars a week delivering the *Star Weekly*." Despite the rationing and the recent Depression, "a lot of kids had spending money," and nearly every boy ran deliveries. "You had to have what was called a wheel—that meant a bicycle—but everybody called it a wheel back then. You made ten cents an hour—big money—delivering. When I was in Grade 8, I was working for a delicatessen on Kingston Road near Victoria Park Boulevard, and people would phone in orders to the deli and I'd deliver them. You had an hour and a half lunch break at school, so I had fifteen minutes to get to the deli, an hour to deliver, and fifteen minutes to get back.* So I put in an hour at lunchtime, school got out at 3:30, and by four I was at the deli and worked 'til seven."

---

* Ted attended Courcelette Road School in Scarborough for 8th Grade—for Grades 1 through 4, he attended Williamson Road School in Toronto. For Grade 9 he went to Malvern Collegiate, and for Grade 10 and 11 he was at Lakefield. Grade 12 he spent at Scarborough Collegiate (they could not afford the $600-per-year tuition of Lakefield for a third year.)

Ted worked four hours a day, five days a week, and ten hours on Saturday. As a result, he got to know the city so well that he could navigate any neighborhood without a map. Some of the orders were sizeable. "You had a basket on the front of your handlebars and a big box would fit into that basket. Some kids had one on the back, but they didn't work that well." It was hard work, but it was good work. It was common for children to be roaming about back then—everybody walked to school. "Getting a job, even at that age, was very important. Working was very important. Nobody had to tell you that you needed to go to school to learn stuff to get a job. You knew that. When so many people were unemployed, it was easier to take school seriously, because you realized that school is the way that you get a *better* job."

At age 13, Ted decided that to get a better job, he would need to strike out on his own. As his son Mike later described it: "[T]his child of the Great Depression startled his parents by running away from home to spend a wonderful summer working on a Great Lakes cruise vessel; he sold carcinogenic orangeade and operated a lottery on deck."[12] As Ted told the story, he'd gotten a lead on the job opportunity from Kenny Matthews, a fellow student a year older than him at Malvern Collegiate. Ted found Matthews to be a fascinating figure due to Kenny's ability to beat nearly anyone in an argument, something Ted badly wanted to be able to do (and a skill that would serve him in good stead in the years ahead).

"He had a weird way about him," Ted said. "He'd learned logic, literally. He'd take a sentence you'd said and show you where the sentence was irrational and why and what rule it was. And I thought this was wonderful, to be able to do this. He became a very close friend. He worked on the *Northumberland* in the summer." Ted asked his mother if he could work on the ship for a summer, as well. His mother decided to consult his grandmother, and old Mrs. Byfield said that she'd probably say no if it was her son, but that after all she'd probably done too much of that with Vernon, and if she'd let him do more of the things he wanted to do, perhaps he wouldn't have turned out to be a drunk. With that, Ted was off.

The *Northumberland*, Ted recalled, "crossed to Port Dalhousie, which was a big beach resort. I worked there for two or three summers, going about the decks selling peanuts and popcorn. There were also chocolates for sale, ranging in price from one cent to 49 cents, which would be a box. It was run by a guy named Benny Atkins, who came from Kirkland Lake. He had about twelve kids himself, and he also hired another twelve or fourteen to work selling stuff and running the hotdog stands on the *Northumberland*. He was very sharp in the way he taught kids: how to make change, how to treat people. Sometimes we'd work fourteen or sixteen hours in a day, but we never felt exploited because we were learning stuff. It was like going to school. He was as good as any teacher I ever had, teaching you to get along in the world."

Ted's mother, however, wanted to ensure that Teddy was in fact getting along well in the world, and so unbeknownst to him, she purchased a ticket to take the *Northumberland* to Port Dalhousie one day early in the summer. Ted had no idea she was on board and covertly watching him as he darted about plying his wares and was rather shocked when his mother confronted him. "You were such a smartass," she informed him. "What are you talking about?" Teddy asked, confused. His mother recounted his performance selling fresh-picked Niagara plums, which were in high demand on the 2.5-hour trip across the Lake. Someone had yelled at Ted: "How do you know they're fresh?" And Ted had responded: "I picked 'em myself this morning!"

Occasionally, more sinister sentiments invaded Ted's sunny summers. He heard people complaining about Jews on the beach, and prejudice was the norm. "Anti-Semitism was a real thing," Ted recalled. He was even told that "gangs of young men would get together and try to drive the Jews off the beach," something he found bewildering, as all the Jewish folks he knew were "magnificent people." This seemed even more wicked when the War ended and the world discovered the Holocaust, a horror so hellish that Ted recalled many people simply refusing to believe that it had happened. Benny Atkins was Jewish, as were many of the kids he'd worked with.

He asked his father the question that so many of the victims had surely asked themselves—*Why the Jews?*—and Vernon told him that he didn't understand it either. All of the Jews he'd ever known, he told Ted, had been "good, honest people." Ted's own experience in journalism later on would confirm this.

• • •

Throughout his childhood and into the War years, the Christianity that would later define Ted's career and have a profound impact on Canadian journalism and politics was largely background noise. Canada was a country with a Christian foundation, but Ted had little first-hand knowledge of what that meant. "Growing up, I knew nothing about God," he said. "We didn't go to church. Sometimes my mother would go to St. Aidan's Anglican Church in the East End, which I liked because they ended the service by singing 'God Save the King." His grandparents were Unitarians, and "my father, like his whole generation, seemed most eloquent when he discussed those things in which he did not believe."[13] For the rest, "God was just there. Everything was there, so Someone had to have made it. But He played no particular role in my life whatever until I went to Lakefield."

Lakefield Preparatory School was an Anglican institution north of Peterborough on the Kawartha Lakes, and it had attracted Ted's attention because, although he was too young to join the Navy, he *could* join the Naval Cadet Corps. The best sea cadets in the country were being trained at Lakefield, and this seemed to Ted like a good path into the Navy. It cost $650 per year in tuition, and his grandmother agreed to put up the money for two years. Ted arrived there in 1942.

Lakefield changed his life. As he described it in his 1965 book defending traditional Anglicanism *Just Think, Mr. Berton (A Little Harder)*: "My first effective contact

Ted as a naval cadet attending Lakefield, pictured with brother John and mother Caroline.

with institutional religion occurred in my early teens when I became a student in Lakefield Preparatory School…Here I dwelt for two unforgettable years. The place established the first positive values of my life—moral, mathematical, literary—and it introduced me to the Christian faith."[14]

Ted arrived at Lakefield totally ignorant of the basic facts of the Christian story. He was immediately intrigued by the twice-daily chapel services, the *Book of Common Prayer*, and the chanting of the Apostle's Creed. He'd never been to Sunday school and had scarcely been to church. "I knew that Jesus was a good man, and that there was something about His dying that was important, but I wasn't sure what it was," he recalled. "There was something about all the kids standing there, reciting Psalms and singing—everybody sang very lustily because if there's no girls, boys will sing ten times better and more loudly—and I immediately fell in love with a lot of the hymns. I thought this was all wonderful."

"At the school," Ted wrote later, "It was impossible to avoid observing several pertinent facts. For example, it was clear that a few people actually believed what Christ had said. One was the headmaster, Mr. G. 'Windy' Smith—one of the finest people I have ever known. It became apparent to us all that our headmaster believed in God and regularly prayed to Him about, among other things, us."[15] Smith was not only no hypocrite, but he was also "far more manly than many Christian clergy are," which was important when running a school full of rambunctious boys. Ted's experiences at Lakefield would shape not only his Christianity, but also his philosophy on the education of boys, which would become significant when he found himself running his own school years later.[*]

Ted [front row centre] as captain of the school hockey team.
Many of the Lakefield friendships would serve Ted well later in life.

The boys had Saturday afternoons free, and they could go wherever they wanted—except for Peterborough. Ted and two other boys—"Jones, Hall, and Byfield"—had become something of a trio. One Saturday in mid-winter, the three attempted to hitch-hike to Bancroft, where Jones hailed from. They got about halfway there before it got dark and the boys realized they couldn't make it back to Lakefield by sundown. They trailed in at 11 PM and got six hard swats across the rear end for their efforts. And that, they thought, was the end of it. But on Sunday morning, an announcement was made at chapel: "Would Jones, Hall and Byfield go to the headmaster's office." Ted was nervous. *They've already beaten us*, he thought. *What now?*

Every boy had dinner with the headmaster at some point during the year, and Windy Smith had decided to have all three boys over at the same time. The boys sat nervously as he said grace. Then he looked up with a smile: "Now! Tell me all about the trip."

"He was trying to show us that this was an enterprising and daring thing to do," Ted marvelled later. "He didn't want the school, or for that matter the Christian faith, to leave the impression that they were against such things. It was in *favour* of such things. That's why we were invited to dinner, and we told him everything that had happened. *That's* genius, and that's what he had. He left an impression, and I realized that he was more than just some person—there was something in him that was considerably above everybody. What was it? I later discovered it was Christ."

After his second year at Lakefield, Ted asked the headmaster if he could join the Church of England, and Smith informed him that he'd first need to be baptized. "What's that?" Ted asked, and Smith

---

* One thing Ted noticed years later is that nearly all the boys who went to Lakefield had good marriages. To his mind, this was because "women were a mystery to all of us. Not women—girls. I think that's part of a normal male upbringing. When you teach them about sex when they're two years old or whatever they're doing these days, you're destroying a wonderful mystery."

did his best to explain. In due course, the teenager was baptized, an event that he would later see as setting the compass of his life.

In the immediate term, however, Ted left Christianity when he left the school after two years, attending church services only occasionally thereafter. The sheer magnitude of Christianity's ironclad demands began to terrify him, especially as the realization that he could not possibly keep them grew daily. "I slipped quietly out into the night, casting a suspicious glance over my shoulder to see if I was being followed," he wrote. "Although I didn't recognize it at the time, in a sense, I was."

• • •

Beyond the Depression, the War, his jobs, and Lakefield, it was his parents' exploding marriage that impacted Ted most profoundly throughout his childhood. There was, of course, the fact that moving in and out of Grandma's house became a way of life. But there was also the fact that Vernon and Caroline could not get along. There were signs of this from the very beginning.

Massive fights were a feature of the Byfield home, and when things erupted, Teddy and Bill would hide out in the kitchen to await the passage of the storm. "Their quarrels were incessant, articulate, violent, and sometimes hilarious," Ted wrote. "Invariably she would blow up and begin hurling things at him. He never fought back, but took to using a card table as a shield while assorted dishes, ornaments, and other missiles went hurtling by. Her aim was hopeless; she couldn't hit anything, let alone a target concealed by some 16 square feet of card table who kept poking his head out from behind, making jokes. Finally she would dissolve in laughter and that would be that."[16]

On one of these boisterous occasions, Bob Knowles, a reporter from the *Toronto Daily Star*, was over for a visit. His presence was apparently not enough to prevent a loud brawl, and he ignored the disintegrating household items and carried on reading until something caught his eye and he stilled the din: "Carol, Carol! Stop this right now, I must tell you something. What you just did defines the difference between manslaughter and murder. I thought you should be aware of this. Did you notice that when you came along that mantelpiece picking up stuff to throw, you bypassed this little one here because it was quite expensive and you picked up this other cheap thing and you hurled that at him?"

Knowles had her attention. "*That's* the difference between manslaughter and murder—the fact that you were able to omit throwing this one piece showed that you were mentally competent at the time. So if you'd killed him with the thing you did throw, you would have been charged with murder, not manslaughter." He turned back to his reading. "Now, carry on, the two of you."

Caroline's charm also ensured that she generally appeared to be in the right even on occasions where she was the aggressor. During one fight, she switched from hurling projectiles at her husband and came at him with a knife, gashing his arm. "There was blood all over the place," Ted recalled, "and he called the cops because he thought she was going to kill him." An enormous police officer arrived at the door, and a relieved Vernon answered the door, his sleeve bloodstained. The officer glowered at him. "What have you done to this poor little woman to make her do a thing like that to you?" he demanded—and proceeded to give the wounded Vernon a good dressing down. The Byfields gave the phrase "nuclear family" an entirely new meaning.

It was ultimately Vernon's drinking that destroyed the marriage. "If he hadn't been drinking so much, they would have been an admirable couple," Ted said. His father wasn't a drink-by-yourself type of guy—he liked drinking in crowds, and the only nasty streak he had was that he'd be occasionally acidic to waitresses after imbibing. But he was drowning his marriage. "There's a story," Ted recalled, "[that] he once arrived home with a gang of reporters, late and drunk, to find she'd locked all the doors. He put a ladder to a second-floor window. 'I will now effect an entrance,' he announced majestically. When he reached the window, there was a loud whang as she hit him over the head with a frying pan. With great guffaws he and the gang drove away in their Model-T Ford."[17]

To her credit, Ted's mother genuinely tried to stick it out. Vernon swore off booze in 1936, and Ted's brother John arrived as a result. (John never witnessed much of the fighting, as by the time he was conscious the attempted reconciliations between his parents were sporadic.) By the time the War started, things had irretrievably fallen apart. Vernon had started drinking again, and the jobs fled with his sobriety. Ted remembers the first split happening in 1939, when his mother secured a job as a telephone salesperson and moved out. To Ted, this was quite simply the worst thing that had ever happened to him, and even at ninety years of age, he struggled to find a comparison for the pain he felt. "My wife's death was the worst thing that ever happened to me. But when I found out that my mother had moved out…awful."

"It was just as if the world came to an end," he remembered. "I mean, they fought, my mother and father, but we were a group, and when they split and Mother went off to work on her own and got her own place to live, which I can hardly blame her for, to me it was the most awful experience because that was *life*. It was yourself, your mother, your father…and now they're not together. I wept for a long time out of uncertainty. It was awful. I don't think parents, even today, realize how much devastation they're causing in their kids' lives if they split up. They tried several times to put the marriage back together but could never do it."

Divorce was still rare, and so for the family to break up in such a public way was a matter of great shame. After all, "there were bad marriages galore, but *they* stayed together." Vernon was a journalist, and thus the Byfields knew a lot of people. Despite this fact, Ted only knew of two or three people who were divorced. It felt as if everything had shifted beneath his feet. "When you're very young, your security is in your mother but also in the idea of the two of them, as a family. The idea of them splitting up was like the end of our world."

After the initial split, Ted wrote later, "four subsequent separations all failed and they eventually parted for good. She married two other men, the last a California lawyer whom she pushed into becoming a judge. She would order him about mercilessly, he meekly and happily obeying. It was her dreamed-of perfect marriage and it bored her to tears. When the judge died she went briefly back with my father. It was less rowdy because they were then in their 70s, but again it didn't work. Yet they continued to be fascinated with one another."[18]

Indeed, Ted suspected that the marriage of Vernon and Caroline Byfield never really ended. "Orthodox Christian theology has always held that a marriage can 'die,' thereby making divorce possible. This marriage, I think, would not have qualified. It never died." Even when she was in her nineties and Vernon had been gone for two decades, she remembered him: "Near the end her mind faded, yet not entirely. 'Do you remember Vernon?' I once asked her. Her face lighted in a broad, appreciative smile. 'Oh,' she replied. 'He was a dandy!'"[19]

For the rest of his life, Ted Byfield would defend the right of children to grow up in a traditional, two-parent home, spilling gallons of ink writing about socially conservative issues and decrying the breakdown of the family. His passion was not philosophical or even religious. It was rooted, fundamentally, in the gut-wrenching boyhood experience of discovering that everything was caving in on him because the two halves of his world were breaking apart.

• • •

In many ways, Ted's childhood ended with the Second World War. First, there was V-E Day, which arrived with the unconditional surrender of Nazi Germany on May 8, 1945. Ted was in Toronto. "All I can remember is a guy standing outside a streetcar stop on Kingston Road with a case of beer handing everybody that got on the streetcar a bottle of beer—opened," Ted recalled. "People were going wild, kissing each other on the street and everything else. It was a magnificent thing, and it was well and truly won. We'd beaten the bastards."

While his parents were in Washington, D.C.—Vernon had a job and he and Caroline were attempting one of their failed reunions— seventeen-year-old Ted headed to Atlantic City to work in a hotel for a few months. The hotel management, he recalled, attempted to be strict with guests, forbidding unmarried couples to register for a room together—they did not want the hotel to get a reputation as the sort of establishment where one might take a prostitute. Thus, if a man and a woman entered a room, one of them had to leave before ten o'clock. The night clerk was schooled in how to ferret out potential fornicators by leaning a matchstick against the door. If the matchstick was still leaning up against the door after ten, it meant that the couple were still together in the room, in which case it was time to call up to the room and announce that it was time for one of the lovers to depart the premises.

While the War in Europe was over, America was grinding forward in the Pacific Theater, and the progress of the conflict was on everybody's lips. Prior to Pearl Harbor, Ted remembered, he and his pals would loudly condemn American reluctance to join the War. Democracy was under threat, the United States was a democracy, and thus the Americans were "chickenshits" for declining to enter the fray—a fervent young Ted even argued this point with his American relations. But after the Japanese awoke the sleeping giant on December 7, 1941, the rising superpower poured her men and machines across the oceans, smashing the Nazis and driving the Japanese from their conquered territories, one blood and mud-soaked inch at a time. American war movies began to play in every theatre, and these films, said Ted, were "all we watched."

The hotel Ted worked at—it is long gone now, and he couldn't recall the name decades later—was one of the smaller ones, as many of the large establishments had turned into hospitals for wounded servicemen. He was working when the news came that the Americans had dropped the atomic bomb on Hiroshima on August 6, and then Nagasaki on August 9. Shortly thereafter the Japanese followed the Germans in signing an unconditional surrender, and on August 15, 1945, V-J Day arrived. Atlantic City erupted in wild celebration. "I was working in the hotel," Ted recalled. "People were dancing in the streets and a lot of people were drunk and a lot of people were singing. The hotel tried to keep order. Girls would kiss anyone in uniform."

The War was over.

• • •

Ted Byfield's childhood had been roiled by the great events of the first half of the twentieth century, and the worldview that would eventually reshape the Canadian political and media landscape was formed by these foundational experiences. The Great Depression taught him the value and essential nature of work and would render him almost incapable of understanding laziness for the rest of his life. He also got his first taste of the exhilarating newspaper business that he would remain devoted to for decades thereafter.

Despite his fierce love for and loyalty to both his mother and his father, his parents' divorce scarred him deeply, and left him with the firm conviction that family breakup was a social tragedy as well as a personal one. When he would write about the wounded children left in the wake of shattered marriages in countless columns and books throughout his career, he was writing from a raw and painful place. His critics often accused him of being a run-of-the-mill reactionary, but if Ted was reacting to anything, it was the feelings of crushing despair he felt in the moment that he realized his beautiful mother had left the family home.

The War left him with an idealized view of what citizenship, sacrifice, and honour really meant. Even in his nineties, he would contrast the men who went off to the War to fight on behalf of the Empire and the children of the sixties who, to his mind, had rejected that noble sacrifice and spat on everything their parents had fought for. The example of the Greatest Generation that he observed and absorbed as a child, he would often admit, was one that spurred much of his life's work. One of Ted's favourite anecdotes encapsulates this.

It was 1975, and he was in the little town of Pontefract, West Yorkshire, recruiting for an Anglican order he had helped found, the Company of the Cross. Ted checked into his hotel just outside town, and as he did so he noticed a sign in the lobby: *Annual RAF Dinner, 17th Wing*, as he remembered it later. Intrigued, he decided to grab a drink and see what was going on. With him in the lobby was a circle of men speaking in German, and one of them saw Ted staring. The man left the group and approached him.

"You're curious," he said.

"Yes," Ted admitted.

"Why?" the German fellow asked.

"Well, why are you guys here?"

"Well, we're here for the annual RAF dinner!" came the reply.

At this point, Ted felt it necessary to point out the obvious: "But...you were on the other side!"

That was true, the old veteran admitted. He and his comrades had been pilots in the Luftwaffe. Just after the War, they had gathered for an annual dinner of their own each year with the men who had survived. But gradually, as the years went on, the reunions began to shrink as the Luftwaffe survivors died. One year, one of the airmen brought an RAF vet with him to the dinner in Frankfurt. The Brit could speak German, and the men had a wonderful time trying to figure out where in the black skies of Europe they had been on certain nights to determine if they'd ever shot directly at each other. The evening was deemed to be such a success that the veterans decided to merge the reunions—on the odd years, they would meet in Frankfurt, and on the even years, in Pontefract.

It might seem odd, the German veteran told Ted, but we have more in common with the RAF fellows than we do with our children. We don't understand them at all, just like the Brits don't understand theirs.

That exchange, for Ted, summed up what the Sexual Revolution really was: When parents woke up one day, and discovered that their children were strangers. "There was a principle," Ted said later, "that you were responsible for losing your life if need be, defending your values and your country. That's what people *did*. Otherwise, you would be made into a slave. First, they went through the Depression. Then, they fought the War. And then, they built the most prosperous society the world has ever known. Now, that's quite an accomplishment for one generation."

And after all of that, Ted said, the rebellions of the sixties were "incomprehensible. We thought it was evil. And I still think it was actively evil. And what, exactly, did the sixties generation accomplish? They say they spread 'tolerance.' Well, they allowed the values that underly any society to just rot. The so-called sixties generation is a tragedy."

But that was all yet to come.

41

CHAPTER TWO

TED BYFIELD, NEWSPAPERMAN

Anything people want to get into the paper probably isn't news.
Anything they want to keep out of the paper probably is.

—Vernon Byfield

I n August 1945, 17-year-old Ted was on the cusp of manhood and needed a plan. With the War won, joining the navy was no longer necessary. At the hotel in Atlantic City, a fellow named Terence who ran a confectionary business in Syracuse, New York offered him a job. Instead, his head filled with romantic notions about pioneer life and living off the land, Ted decided to try farming. In high school, he'd studied Ontario's clay belt, a huge tract of land across Northern Ontario that some speculated might be arable. He took the CNR train north as far as Cochrane, hopped off, and hiked five or six miles through the bush until he reached a ravine.

This, he thought with satisfaction, would be a perfect—albeit highly impractical—place to farm. He scrambled into the ravine, filled six heavy jars with soil for samples, and hiked back. As he lugged them towards a bridge across the ravine, he began to have sweaty second thoughts. By the time he reached it, his mind was made up. He heaved the jars back into the ravine along with his farming plans, hopped back on the train, and headed to Syracuse to see Terence and ask for a job. It might not be adventurous, but it was work. A job meant money, and money meant independence.

He hated it. For twenty dollars a week, Ted and other salesmen went to different stores to flog their confectionary wares, and he was certain that there must be more to life than "just going around selling biscuits." On Saturdays, he used his earnings to go to the movies, and one December afternoon he realized what his life was missing. *The Philadelphia Story*, starring Cary Grant, Katharine Hepburn, and Jimmy Stewart, was a romantic comedy, but Ted was fascinated by the portrayal of the newspaper business. This, he decided, was the life he wanted—and he was in luck. His father was working as a reporter for *The Washington Star*, and Ted headed to D.C. to join Vernon and his mother, who were attempting another short-lived reunion.*

Ted had never connected his father's journalism to the glamorous lifestyle in *The Philadelphia Story*. He informed Vernon that he'd decided to become a reporter. Vernon asked him if he knew what he was doing. "No, I don't," Ted replied. "But I like the look of it." In that case, Vernon said, there was something Ted should be aware of. He told his son the story about the newspaperman who married a prostitute. "What happened?" Ted asked. "Well, in six months he'd dragged her down to his level," Vernon replied.

Vernon worked at the *Star*, so Ted headed to *The Washington Post* and got a job as a copyboy on January 1, 1946. He was a gofer who took typed stories from one section of the paper to another, ran errands, and did whatever he was told. It was just as he'd imagined it. "*The Post* newsroom was the most romantic place I'd ever seen," he recalled. There were sixty people working

---

* *The Washington Star*, which went through several name changes over the years, was published as an afternoon newspaper in Washington, D.C. between 1852 and 1981.

in two enormous rooms—forty reporters, twelve copy boys (and girls), and twenty editors. There was the city desk editor, three assistant editors, and police radios from Virginia, Maryland, and the city cops.

Everything was in full swing round the clock. There was the haze of cigarette smoke (almost everyone smoked), the splattering coffee, the police radios barking in pseudo-code and reporters scrambling in response, hidden whisky bottles sloshing as desk drawers were slammed. There were "eight guys on the White House and Congress," covering the inner workings of the world's rising superpower. "I just fell in love with this business," Ted said. "This was *reality*. This was where things *happened*." Ted watched the reporters and revered them. That first year, one of them won a Pulitzer Prize, and Ted dreamed of joining their ranks. In the meantime, he balanced enormous coffee orders, "keeping track of three with cream and sugar, two with sugar only…"

His mind was made up: He was going to be a newspaperman. To accomplish this, he was informed by the powers that be at *The Post*, he would need a four-year degree. He registered at George Washington University for two courses: political science, which he found interesting, and English literature, which he did not. The assigned reading was Nathaniel Hawthorne's *The Scarlet Letter*, which he found a confusing waste of time. The campus was packed with "about a thousand kids, all war vets" taking advantage of the GI Bill. "These guys never dreamed they'd have a college education, and they worked hard," Ted recalled. "The profs said these were the best workers they ever had." They'd gone from the front lines of combat to the front row of the class, and they were eager beavers to a man.

Ted set out to learn the trade. Vernon coached his son during the evenings, teaching Ted how to read the paper. For six months,

Vernon had Ted read newspaper clippings, and then asked him to explain the placement and wording of sentences and to note where interview subjects worded their answers in a way that indicated more was going on. He taught Ted what a "lede" was. "I'm the cop and you're the reporter," he would say. He'd do a mock interview, have Ted write the story, and then show him what the reporter had actually written in the clipping. It was an excellent way to learn, Ted recalled, and illustrated clearly "where I was woefully deficient." Years later at the *Alberta Report*, Ted would still be using the tricks Vernon had taught him, combing news articles to see what the reporters had missed and where the real story might lie.

When Vernon thought he was ready, he'd send Ted off to ask questions, zeroing in on what other journalists might have overlooked. "He'd say: *If they'd asked this particular question at this time, it would have been a great story.*" Ted started to turn in stories of his own at the city desk. His work inevitably ended up in the wastebasket.

Under his father's tutelage, Ted discovered a different side of the old man—his razor-sharp street smarts. Once, he told his son that he'd discovered, upon studying the public accounts, that a large sum of money had likely been stolen by a senior cabinet minister. Ted was impressed:

> "Great story," I said.
> "Never wrote it," he said.
> "What!" I gasped. "Why on earth not?"
> "For one thing, there was a slim chance it wasn't true. He would have denied the story, of course, and there would have been a major libel action. It would have been messy."
> "So what did you do?"
> "Just one thing," he said. "I let him know that I knew. He was in office for the next eight years or so. And almost

every major story that broke from his department, or even from the cabinet itself, somehow found its way to me first. So instead of one major story and a libel suit, over time I got ten or fifteen major stories, and no libel suit. So you see, it's sometimes better not to write what you know."

In the meantime, Ted was a copyboy—and there were a number of gorgeous copygirls. He was terrified of them. "I, of course, fell in love with them, although I never did anything about it," he remembered. "One was a beautiful girl from Florida. I would have really liked to take her on a date but didn't dare ask her. And then there was Frederica (Freddie) Rubenstein. She was a tiny little Jewish girl, smart-assed and hilarious." He spent time with her in the suburbs of Washington, hunting with a .22 in the patches of forest that had briefly escaped the axe. Once, she pointed the loaded gun at his head. "I said: *You shouldn't do that—it makes me nervous.* She just laughed. I was always too frightened to try anything with her, and I think Freddie may have been disappointed in this regard. She was two or three years older than I was, but I liked her a lot. She was fun to be with, and I wasn't afraid of her after awhile."

Vernon and Caroline pictured together one last time shortly before Vern's death in 1977. Their persistent (but unsuccessful) efforts to reunite led Ted to suspect their relationship stubbornly refused to end.

Ted didn't meet anyone of importance while in D.C., but his father looked like a senator, and so Vernon used to take his wife and sons out for dinner on Sunday. He rarely paid. He'd chat with the cashier briefly, and then stroll out with his family. "My mother would be sick in case he'd get caught, but he never was because nobody was ever sure if he'd paid the waiter. It was always an uncertainty. He looked so dignified that he got away with it." He gave Ted tips, too. Ted held the knife properly, as he'd been taught at Lakefield. Vernon informed him that this was all wrong. "Hold it like a dagger," Vernon instructed. "They'll think you have money."

It was a heady business, and Ted felt like he was at the crux of everything as ink-stained reporters and editors raced about, filing history's first draft. During his short time at *The Post*, journalists were busy eviscerating Harry Truman, who was so unlike the "suave, polished FDR," pillorying the president for taking a harder stance on Russia. History, Ted would later observe, proved Truman right.

Decades later, squinting back at the blur of those hectic days, he vaguely recalled the first rumblings of African American discontent that would become the civil rights movement as well as the stirrings of feminist revolt. The feminists, of course, would become his ideological foes in the years to come when he ran his own magazine. There were major strikes in steel, coal, and even in the music industry, the beginnings of the great labour upheavals. The biggest story of his tenure was a gruesome one—the magnitude of Hitler's Final Solution slowly coming into focus.

• • •

Ted finally got a break with a story of his own when a Brooklyn bus driver came to the end of the line and kept driving until he hit Florida, where he turned himself in. Nobody could explain why he'd done this, so Ted headed down to the Washington depot to ask the bus drivers why their colleague had snapped.

The bus drivers were more than happy to fill him in. He'd stolen the bus, they informed Ted, because bus passengers were the worst people in America. They regaled him with tales of the various horrors that passengers perpetrated on buses. Ted scurried off, wrote the story, and turned it in, expecting nothing. His article turned up on Page 1 of the Sunday papers with the name "Ted Byfield" under the headline. He wasn't identified as "Post reporter," because that was against regulations. But still—teenaged Ted had landed a front-page story in one of the best newspapers in the world. He was ecstatic.

By this point, Ted had concluded that university was not for him. The vindictive clergyman of *The Scarlet Letter* had become unbearable. "I simply couldn't get into it. I knew some clergymen from Lakefield, and none of them were like this. I thought it was crap." He also disliked the professors—his blunt conservatism was already budding then—and suspected, perhaps unfairly, that the academics "seemed to be putting on academic airs." He asked the city editor why he couldn't be a reporter until he got a degree, especially now that he'd gotten a story published on the front page. The editor informed him that they were "trying to elevate the profession."

Ted decided this was stupid. A degree meant "four years of Nathaniel Hawthorne." He could write and he had a front-page story to prove it. He decided to seek a newspaper with less stringent standards. He'd joined *The Washington Post* in January of 1946, and in August of 1947, he struck out on his own again. To the everlasting dismay of generations of progressives, Ted Byfield headed back to Canada.

• • •

Ted hitchhiked to Toronto to see his grandmother, and then took a train to Ottawa. He'd worked briefly as a copyboy at the *Ottawa Journal* in the summer of '42, the year he went to Lakefield. Five years later, he was back, asking for a job as a reporter. The editors at the *Journal* knew Vernon Byfield, and figured Ted was worth a try. "All of a sudden I'd saved myself four more years of Nathaniel Hawthorne. I was a real reporter."

Ted started with obituaries—all fresh reporters started with obits, as it taught them how to follow a pattern and do interviews. If a reporter came on and claimed to have experience, the editor would give him a story that had the word *cemetery* in it. If he couldn't spell it, they'd know he was lying, because the word *cemetery* turned up in nearly every obituary—and almost always got misspelled. "I was going out, writing obits, and going out drinking—all the reporters drank, so I had to drink almost recklessly to be a reporter," Ted remembered. "There was a girl named Barbara whom I liked, but she was a lot older than I was. She was too old for me, but I wasn't frightened of her."

"Charlie Lynch, the city editor, was one of the toughest buggers I'd ever met, frightening beyond words," Ted recalled. "He was—some said—crazy. He'd huddle in the corner—he had a telephone in the very corner of the office—and he'd huddle there and whisper into it. He had a cackle for a laugh—*heh, heh, heh*. Like something out of Dickens." He was a big man but walked hunched over. When the reporters greeted him in the morning, he'd glare and snort: *HUH*. Lynch had an unshakable faith in the ability of his staff to screw up his day.

Lynch would come in with his assignment book with the names of his reporters written next to their assignments. "I remember one saying INT SP AMB. I said: *Mr. Lynch, I don't know what this means*. He said: *You're going to have to start reading the paper*. I went and asked Barbara and she told me it meant I had to interview the Spanish ambassador. "You're supposed to know that from INT SP AMB." Upon consulting the paper, Ted discovered that a new Spanish ambassador had been announced. This was the sort of thing he was expected to know. It was a steep learning curve, but it was not something he would have gleaned from Nathaniel Hawthorne.

There was much to learn. Ted had been showing up wearing a sweatshirt. Lynch informed him that he needed to learn how to dress properly. A reporter should be wearing a suit and tie. Ted, who was rake-thin, borrowed some money, headed to a department store, and suited up. If he was to be a newspaperman, he needed to look like one. Years later, when the golden age of newspapers was finally over, he recalled the milieu of journalism in those days:

> Journalism over the years had acquired much in common with a cult. It determined the way one dressed (trench coat, fedora, rumpled pants, cigarette hanging from mouth); the way one talked (clipped sentences; males addressed by surname: "Zat you, Peterson? This is Byfield. Gimme rewrite.") Its drinking habits were excessive by almost any standard, but leaned towards beer, since anything else was usually unaffordable.
>
> Paradoxically, however, the cult's politics tended towards the conservative. This derived from their habitual cynicism over almost any centre of authority. Of big business, journalists were deeply suspicious; of big government even more deeply suspicious. Lord Acton's doctrine—"power tends to corrupt, and absolute power corrupts absolutely"—they embraced as a kind of creed. They had another dogma. If you had asked them: What about people's right of privacy, something they invaded habitually, they would have answered that there was no

such thing. If it's news, whatever it is, the people have a right to know. Question: How did people acquire that right? Answer: By learning to read.

Yet beneath all this pseudo-barbarism, there existed a functioning ethical code. Promises not to quote were taken very seriously. Women must be treated civilly, even on occasion chivalrously, both in your life and in your copy. No obscenities in front of women. No off-colour stories. On the other hand, the stealing of public documents concealed by government was not only allowable, but highly admirable. The government should have no secrets. Everything was fair game for 'the press,' as it was then called.

There were other curiosities. Shortly after I got my first newspaper job, for instance, I asked my father what exactly news is. "Anything people want to get into the paper, probably isn't news, and anything they want to keep out of the paper, probably is," he replied.

A couple of other idiosyncrasies of this strange craft are noteworthy. Journalists considered accurate spelling and correct grammatical structure vitally important. Persistent spelling errors could get you fired, and flawed verb-subject or pronoun-antecedent agreements would be met with anger and contempt by editors. They believed, that is, in structure, not just in the structure of language, but in the structure of society as well. There was a right way to do a thing and a wrong one, admirable ways of behaving and contemptible, fact and fantasy, true and false.

This meant that Ted's most pressing problem was that he couldn't spell. Lynch was forever correcting his mistakes. One day, he snapped. "You've misspelled *Niagara*. If you misspell anything else, I'll fire you." In the next piece Ted submitted he'd misspelled *Saskatchewan*, and Lynch lost it. "That's it. Go away. Come in tomorrow and pick up your cheque." Ted was crushed. He'd blown his chance at a job in journalism over *Saskatchewan*. He showed up the next morning to pick up his cheque from the managing editor, who had also been friends with his father. The editor looked him in the eye. "Ted, I've talked to Charlie; we're going to give you another chance. But I'm telling you this—if you misspell anything, your life is in danger."

After years of ignoring teachers' warnings about his spelling, Ted suddenly became a precision fanatic. Later, he discovered that his firing and rehiring had been a ruse cooked up by the editors to cure his sloppy habits. It worked.

As Ted remembered it, there were three phases to Lynch's training. The first was that he wrapped his words in barbed wire and bashed you over the head with them incessantly. The second was that he worked you round the clock, handing you nocturnal assignments nightly so that "you were perpetually half dead." In phase three, Lynch now approved of you, but you were expected to use your imagination to secure good stories so as to avoid a demotion back to phase one. "It was a very good training program. You find out more about politics covering a single election than taking two years of political science. Practical knowledge. Journalism school is a waste of bloody time."

As 1947 wore on, Ted got more assignments. In November, there were municipal elections, and Ted was sent to cover meetings in Gloucester township. It was a suburban township: half rural, but the city was growing and the electorate was becoming urban. "I wasn't covering the election, only the meetings," Ted recalled. "The night of the election, the guy who was supposed to be covering it was drunk, so they threw me on it. I said: *The polls have been closed for hours. It's 11 PM. What am I supposed to do?* Cover it, they ordered."

"I called the winner and the loser at home. The defeated guy said that the winner was crooked, that he'd been ferrying people to the polls." This was the way city folks behaved, and not the way things were done in Gloucester, the loser bellyached. Ted phoned the winner back. "He came smashing back at the loser, and I had all kinds of great quotes—wrote them down, turned them in. We destroyed the *Ottawa Citizen* for election coverage. They didn't have any of that."

Ted's story ran on the front page under the headline "Charges fly after Gloucester upset." Lynch put the paper down on his desk, smacked it with the palm of his hand, and declared happily: "*That's* the way you do it, Teddy boy!"

After that, Ted got one good story after another by working his tail off. "I was on weekend duty and I took it seriously. Usually, you just checked with the cops, and when I asked them what was going on, they said they were using three cars to evacuate people. The Rideau had come over its banks and was flooding one of the suburbs. I called the photographer, and he got out there right away. The bloody *Citizen* missed it. We had a big headline on the flood, and the *Citizen* didn't have it at all." Lynch approved. "That's a magnificent job—you were right on the ball, Teddy. I always knew you had it. Have an American cigarette." This, Ted said, was the highest compliment he could pay you. An American cigarette was Lynch's version of the Pulitzer Prize.

In June of 1948, Ted got sent to Cornwall to cover a strike of the Canadian Seamen's Union, a Communist outfit (it would eventually collapse almost entirely due to its Red connections). A scab union, the Canadian Lake Seamen's Union, was rendering the strike ineffective by running the steamship lines on the Great Lakes through the Cornwall Canal (before the St. Lawrence Seaway was built), and trouble was brewing as CSU members lost their jobs. The CSU's thuggish tactics included savage beatings—they would swing from the bridges and land on the boat decks, maul the scab crews, and then leap off at the next opportunity.

Ted headed onto the boats to interview recipients of this treatment, and his coverage was not welcomed by the Communists (a trend that would last for Ted's entire career). "Two goons from the CSU met me on the street in Cornwall and told me that the Union agent wanted to talk to me," Ted recalled. "*Fine*, I said. He wants you to come up to his office, they said. At his office, they informed me that I was writing stuff in the *Journal* that was not helping the union at all. Well, I said, I'm just covering the story. You're covering the story in a certain way and we don't like it—if you want to save your face, you better not do it, they told me. Which made it pretty clear they planned to beat the shit out of me." Having spent some time interviewing men after the Commies had given their face a working over, Ted wasn't sure what to do. He phoned Tommy Lowrey, the managing editor at the *Journal*.

"They can't terrify me!" Lowrey roared. Ted was disconcerted. "You? It's me they're threatening!" Lowrey courageously decided that Ted's coverage would continue.

Several of the union goons, including the head thug himself, ended up charged with a collection of crimes. One charge, Ted recalled, was the "seizing, retaining, or otherwise forcing of a human being." He wrote the story, which was mostly a recap of news he'd already reported on. Then he had an idea. Speaking to the Crown attorney, he asked if the charge amounted to abduction or kidnapping. The attorney replied thoughtfully: "You could call it kidnapping, because they were making demands of certain individuals."

Ted did—and he was the only one. While stories in the *Citizen* and other papers referred obliquely to "seizing and retaining," Ted's headline read: "Kidnapping charges in Cornwall riots." Ted was a hero—although fame was fleeting in the newspaper business. "You'll screw something up in short order and then you crash again. But for the moment, I was the king of the world."

• • •

54

Just before he left for Cornwall, Ted noticed a new girl in the women's department. Ted found her extraordinarily attractive, and desperately wanted to date her. There were only two problems. "I was shy, and stupid, too." There were two desks in the little cubby hole of the department, and the other was occupied by another girl, Bobbie Turcott. He decided to be clever and ask Bobbie out for a beer, and then, as an afterthought, casually invite her colleague to join them.

Bobbie turned him down—she had a date that night already. Ted recalibrated and turned to her friend. "Well, maybe you'd like to go out for a beer?" The girl declined, informing Ted that she knew nothing about him other than the fact that Bobbie had just turned him down.

Ted left, defeated. After a moment, he headed back to the office. Bobbie had left, but the new girl was still there, typing. "Listen," he told her. "I don't know whether you believe me or not, but it happens to be the truth. I wasn't interested in taking Bobbie out, except if maybe you could come with us because I'd really like to take you out for a beer." In that case, the girl replied, I'd better come.

Virginia Luella Nairn was nineteen years-old and, like Ted, a child of divorce. Her American father was a highway builder and her Canadian mother had been working as a schoolteacher in Florida when they met and moved to Albuquerque, New Mexico, where Virginia was born on March 26, 1929. When her father got his leg blown off in a demolition accident, they moved to Greenfield, Nova Scotia to be near her mother's family. Her mother left her father and moved to Ottawa; her father moved back to Florida. Virginia—Ginger, to anyone who knew her—was left in the lumber town to be brought up by her grandparents and uncles, whom she adored.

Her grandmother was a very pious Baptist, but Ginger wanted to spend her time with the men. Whenever she could, she headed

Virginia Nairn around the time Ted met her. After witnessing Ginger dump a beer over a disagreeable pub patron Ted became smitten with admiration.

out with the loggers for the day. To her grandmother's horror, she soon began to speak like them, displaying an ability to swear with great proficiency. For the rest of her life, Ted recalled, you didn't know if you were going to get the logger or the lady when she opened her mouth. Her uproarious sense of humour was forged in the lumber towns of Nova Scotia, much to the dismay of upper-crust women who had a decidedly different view of what it meant to be a lady.

When her mother remarried into a wealthy establishment family in Ottawa (bagging a chemical engineer widely considered to be the most eligible bachelor in the city), she decided that Virginia ought to be raised like a lady, not a logger.* Finishing schools and debutante balls followed, but despite her mother's pleadings, she refused to either "make a debut" or marry up. Instead, she scored scholarships to study Latin, Greek, and German at the University of Toronto, studied political science and economics, and began working for the communist rag, creatively called *Campus*. Her grades were high, although the dean of women was forced to request that she stop smoking her pipe at official university functions. She even dated a left wing activist who worked with the Co-operative Commonwealth Federation (CCF), before taking a summer job at the *Ottawa Journal*.

Enter Ted Byfield.

---

* This marriage would produce two more daughters for Frances Lyons.

Ted and Virginia at their first home in
South Porcupine, Ontario.

Twenty-year-old Ted was smitten immediately. "I was just floored by her, infatuated beyond description, from the moment I saw her. She had a lovely laugh. She could quote poetry. Not to show off—we'd be discussing something, and she'd run a line from Shakespeare that fit in exactly with what we were talking about. I was so taken that I thought: *I need to get this woman.*" Characteristically, he threw himself into winning her heart. As their older son Mike put it years later: "His immediate enthusiasm for her eventually triumphed over her initial distaste for him."[1] He pursued her relentlessly.

"We had the summer together," Ted recalled. "We were interested in all the same things. When we finished work, we'd go down to the pub and drink beer, and then I'd walk her home, which took half an hour. I was just enthralled with everything about her." Ginger also occasionally had the use of her father's car—she could drive long before Ted could—and sometimes they'd drive somewhere they could look out over the city and talk. They would spin wild schemes, most of which went nowhere. But it was good to be young and in love and feel that the world was at their feet—and that anything might be possible.

When Virginia's mother discovered that a lowly newspaper reporter was courting her daughter, she was horrified. It was immediately decided that what Virginia needed was more time at the family cottage in Gatineau, and that she should forthwith spend her weekends there, where, importantly, Ted was not. Neither Ted nor Ginger were easily dissuaded. Ted worked every second or third Saturday, and so on his free weekends he would walk the eight miles to the west side of the Gatineau River, arriving near evening. He would shine his flashlight at the cottage on the other side, and Ginger would paddle over in a canoe. "We'd spend the evening together, talking and drinking whisky, and then she'd get back in the canoe and head back before daylight." In the dark, cool nights of summer, they talked about everything, laughing, enjoying being together, and sipping liquor from the bottle. For Ted, it was magical.

But all good things come to an end, and disaster loomed. Come September, Ginger would be heading back to the University of Toronto, where Ted was certain she would return to her socialist boyfriend. "His father was one of the senior people in the steel-worker's union," Ted said. "He was very much of the Left, and I was very much of the Right because of Lakefield. I knew if she ever got back to university, she'd get back with him—so how did I prevent that? He went down to visit her in Ottawa for one terrible weekend. Very stressful. Before she left, I said to her: Look, I'm going to move to Toronto, and I'm moving there because I want to be near you. I'm going to meet you on October 11, on the pier at the Eastern Gap at 8 PM, and we'll figure out what to do." She promised she'd be there. Nonetheless, Ted was doubtful.

Shortly after her return to campus, Ted called her residence (they were extremely strict about boys showing up in those days), asking if she was still going to meet him. She told him she wasn't sure. Desperate, Ted informed her that he'd quit his job at the *Journal* to be close to her, and that if she didn't show, he'd turn up and break every window in the residence. Ginger, chagrined that her summer fling refused to be flung, agreed to show up. (She later told Ted this was because she knew he'd actually follow through on his threats.) They met on the pier and walked out to the lighthouse, talking. It was October, so there wasn't anyone out and about except for a fellow who appeared to be walking his dog. Ginger and Ted ducked into a pub to discuss what they were going to do.

Things were proceeding well when the door burst open and the dog-walker—Ted's left wing rival—stormed in. He'd been stalking Ginger and her stalker to ensure that she would be protected from the lunatic she'd gotten involved with in Ottawa, trailing her to Centre Island and then into the hotel pub. Ted acted swiftly. He'd been one of the five reporters covering that year's Progressive Conservative convention, where George Drew had been elected leader. Ted pulled a handful of George Drew buttons and ribbons he'd kept as souvenirs out of his pocket, and graciously offered them to his socialist competitor. "Here, I brought you a present."

The boyfriend blew his stack. "He flew into a rage and walked out the door and lost the game right there," Ted chortled decades later. "So we went on planning. I needed a job, and I couldn't get one as a reporter because I didn't have enough experience yet." During the day, he worked at a power station on St. Claire Avenue West; at night he loaded trucks for Coca Cola.

"We put together a plan for a monthly publication for the students that would be conservative," Ted said. "She agreed that this would be a good idea, the socialist boyfriend having now departed." Ted cautiously inquired about her ideological promiscuity, and Ginger replied laconically that since she was dating a conservative, she was a conservative. The years ahead, Ted later observed, would prove that Ginger was conservative by nature— and she would become the unlikely den mother of Canada's conservative journalists when *Alberta Report* was launched decades and several provinces later.

To help him along, one of Ted's contacts in the Conservative Party of Ontario gave him the names of several construction contractors, who agreed to take out ads. Ted and Ginger put out two editions of the paper, and Ted told the story of his run-in with the union goons in Cornwall. The union promptly threatened to sue. They didn't need to—as they were working on the third edition of *The Reporter*, Ginger began to run out of time to work on the paper, and Coca Cola laid Ted off as the Christmas season ended. He needed another job.

• • •

Fortunately for Ted, Vernon Byfield's contacts came through for him once again. His father was back in Toronto and connected him with Charlie Bruce, the head of the Ontario wire for the Canadian Press. Bruce told him that Roy Thomson (who would become 1st Baron Thomson of Fleet, the Canadian-born British proprietor who would emerge as one of the great moguls of London's Fleet Street) was looking for editors in Timmins. Where was Timmins, Ted wanted to know. In Northern Ontario, Bruce told him. Thomson did his hiring in Toronto and had an office in the back of the Nova Scotia Building.

"Who's Roy Thomson?" Ted asked Vernon. "A cheap crook from Northern Ontario," his father replied. Ted told him that he might have a job available. Vernon asked him how much he was making at the *Journal*, and Ted told him thirty-three dollars a week. "Then tell him you were making 38 and he'll give you 30," Vernon told him.

Thomson had purchased the *Timmins Daily Press* in 1934 for a down payment of $200, and over the ensuing decade and a half had amassed a string of newspapers and radio stations across Ontario, including *Northern Daily News* in Kirkland Lake. He ran them out of Toronto along with companies as varied as ladies' hairstyling businesses and an ice-cream cone manufacturing operation. In the 1950s, the owner of 19 newspapers, he began his first foray into the British business, eventually moving to Edinburgh. In the meantime, he was looking for small-town reporters.

Ted met Thomson—"this affable guy with really thick glasses"—at the Nova Scotia Building. He seemed impressed with Ted's résumé. How much were you making in Ottawa? he asked. 38 a week, Ted told him. I'll pay you 30, he replied. When can you get to Timmins? Thomson bought Ted a train ticket, and he was on his way that evening.

"I was news editor of a newspaper with reporters, four desks, a managing editor, and a circulation of 11,000 a day," Ted recalled. "I was thrilled. Gin was thrilled. The train left Toronto at 11 PM.

The coaches were filled with men. A few groups were drinking from a whisky bottle, which was absolutely forbidden. Some of them were singing and laughing and having a good time—miners, headed up North." Ted asked how they'd gotten the whisky. From the conductor, they told him—the man who was supposed to be enforcing the no-drinking rule. "This was a part of Canada I had not experienced, coming from Toronto and Ottawa. I was heading into an area of Canada I knew nothing about, and it thrilled me. I was fascinated by the North. It wasn't the city; it wasn't the country; and it was filled with all sorts of interesting people."

Ted got off the train the following morning in Timmins, and a squat little fellow was walking about, squinting at people. Finally, the only ones left at the station were Ted and the squinter. Ted approached. "I'm looking for a Mr. Gunn." He replied: "I'm Mr. Gunn. I'm looking for a guy named Byfield."

"Well, I'm Byfield."

"You're not Byfield."

"Yes, I am Byfield."

"Vern Byfield?"

"No. That's my father. They hired me, the son."

Ted scarcely had time to get settled. "I became news editor, which meant you picked the stories they were going to run that weren't local and wrote the heads for it. I came to work the next morning and I was hopelessly slow, but they got it out anyway. The next morning I came to work around 2 AM, and the deadline was around 11. I was having the time of my life. There were about six or seven guys in the editorial department, and it was a good paper. I loved Timmins—even the cold. There were 28 mines, so it couldn't be a company town, and a seat in a beer parlor for every man in Timmins, a city of 28,000." The pubs for men admitted only men; the women's beer parlours were conveniently mixed.

Ted began to write love letters to Ginger, assuring her that the *Timmins Daily Press* operated out of an establishment that "was a little like the *Globe and Mail* building" (which, when she laid eyes on it, elicited much scoffing). She folded up the little campus paper she and Ted had begun and came to Timmins for the weekend to visit him. Ted got her a room in the Goldfields Hotel. "There was no sex. Kissing, and that was it. That remained the rule until we were married." Naturally, the already eager Ted was even more determined to tie the knot. He didn't want her to go back to Toronto, where some campus rake could set his sights on her. Fortunately for him, Ginger had gotten trainsick on the way to Timmins and was in no hurry to head back.

There was one obvious solution. The *Timmins Daily Press* needed reporters, and Ginger applied for a job. Jimmy Gunn, an editor who somehow managed to survive a bottle of rye a day, informed Ted that hiring his girlfriend was impossible. Ted was confused by this. "We'd like to get married, and if we had two incomes, we *would* get married." Gunn was firm. "We will not hire her unless you *are* married."

As it turned out, Timmins had been rocked by a salacious sex scandal just a few months before Ted and Ginger had arrived. The building which housed the *Timmins Daily Press* had an apartment for the publisher on the top floor. The publisher had begun an ill-advised affair with the wife of the newspaper's top advertiser. One night, this fellow turned up at the apartment and discovered them together. Livid, he began to thrash the publisher, who fled into the bedroom with his paramour. This, understandably, did not cool the jilted man's rage, and he decided to call the chief of police. "Will you please come up to the third floor of the *Timmins Press*? There's something quite awful you must see."

Following that, he called the Crown attorney, the district judge, and the city councillors. As each man joined the growing crowd outside the bedroom, he would fling the door open and demand that they peer in and witness the crime as his wife and the publisher shivered within. The news spread, and the wife's lawyer arrived, asking if he could do one thing for his client. "What's that?" the husband glowered. "Loan her my raincoat," came the reply.

This was not the sort of publicity the *Timmins Daily Press* needed, and Jimmy Gunn was determined to ensure that the newspaper was henceforth not associated with even a whiff of impropriety. Ginger could have the job—so long as she and Ted got married. The couple procured a marriage license the following day and had to wait three days by law to tie the knot. They phoned her parents on the second day so that there was no way for Ted's incoming in-laws to stop the wedding unless they hired a private plane. Ginger's mother was appalled at her daughter's decision to marry a lowlife reporter. "If you were half a man, you'd send that girl home," she told Ted.

"I'm not half a man, I'm a whole man, and she stays here," Ted replied unrepentantly, feeling both extremely triumphant and slightly sorry for her.

Ted's mother was weepy. "Oh, Teddy, you're so young!"

Vernon was more to the point. "You know something? This is the only smart thing I've ever seen you do." From that point forward, his comment planted him firmly in his daughter-in-law's good graces.

Ginger's stepfather tried to talk her out of it. Did she know how serious this was? She did. Was there any chance she could be dissuaded? No. "Well," he said. "Best of luck!"

He missed the last available plane and couldn't make it to Timmins in time to halt the nuptials.[2] The following morning, the *Timmins Daily Press* staff put out the first edition—it had to be on a train going south by noon—and during the break before the afternoon edition had to come out, they rushed over to the United Church. The composing room foreman was the best man, and the society editor stood in as bridesmaid. "We rushed back, the manager had prepared a nice little lunch for everyone upstairs, we swallowed the sandwiches, rushed back downstairs, and put out the second edition," Ted remembered.

Thereafter, Ginger enjoyed telling people that they'd "had to get married," neglecting to mention that it was the carnal activities of the publisher and an advertiser's wife that made it so. To the great confusion of everyone, their first child—their son Mike—didn't show up until a year later.

Ted's nineteen-year-old bride turned out to be a crack reporter. "She covered Ansonville-Iroquois Falls," Ted said. "She headed out on the train in the morning and came home on the last train at night. She'd have to get enough to cover at least two pages of the paper. That meant writing about twelve stories before she went to

The *Timmins Daily Press* newsroom in 1949 [Ted seated rear left, Virginia front right foreground]. Ted's nineteen-year-old bride turned out to be a crack reporter.

bed. She'd gather all of these stories while out of town, and then write them and submit them in the morning—every week. Nobody would ever ask anyone to write like that anymore. She covered police, fire, and accidents for awhile. They had a half-volunteer department. I remember a fire engine going by on the street, sirens wailing, men hanging off the outside. As they passed, they were all yelling *Hello Ginger! Hello Ginger!* It was wonderful to be married to a famous wife. She was very, very sharp."

Decades later, Ted looked back on this hectic honeymoon period as one of the best times of his life. "It was just fun, from that point on. She could quote poetry all the time. Man, I loved that. No matter what situation we'd be in, she'd have the proper verse. It was just a wonderful thing to even be married to her. There was never a period of disillusionment."

• • •

One reporter attracted the envy and admiration of the rest: Don Delaplante, a former alcoholic who wrote for the *Globe and Mail*, the *Telegram*, and other publications. To observers, he appeared to be more than a journalist covering events—he was a catalyst for them. He covered Northern Ontario and would drive from town to town. As Ted remembered it, stories would simply break in his wake. "He'd come into Timmins, and everyone would wait for something to happen."

"He drove into Sudbury on a Saturday afternoon, and a guy promptly shot a bunch of cops in the street," Ted recalled. "He drove into Larder Lake, and that same day someone stole $90,000 worth of gold bullion that was sitting on a cart on the railway platform. He got the whole story exclusively. He'd sit behind his typewriter, write a sentence, and then clap his hands and exclaim: 'This is *really* good.' He wasn't arrogant, he was just rejoicing that he'd been able to put together such a great sentence. He never drank—he'd just sit in the pub. He was one of the best journalists I ever knew."

Although he'd more or less abandoned the Christianity he'd found at Lakefield, Ted's habit of running into muscular and strong-minded Christian men continued. At Lakefield, it had been the headmaster. In Timmins, it was a man known as "the dean." As he later described the meeting:

> [A] tall gentleman of military bearing appeared one day at the counter of the Timmins Press and was immediately referred to in whispers by the rest of the staff as "the dean." He was Very Rev. Cooper C. Robinson, dean and later bishop of Moosonee. I was told he wanted to see me.
>
> "Ah," I thought, "one of the local clergy with an item for the paper." I walked into the outer office.
>
> "Are you Anglican?" he demanded.
>
> "Well, I don't know."
>
> "You don't know? What do you mean, you don't know? Either you are or you aren't."
>
> "Well, I suppose I am."
>
> His reply was immediate: "Why were you not in church on Sunday?"
>
> "I didn't make it on Sunday," I said.
>
> We agreed I hadn't made it for quite a few Sundays.
>
> "Very well, then, get there next Sunday or you should stop calling yourself an Anglican." He paused and added soberly, "Or, for that matter, a Christian."
>
> This, I was later informed, was the way things went with the dean. He had been a missionary in the Orient most of his life. At Timmins, he was accepted as a fact of life—abrupt, direct, hearty, generous and, on one or two occasions, two-fisted. Once he was said to have dragged a

wife-beating miner into the street to "knock some sense into the man." The man was later presented for confirmation. Whether the story was true or not, it was always told with great affection around Timmins.

That Sunday I returned to church, though not to the faith. I didn't have the intestinal fortitude for that, but I also had too little to face the dean's questions. My attendance was occasional.

I came, however, to know the dean and I remember well the conversation I had with him the night the Korean War broke out. To most of us, it looked like the Third and Final World War was now underway. Since he knew Korea, I was anxious to hear what he would say.

He leaned back in his chair as if he was discussing some routine of parish life. "Imperialism," he said. "It's just imperialism again. The old imperialism. Now it's Communist imperialism. That's the latest thing."

"But what you call 'the latest thing' could bring the whole world to war."

"Yes, that's right," he said.

"But it could be an atomic war. It could destroy civilisation."

"No doubt about it," he said. "Another dark age in that case. It's all happened before."

"But what can we do about it?"

"We must do everything we can to prevent it," he said, "and it's not impossible we'll fail. Our Lord was never very optimistic about the future of the world, you know."[3]

Ted would remember that lesson for the rest of his life, and it would be the source of his cheery, preternatural calm in old age—after most of his gloomy prognostications about the moral collapse of the West had come to fruition without denting his good humour. The dean believed that life was short, eternity was long, and that Christ had died to take the fear of death from His people. Ted remembered being as shaken by the dean's calm in the face of possible global catastrophe as he was by the spectre of war itself.

In the meantime, Ted's time at the *Timmins Daily Press* proved invaluable. "We could experiment. You confronted all the same issues as the big papers, but you had to figure them all out." Working for Thomson, Ted said, was like going to school. His papers created great reporters, but because he paid them so badly, they inevitably left for greener pastures once they'd accrued enough experience—a scenario that would play out at Ted's own magazines decades later.

• • •

For Ted, greener pastures meant Sudbury. Once he and Ginger discovered they were expecting their first child in the fall of 1950, Ted realized he needed to make more money. The *Sudbury Star* offered him $60 a week, and he and Ginger left Timmins in October.

Ted worked as a reporter in Sudbury for scarcely a year before deciding to pursue his dream of owning his own newspaper. Many reporters fantasized about running their own show, but Ted's dream soon turned into a nightmare. Ginger had covered Iroquois Falls and Ansonville, so Ted hitchhiked there from Sudbury to scope it out and then returned to move the family. He called his weekly newspaper the *North Star*, and it was a disaster. Again, a pastor surfaced to remind Ted that temporal things were not all that mattered:

Ansonville was the suburban overgrowth of the neat little Abitibi Company town of Iroquois Falls. Here we published a 16-page weekly tabloid. Even then the venture looked precarious. Now I know it was insane. The paper lasted six months…Throughout the disaster I learned how fickle were the fancies of the world. When the paper began I was popular with everyone and met friends on every street corner. My prestige began to decline as the business began to founder. At the time of its final bankruptcy and demise it is no exaggeration to say I was a virtual outcast—destitute, depressed, separated from my family, my savings gone, and the most enormous effort of my life a total failure.

The rector of the local parish was Rev. M.C.D. Hutt, a gentle man with a fine sincerity and a crisp sense of humour. In the early days when I was still locally important I saw very little of Mr. Hutt. He had invited me to church, but I rarely went.

Throughout the decline, however, he made a point of seeing more and more of me. His wife helped care for our child. He made his old car available whenever possible. In the last frantic week, he was in the office every day preventing me from feeling totally abandoned by both man and God. In his religious enterprise I gave him little encouragement. Yet his assistance remained as steady as a rock until the last day I was in town.[4]

By December of 1951, Ginger was pregnant with their second child, they were living in the basement of an old house, and heavy rains had washed a foot of water into their living quarters and sent the family fleeing to the make-shift newspaper office. Ted was writing the entire paper himself, with occasional help from Ginger as she tried to balance their failing venture with their growing family. Vernon Byfield arrived to help Ted save the paper, but to no avail. The *North Star* folded around Christmas, and Ginger took their son and headed to Mississauga to stay with an aunt and uncle while Ted and Vernon closed up shop.

For Ted, it was rock bottom. Vernon returned to Washington, and Ted boarded the bus to join his family. He had sunk their savings into the *North Star*, and now had just enough money for a bus ticket to Windsor, with stopovers. He stopped in at different newspapers, asking for work. There was none to be had. At the *Windsor Star* at the end of the line, the managing editor told him that the *Winnipeg Free Press* was looking for reporters. Ted had a bit of extra change (and a return ticket to Toronto) in his pocket, so he put his quarters into a payphone (*bong, bong, bong*) and called the editor of the *Free Press*. Sure enough, there was a desk spot for a fact-checker and news coverage if he could get there. He'd make over sixty dollars a week, which was more than enough to live on.

Ted had no money, and he needed a railway pass to get to Winnipeg. Journalists could get free transportation—coach class, not sleeping car—on any train in Canada. It was PR for the railways, and the newspapers just had to apply for it. But the *Winnipeg Free Press* didn't like the railways, which, in the view of management, had been exploiting the farmers. Thus, they didn't allow their employees to utilize the passes. Ted was in Windsor, and he needed to get to Toronto and then head to Winnipeg. It was the middle of January 1952, and icy cold. He took the bus to Hamilton and got out to hitchhike. His family was in Cooksville, and Ted figured someone would pick him up along Lakeshore Road. He had to keep walking, because if he stopped, he'd freeze. Every ten minutes or so, a car passed with a blast of wind. Nobody stopped.

When a car finally did pull over, it was a cop. "Who are you, and what are you doing?" the officer demanded. Vernon had always taught his sons one essential rule: "Never, ever lie to the cops. Cops know liars, and you can't trick them." Ted spilled his guts, the cop listened, and then he told Ted to get in. The doors locked, and the cruiser headed towards Cooksville. It was a quiet drive, and the officer ignored Ted's attempts at conversation. They met a cop driving in the other direction and pulled over. The officers had a hushed exchange, and then Ted was told to switch cruisers. The new officer turned to him. "Exactly where do your aunt and uncle live?" Ted told him and tried unsuccessfully to start a conversation. The officer ignored him until they pulled up at the door of his aunt's house. "Good luck in Winnipeg," he said, and drove off.

From that point on, Ted rarely—if ever—wrote a story that reflected badly on the police—and always felt terrible when he did.

• • •

The cops weren't the only ones to give Ted a break. At the train station in Toronto, he hunted down a PR representative and explained that he needed to get to Winnipeg. "Oh, the *Free Press* won't get you a pass," he was informed. The man looked at Ted, perhaps sensing his desperation. "In a hurry?" Ted shook his head. "I got nowhere to go." The man disappeared and re-emerged ten minutes later with an envelope. "Here's your ticket to Winnipeg." It was another good turn Ted was forever grateful for. "When you're hard up and can't support your wife and kids and someone does you a favour, you never forget it."

It was a beautiful train ride with a wonderful view of the Lake. "I had a Toronto mindset," the man who would become known as the arch-defender of the prairies recalled. "Winnipeg was nowhere, and Canada was three cities: Montreal, Toronto, and Ottawa. Everything else was sort of Peggy's Cove. I discovered there was more to Canada."

"I was about to discover the West."

CHAPTER THREE

INTO THE WEST—
AND THE CHURCH

After years of insipid religion, this Christ came to us like a drink of cold water in a desert. Here was a God to believe in, a faith to follow. And so we followed it that first Christian Christmas in 1952, followed it to the church and from there through the creation of schools, magazines, books, wherever it led. Of two things we can testify. We have never measured up, and we have never been bored. His mercy, as the Jewish poet said, endures forever."[1]

—Ted Byfield

In February of 1952, Ted arrived at the Canadian Pacific Railway station in Winnipeg to freezing cold, blowing snow, and a dilapidated hotel across the street that resembled a shack. At the *Winnipeg Free Press*, an editor lent him twenty bucks for lodging. He found a room on Ruby Street about a mile west of the paper and showed up for work the next morning. "It was a big city room, probably a quarter of an acre, and they must have had fifty desks," he recalled. "It reminded me of the *Washington Post*." Founded in 1872, this was no small-town newspaper.

The *Free Press* was a prominent city institution—the rival *Tribune*, founded in 1890, wielded only a fraction of its power. As Ted described it:

The whole place was Dickensian, like the fictional Telfer's Bank in *A Tale of Two Cities*. As with Telfer's, the *Free Press* was highly profitable, but behaved more like an institution than a business. Also like Telfer's, it had its habitués, people with "news" they wanted printed who seemed to wander in and out at will—like the strange little Englishman with his monthly press release on his plan to restore the Anglo Saxon dominance in the West's non-aboriginal population through the English-only colony he was proposing somewhere on the shore of Lake Winnipeg. Then too there were the redundant employees—like the staff telegraph operator, long supplanted by the teletype machine, but kept on anyway because he had only three years left to retire, or the building's elevator operator, similarly retained because he had only two. And besides, push-button elevators were probably only a passing fad anyway.

Such was the *Free Press* of the 1950s, which would preside for nearly eighty years as a rock-like presence on downtown Carlton Street, and prior to that for forty years at various addresses in the rapidly growing downtown area. When it began publishing, the province of Manitoba was two years old. The city of Winnipeg with a population of 1,464 would not be incorporated for another two years. This gave the *Free Press* something of a proprietary attitude towards the province. The *Free Press* saw itself as more or less owning Manitoba. That it should pretty much govern it was the paper's rarely challenged assumption for the first half of the twentieth century. Meanwhile, the lethal prose of its historic editor John W. Dafoe saw it widely regarded nationally as the preeminent voice of the whole Canadian West.[2]

Ted later recalled his first day at the *Winnipeg Free Press* in vivid detail:

I was not a happy person when I assumed my new job on what was known as "the rim of the desk" in the editorial department. I was one of six sub-editors, seated on the outer circumference of a huge semi-circular table. We were pencil-editing copy and writing the headlines for the stories in that day's paper. In the centre of the semicircle, facing all six of us sat the "slot man," our boss, who must fire me if I couldn't do the job. I was frightened and had good reason to be.

Twenty-three years old, I was Toronto-born and raised (not a plus in Winnipeg, as I soon discovered) and had spent five years in the news business…I needed a job, and the *Free Press* was trying me out in one. The *Free Press* was paying me sixty dollars a week—forty-five of which went to my wife. I lived in one rented room with a hot plate to make meals. We could survive. But how could I put my family back together again? Moving our furniture halfway across a continent plus railway fares would cost around five hundred dollars. It would take me at least six months to save that. So even if I could do the job, I still had a huge problem.

I looked at the other five people on the rim—three men and two women. They were courteous enough, even friendly, but for one. The man sitting beside me, about my age, seemed at first a rather severe person—tall, grave, who looked straight in your eyes when he spoke. But speaking evidenced his striking disability. He had a serious stammer. You could easily understand what he said because he spoke so slowly and painfully as he struggled to enunciate. But the stammer was only one of his two chief distinctions. The other, I soon discovered, was his quick perception of absurdity. His comments on the passing scenes, though laboured, could be hilariously funny. He [might] be a little slow getting it out, but what he said was well worth waiting for.

His name was Bob Saunders. Like me, he was a Toronto boy, so we would endure this handicap jointly. Because of his stammer, he had never served as a reporter. But he was one fine copy editor, I was told, and early on I found out something else about him. Everyone in the place was obviously fond of him. He was cherished, even loved in the sense of *philia*, the kind of love that binds a regiment together, or a ship's company, and rarely (though I have known it to happen), the editorial staff of a newspaper.

I had by now handled my first story, but before returning it to the slot man, I decided to take a chance on this Saunders. Would he look at it for me? He went over it quickly, particularly the heading. "It's f-f-fine," he said. "They'll l-l-like it." A great burden fell from me, and I looked at Saunders. He was grinning. He had apparently suspected my desperation and knew he had to a degree relieved it.

I went for a beer with him after work, and talked to him pretty well every day thereafter, gradually unfolding to him my tale of woe. Would the company loan me the money to move my family to Winnipeg, I wondered. He told me to ask the managing editor Ted Dafoe, and that Dafoe would send me to one Malone.* "He's the office oag-oag-ogre, the m-m-money man," said Saunders, adding that he suspected, however, that this parsimonious reputation was

---

* Ted Dafoe was John W. Dafoe's son and managing editor of the *Winnipeg Free Press* from 1944 to 1952. He retired from the *Free Press* in 1962.

a mask to keep destitute people like me away from him. In fact, some had found the Ogre very kind.

Things went exactly as Saunders said they would, and I was now seated in front of the Ogre himself. Richard S. Malone was curt, decisive, categorical, and firm. But not cruel nor belittling, and in no sense a bully. Just tough. He had a military background, having risen to the rank of brigadier during the war. "I'd like to help you," he said, "but it's an ironclad policy with us. We don't loan money to new employees."

"Then what can I do? I like it here. I like the paper, I like the people, and I like the job. But if I can't get the loan, I'll have to quit. I can hardly abandon my family."

"An ironclad policy," said Malone, coughing.

"Without the loan, I can't stay," I said.

The Ogre leaned forward over his desk, peering directly and fiercely at me. "Are you saying," he sounded each word carefully, "that if we don't loan you the money, then you're going to quit?"

"What else can I do?"

"Please answer the question."

"Yes," I said, as loudly and as assertively as felt safe.

Malone breathed what seemed a sigh of relief, sat back in his chair and pronounced: "Well in that case, we'll loan you the money."

Ogre or not, I felt like kissing him. Fortunately, I restrained myself, shook hands with him, and said: "Thank you very much, sir, I deeply appreciate it." I took my leave, but I had to use the stairwell, not the elevator. I didn't want anyone to see the tears streaming down my face. I spent a dollar on a payphone call to my wife, Virginia. "Gin! Gin!

Gin!" I cried. "They're giving us the loan. We can put the family back together again." Now, both of us were in tears.

When I related all this to Saunders, he did not appear surprised. That was their reputation, he said. They were forever referring to "ironclad" policies, especially when they [were] about to break one of them.[3]

For the rest of his life, Ted would credit Saunders, after God, for bringing him back to Christianity. They talked constantly. "In deference to his speech handicap, I felt it might be easier if I led the conversation," Ted wryly remembered. "Only gradually, however, did I realize that I was deluding myself. I wasn't leading anything.

The family unit in 1961: Virginia and Ted with [clockwise from top left] Philippa, Mary Frances, Michael, and Link.

78

Unobtrusively, the stammer notwithstanding, Saunders edged our talks onto the subject he obviously wanted to discuss with me. That subject was God. I soon realized that Saunders was deeply Christian, and that this was a quality that had hitherto escaped me."[4]

In the meantime, there was only a handful of night staff on call at the *Free Press*, and Ted often wandered into the office at night. Nocturnal beat reporters were general assignment folks who covered whatever they could, and Ted told the management that he wanted to join them. "Look, I'm broke, I send all my money to my family, I've got nothing to do. Give me an assignment and I'll write it and turn it in." He also hated editing copy, which he found boring. Reporting was what Ted was good at, and it was what he wanted to do. He took the initiative, writing the stories the *Free Press* wanted to cover but didn't have enough staff for. In the morning, the city editor would grill him on the details.

"They'd have to take me off the rim of the desk to answer questions about the copy," he said. "This was beginning to piss off my supervisor, because the city desk was using one of their employees for one of their jobs. So, I became controversial." Not, one is tempted to observe, for the last time.

Ted's talent for finding the right story surfaced soon after. Skinner's, a hot dog stand, had burned down, and it was rumoured that the fire department had been occupied at their St. Patrick's Day party during the blaze and that the firefighters had been too buzzed to respond to the call. Ted checked with the fire chief, and the man begrudgingly affirmed that this was true, but wondered aloud whether it had been much of a loss, if you really thought about it. Plenty of folks did think about it, and a verbal brawl ensued, carefully covered verbatim by Ted. The story ran on the front page, and the *Free Press* gave it a ring of shamrock green to fuel the fire. Everybody was wildly entertained, and Ted's career at the paper was off to a roaring start.

Scarcely a week later, Ted came across a story from Minneapolis noting that an exotic dancer going by the name of Dark Venus was to be deported by the United States for violating lewdness laws. To get rid of this woman, Ted realized, the Americans would likely have to ship her to Winnipeg, the closest city on the Canadian side. He called U.S. Immigration for confirmation. Dark Venus would be arriving by air at 4 PM the following afternoon. He called Trans-Canada Air Lines and was told that she would be met by Canadian immigration officials.

He called the city editor. "We've got to interview the Dark Venus." This required some explanation, but the details stoked the editor's enthusiasm. Ted left the rim of the desk early with a photographer to track her down.

"What kind of dancing were you doing?" Ted asked innocently.

"Oh, I don't know, the sort of thing you always do," replied the stripper vaguely.

"Was it exotic?" Ted asked.

"Certainly," she said.

"Was it interpretive dancing?" he asked helpfully.

"Yes, yes, I was into exotic interpretive dancing. The Americans didn't get it. I just wasn't appreciated," Dark Venus mourned.

The *Winnipeg Free Press* put her up in a hotel room for two nights. To augment the story, the photographer asked the persecuted artist to hop in the tub and pile bubbles round herself so that just her head was protruding. Ted wrote the story and submitted it with the photographs. The next morning, Ted arrived at the office to find Malone and several other men clustered around a photo. Malone shook his head thoughtfully. "Not enough bubbles. Add bubbles, and we'll run it." The story broke the next day, and Dark Venus was promptly hired by mafia boss Charlie Mazzone, who ran an illegal cabaret on Pembina Highway.

This was not the sort of story that Ted Byfield, later renowned as a fierce moralist, would become known for in the years ahead—but the same irreverent sense of humour and tabloid instincts would permeate and define his entire career. He checked on the deportee a few days after the story ran to ensure she was surviving. Mazzone, who brought in performers such as Louis Armstrong and Bob Hope to the Rancho Don Carlos, was paying her the astronomical sum of a hundred dollars a week. As Bob Saunders later wryly observed: "I did not, at that time, notice that Ted had any strong religious convictions."

But Ted's reputation as a man who could get eyeballs on a story grew. He was taken off the rim of the desk and put on the reporting staff. It was an enormously successful beginning to a conventional journalistic career that would be derailed within a decade by his commitment to Christianity.

The Byfield byline began to show up regularly on the front page of the *Free Press*, and Ted soon gained notoriety as a journalist. Ted's ethic was simple: Get the story, no matter what. Covering City Hall, he and others used to sit on the floor of the bathroom, where murmurings in the adjacent committee room could be deciphered if one strained hard enough to hear through the vents. "Crazy stuff went on," he recalled with pleasure. "Marvelous fun, though." As Dafoe later put it: "[Ted] enjoyed stirring things up. He would sit there cackling away as he typed, laughing to himself...even at his most serious he seemed to be having a good time."[5]

Liberal journalist Boyce Richardson, who worked with Ted for a time, recorded his impression of Ted during this period in his 2003 *Memoirs of a Media Maverick*. In a cast of reporters replete with many eccentric characters, Ted still stood out:

> The lead reporter on city hall was Ted Byfield, a skinny, intense religious fanatic who looked slightly scarecrowish in the rough grey woollen suits he favoured. The son of

an improvident, maverick newspaperman, about whom he never tired of telling hilarious stories, Byfield seemed to have no problem combining his strict religious beliefs with a completely amoral attitude towards his work. He didn't care how he got a story, as long as he got it.

He would listen through keyholes, eavesdrop on conversations, and generally use methods that I thought somewhat *infra dig*. He was extremely clever, and in a few minutes could turn out an amusing article about a council committee meeting, without benefit of notes. When the mayoral elections came around, it was Byfield who persuaded Stephen Juba, a guy from the wrong side of the tracks, to run against the pompous mayor George Sharpe, for whom Byfield had an amused contempt. Sharpe was a stuffed shirt who sometimes made ludicrous errors about Winnipeg's ethnic communities, which he knew nothing about. On one occasion he joined a Ukrainian group, as the mayor was required to do once a year, to celebrate the birth of the poet Ivan Franko. Sharpe was holding forth about the evils of communism and the poet's noble dedication to freedom, when he realized from the puzzled audience reaction that he must be talking to the wrong group: instead of addressing anti-communist Ukrainians who had arrived as refugees after the 1917 revolution, he had strayed into a meeting of the pro-communists, whose parents were refugees from the failure of the 1905 revolution.

Byfield orchestrated Juba's campaign, planting quotes with Sharpe, then running to tell Juba, "Mayor Sharpe says you are a..." He would suggest a smart riposte for Juba, then run back to tell Sharpe, "Juba has just called you a..." Juba won, to everyone's amazement, and Winnipeg had him as mayor for generations thereafter.[6]

Ted's memories of the Juba campaign contradict none of this. For years, City Hall had been more or less controlled by River Heights, a swanky community south of the Assiniboine River where the money resided. Steve Juba, who was from the North End, had already lost two mayoral elections when he decided to run on what he called "the liquor ticket." Winnipeg, he announced, was a proper city now, and thus needed proper cocktail bars. "The city, of course, had no authority to open cocktail bars," Ted recalled with amusement. "But Juba was smart enough to realize that people either didn't know that or didn't care."

Ted liked Juba and told him he would help him get elected. While they were chatting at City Hall, *Tribune* reporter Jimmy Hayes walked in and Ted called him over. "Sit down, Jim. I've just joined Juba's press corps."

"Have you now?"

"Yes."

"I think I'll join George Sharpe's."

Jimmy headed down the hallway to the mayor's office and told Sharpe: "I'd like to help you with your election campaign,

Ted with Steve Juba sporting a St. John's toque. The Winnipeg mayor's advice to Ted: "Don't think 'buy.' Think *scrounge.*"

if I could." Sharpe informed Hayes that he'd already hired an ad agency, and that while he appreciated the offer, he wouldn't be needing any help. Hayes headed back down the hall and found Ted. "I've just joined Juba's team along with you." With that, Ted noted, the election was virtually over—both of Winnipeg's major newspapers had tossed their hat in for Stephen Juba.

Despite this political interference—the supposed impartiality of the press back then was as laughable as it is now—one of Ted's favourite stories involved exposing a quid pro quo between Winnipeg's aldermen and the Pointe du Bois powerplant. Each year, aldermen were given a free trip to Pointe du Bois where they'd go fishing and stay in a dormitory. When it was the turn of Gerson Harvey, referred to by Ted as "a renowned jackass," to receive the weekend retreat, Ted called up City Hydro, which ran Pointe du Bois, and asked who had funded the weekend.

We did, they responded. *Every alderman gets one trip a year.*

Where is the authorization for this? Ted inquired with great concern.

What? came the reply. "I said: Come on! You're handing money to politicians for no reason at all? What is it, to make them more conscious of electric power?"

Ted told the rep to call him back once he had more information on whether the trips had council approval. No call was forthcoming. Ted wrote him a note explaining that in his view, there was no authorization for these fishing parties, which had been going on for years. "This means you're putting money into politics. This has never been approved by council. This has been a secret."

Ted got an alarmed phone call shortly thereafter. "What are you *doing*, Byfield?"

"I'm writing a story," he replied serenely.

As if to assist him, the bus carrying Alderman Gerson Harvey went off the road Sunday on the way back, and the *Free Press* had a story in Monday's paper. "I wrote: 'Harvey's bus went off the road, spilling the best-kept secret,'" Ted chortled later. "Council met Monday night. Everyone in town was talking about the big parties the aldermen were having. People were saying they should have to pay it back. The finance member stood up and demanded that something be done. Everyone was livid because they'd agreed not to talk about it. They ended up physically fighting each other, pushing each other around. They were just in a blind fury."

Ted documented the fray, happily taking photos through the door. One particularly poignant snapshot depicted the finance member grasping a colleague by the tie, screaming into his face. This was all unfolding behind a glass window with the letters "Council Chamber" stencilled solemnly on it. It could not have been a more perfect framing. The scandal dragged on for months—and as it turned out, the only member who hadn't taken a free fishing trip was the Communist alderman. "I never had so much fun in my life," said Ted.

The game of cat and mouse between the press and the politicians was a prime part of public life. Once, when Ted was going on holidays, he took his temporary replacement with him to the mayor's office. The man was a senior reporter who had never covered city hall, and Steve Juba decided to test him. He gestured in front of his desk: "Walk from that point to that point." After he'd done so, the reporter was confused. "I don't understand, mayor."

"What's the third letter from the top on the pile of my desk?" asked Juba.

"I beg your pardon?"

"The letter on my desk," said Juba. "Who's it from?"

"I didn't look at the letter on your desk!" the reporter protested.

"You'll never make it on this beat," said the disgusted mayor.

Indeed, politicians expected journalists to operate with loose ethical standards. Winnipeg's city clerk, George Gardner, once informed a group of gathered reporters that he'd figured out how to outfox them. "I can get anything in the paper I want," he informed them. "I want it in there, I get it in there. I can also keep anything out."

"Can you now, George," said Ted.

"You bet. I've got the whole key," replied Gardner.

"Explain."

"If I want to keep something out of the paper," said Gardner, "I bind it up in a book and hand each of you a copy of the book and I say: *This is a project the city is working on. Could you give it a little publicity?* Not one sonofabitch among you will take a look at it. I've kept it a secret by handing it to you."

"How do you get something *in* the paper?"

"I mark it confidential and leave it on my desk and leave my office for five minutes," said Gardner. "Someone'll be in there and pinch it."

Ted would meet many renowned politicians in his day, covering speeches by Tommy Douglas and getting to know John G. Diefenbaker, whom he described as "a delight to cover, because he was such a character." During the 1957 federal election campaign, which would result in Diefenbaker becoming prime minister, Ted distinguished himself with a front-page story that would win him that year's National Newspaper Award. During an altercation between an angry farmer and Liberal Minister of Trade and Commerce C.D. Howe, the farmer demanded to know how he was supposed to make ends meet with plummeting crop prices. Howe poked the farmer in the belly and told him: "You look pretty well fed." Ted snapped a picture, got the story, and thus, according to some, played a small role in the Liberal government's downfall.

Within five years, he was the highest-paid reporter on the *Free Press* staff. There was every indication that Ted Byfield would become a prestigious and even nationally known journalist. He did, of course—but for distinctly different reasons than anyone suspected.

• • •

Concurrent to Ted's blooming career at the *Winnipeg Free Press* was Bob Saunders' relentless mission to convince Ted of the truth of Christianity. Saunders knew Ted wasn't religious and looked for opportunities to refocus the young journalist's attentions. "Once he inquired if I was Anglican and when I said I was, he asked me to be godfather to his son, Link," Saunders remembered. "He assured me that this was a mere formality and that I wouldn't actually have to *do* anything."

Saunders was good company during those first lonely months, and like Ginger, he could quote reams of poetry at the drop of a hat. Saunders invited him to come to church, and after persistent invitations, Ted relented. As Saunders remembered it: "One day, he spoke to me about some concern he had. I had been a Christian for five or six years and I suggested he pray about it." He also gave Ted some books to read, starting with *The Screwtape Letters* by the great Anglican C.S. Lewis. Uncomfortably, Ted began to reach a difficult conclusion: Christianity was either the most important thing, or it was meaningless. What it could *not* be was mildly important.

Grappling with this, Ted began to pray nightly. "My wife thought I was nuts," he recalled. "She later told me she thought I was crazy. But at the same time, my behaviour was becoming more amenable. I didn't sharply rebuke her or do other things people do when they're outraged. She said: 'I could see you changing, and for the better, so I thought I'd better pay some attention to what you were doing.'"

He and Ginger read Lewis's *Mere Christianity* together and initially, Ted recalled, "she fought every paragraph." When Ted started attending church, Ginger briefly considered leaving him. "It seemed very extreme," she remembered. "I had nowhere to go. I guess Ted argued me into it—Ted and Lewis. I couldn't really argue with Lewis."[7]

For Ted, the great 20th century apologists of the Christian religion were a revelation. He found C.S. Lewis extraordinary—the man seemed to know just what he was thinking. He'd read through a paragraph, think it over, and come up with objections. He'd then move on, and Lewis would begin the next paragraph by informing Ted that he was probably thinking of such and such objections—and, invariably, he was. As it turned out, Ted was not the first fellow to ask such questions. Ginger also began reading Lewis, and, for the first time was confronted by the rational case for Christianity. "I didn't know that existed," she told her husband.

Ted headed back to church in May of 1952, and when he walked into St. John's Cathedral in the North End of Winnipeg, he was not yet a Christian. "I had accepted three principles as true," he wrote later. "There must be a God. He must be good. Men, myself included, were bad. This was my entire theology. It did not constitute, I knew, belief in the Christian religion. But nevertheless it was time, [Saunders] had said, to go to church...Inside the heavens did not open. Nor did I expect them to. The setting, the congregation, the service, were much what they had been everywhere else. There was, it is true, an odd feeling of coming home again. But feelings were something I had forearmed myself against."[8]

The rector of the Cathedral was the Very Reverend John Anderson, whom Ted described as "a very erect person." Anderson was a good-natured man with flecks of black dotting his face—these were bits of the landmine that had blown up his Jeep during the War. He'd returned from Europe a decorated chaplain, and he knew how to handle men—including the trench coat-clad reporter who styled himself a hard-ass. On that Sunday in May, Anderson preached on the folly of men's desires for worldly fame and recognition. Ted recognized much of himself in the preacher's words. It made for uncomfortable consideration as he made his way home.

As Ted struggled through his questions about Christianity with Saunders and several other friends, he began to consider the cost of becoming Christian. He knew himself well enough to suspect he would be unable to keep his mouth shut if he did. "The role of gospel-thumper was not one I particularly yearned to play," he wrote. "You would very rapidly acquire a stigma within sophisticated company. I might, like [Saunders], be subtle about it. But I did not have his gift of subtlety and nothing like his patience. This fact would tell and ultimately I would be branded as a kind of religious nut. There would be whispers, snickers, and so on, and I could write off any possibility of a future in the newspaper business. Who was going to entrust any responsibility to a hot gospeller?"[9]

Ted decided to ask God for a sign. "If Christianity is true, if I ask for direction, I'll get it," he thought. "When I go to church next Sunday, I'm going to ask God if somewhere in that service, somehow, He will tell me what He wants me to do." The following Sunday, Ted plopped into the pew. Throughout the service, there appeared to be no discernible requests, demands, or messages, not even in the songs or the Scripture readings. As the service ended, Ted resigned himself to the fact that he would go home empty-handed.

Then, the Rev. Anderson remembered something. "Oh! Sorry, I was to make an announcement. I forgot. We very badly need more men in the choir." The choir had a few boys, fifteen faithful women, and only four or five men. The parish wanted this to change.

This was alarming. "I loved singing," Ted said. "But I didn't want to wear all those skirts. I mean, I'm a tough newspaperman, and all those robes they wear? I remember walking down Main Street on my way back from church, thinking: What would they say at the office about singing in a church choir? And this other voice kept on reminding me that I'd asked what He wanted me to do."

Ted described this struggle in *Just Think, Mr. Berton* (although he omitted the detail that he'd asked God for instructions):

JUST THINK, MR. BERTON
(A LITTLE HARDER)

by Ted Byfield

1.50

I knew a great deal about singing. I received my early training in a place called the Chatter Box Bar & Grill on Ninth Street in Washington, D.C. The proprietor used to play the piano every night and all present would sing things like "Loch Lomond" and "The Road to Mandalay." Shortly after I left the city the Chatter Box had a moment of fame: one of the customers shot dead a fellow customer right outside the door. I often wondered if what motivated the killer was the outrage to his aesthetic sense caused by the row that used to go on inside the door.

I did my post-graduate work at the various assemblies of the Ottawa Press Club in Ottawa. And in Timmins, Ontario, I attempted several times to offer vocal selections to the patrons of the Lady Laurier Hotel across from the Timmins Press until requested by the management to cease. The Ontario Liquor Act forbade that kind of entertainment, it was explained, and the customers didn't seem all that keen to have it provided. All this wealth of experience, however, I felt conscience-bound to bestow upon the Cathedral choir.[10]

Conscience aside, Ted badly wanted to avoid the robes. For two evenings, he paced about, and finally worked up the courage to knock on the door of the rector's house. "I'm sorry," Ted told him. "I have to join the choir." He emphasized his lack of credentials, but Anderson told him to call the choirmaster, Harold Christie, anyway.

"I would like to volunteer," Ted told Christie.

"Wonderful, we need men very much. What experience have you had?"

"Bathtubs," Ted said.

"Bathtubs are fine," said Christie encouragingly. "Some of the best singing is done in bathtubs. Are you a tenor or a bass?"

He told Ted to show up Friday night for practice. When Ted didn't show, Christie called him. "I thought you'd come," he admonished.

"Well, I didn't," said Ted obviously.

"Next week?" asked Christie.

"Yes."

"I'll pick you up."

Despite his halting start, Ted was soon enraptured by the choir, discovering Bach, Haydn, and Handel. He didn't know if he was a tenor or a bass, and so Christie stuck him between two men to try him out. All his life, of course, Ted had been singing melody. Now, in more ways than one, he was singing a different tune. He found that he loved it, and the next Friday, he donned his cassock again. By the third session, the choirmaster felt confident enough that Ted would stick around to inform him that his pronunciations were awful and that he needed to stop singing in his speaking voice.

By the fourth session, the choirmaster asked him to recruit more men, and Ted's doubts resurfaced. Here it was—the moment he traipsed around the office, a fisher of men from the Cathedral, trying to reel in his colleagues through the choir. He did it anyway. "To get men in the choir you had to convince them that this was a respectable thing to do—putting on a cassock and all that," he recalled. "Didn't seem very manly." But Ted's talents as a recruiter were already impressive, and men starting trickling in. Soon, he said, "we began to sound a bit more like the Red Army Chorus. It was an excellent way of engaging people on the Christian faith—getting them to take this tangible step." Seventeen men ended up joining by Christmas—five eventually became Anglican priests.

As Ted described one of these unlikely conversions in 1965:

> Gradually, the Cathedral choir began to fill up with men. We were a strange lot. At one point we included five newspapermen, plus a mixture of acquaintances from the Clarendon and Aberdeen Hotels. A young fellow who was a night police reporter brought with him one day an old school friend, an army officer, deep chested, swarthy, black-haired, dark-eyed, and with a laugh so hearty that he used to fall backward into a chair, lift his feet off the floor and roar to the ceiling until the room shook. He was, he assured us, no Christian. But he liked to sing. That's why he'd come into the choir. But God's ways are mysterious. Discussion followed argument. There were pleasant fall Saturday afternoons. There was a Christmas. In spring, he made his mind up and he, too, was confirmed. He is now the Reverend Dick Cawley, rector of St. Thomas', Lockport, Manitoba.[11]

"After that, spurred on by his customary ardent nature, Ted flung himself into promoting the Christian religion," Saunders remembered sixty years later. "Five or six of us would meet weekly at his apartment for prayer and discussion. Most members of this group were friends of Ted's, but not many were from the *Free Press*." Many of these men were choir members, and together they discussed how to bring others to church with them. They called it a "cell group"—and

Ted was sure to emphasize later that the Communists had cribbed this concept from the Christians, not the other way around.

As Ted's son Mike remembered those gatherings: "Through my seven-year-old eyes, his new circle of friends appeared a boisterous, exceptionally happy bunch. Their favourite activity was arguing and drinking in the spartan men-only beer parlours of the time. They passionately admired C.S. Lewis...[who] reawoke my father's boyhood faith and defined it further. He also initiated within him a powerful dislike for the secular philosophy then waxing overwhelmingly influential—liberal humanism. The Byfield group's animal high spirits and intellectual vigour were rooted in the tradition of the English medieval church, a tradition that glorified God's law as manifest in man and nature."[12]

Ted's Christianity, for all the later accusations of heartlessness levelled at him by progressives who believed that compassion was the government's business, was more than mere lip service. He and Ginger not only read the Bible but sought to apply it to their lives in practical ways. When he encountered men with nowhere else to go—drunks, jailbirds, and other riffraff—he began to take them home. He'd introduce them to the cell group, invite them to join the choir, and take them to church.

"Some of the men we brought in were in a terrible state," he remembered. "They had no place to go; they were living on the street. Older people, most of them. You can't read the New Testament and try to apply it without realizing that when God puts people like that in your path, you're supposed to do something about it. So I began bringing them home. There was quite a few of them."

The experiences these men shared helped shape Ted's emerging worldview. His much-maligned position on corporal punishment, for example, was informed by a fellow named Jerry who, with two others, had beaten up a storekeeper on the east side of the river north of Selkirk. Jerry received a sentence of six months and six strokes of the lash—one of the last times this punishment was administered in Manitoba. Jerry was 17 or 18 with no place to go. "Gin and I discussed this at some length and we both came to the conclusion that we were supposed to do something to help Jerry." He got a job at a store and lived with them for six months.

In a column published years later in the *Alberta Report* titled "The case for the lash: Mercy is not love," Ted described what Jerry had told him upon his release from prison: "In many respects, his life in jail was actually easier than it had been at home. But the whipping, that was something else. After several days in jail, he had been led into a room where several guards were waiting for him. He was stripped down to the waist, bent over and struck six times across the back with what looked like a belt about four feet long. He remembers that it had round holes in it. He had begun relating

One of the cramped attic/apartment gatherings on Winnipeg's Alfred Avenue. [Clockwise from top right] Shirley Hogue, Fran Sutton, Gail Burden, Virginia, Ted, Nancy Cox, Eric Cox, Bob Sutton, Dick Cawley, and Joan Perry (later Cawley).

this story with characteristic jauntiness. But as the memory of the gruesome ghastly experience refreshed his mind his tone changed. It became very cold and decisive. 'Never,' he said, 'never, ever do I want that to happen to me again.'"[13]

Jerry tracked the Byfields down twenty years later in Edmonton to thank them. He had a successful career as a builder and was married with children. He told Ted that the lashing he'd taken after his crime was the best thing that had ever happened to him. "It saved me," he said. To Ted, this was evidence that going soft on crime was, in fact, one of the many compassionate cruelties of the emerging liberal era.

Jerry was one of many who found their way to the Byfields' doorstep. There was a drunk who frequently broke into houses and was in and out of prison before a judge tired of him and handed him a federal sentence. There was a Ukrainian fellow who showed up at the *Free Press* looking for a meal and stayed with the Byfields for six months (he ate raw garlic in his room that Ginger assured him was odourless but could be smelled from the street.) "I had very little to do with Ted's work with convicts from the provincial jail at Headingley, but I do remember hitchhiking to Headingley once to talk to one of the convicts Ted was helping," Saunders recalled. As always, Ted dragged everyone along with him.

"We had a whole chain of people who came to live with us," Ted recalled. "When the Hungarian Revolution broke out, we had four Hungarians living with us. There were appeals on the radio for people who would take Hungarians into their home. They fled over the Austrian border to escape the Russians and were shipped to Canada and the United States. It was one of the best immigrations we ever had. These were all very talented people, and they were all Christians." The Byfields did their part. "At various times we had living in our house a Hungarian tank commander, a watchmaker, several students, and a quiet, sad-eyed, middle-aged woman who, we were later surprised to learn, was a prostitute."[14] Ted and Ginger had thought she was a cleaning woman. Ted was not judgmental—he, after all, was a journalist.

• • •

The year 1952 would prove pivotal for Ted and Ginger Byfield. It was the year they became Christians, and this fact would have profound implications for Canada. The two of them would become the media vanguard of the backlash to the moral revolution unfolding across the nation in education, media, and politics in the decades ahead. Unlike so many Christians, their extraordinary careers would be fundamentally rooted in the fact that they took Christianity seriously and applied it practically.

His colleagues would be stunned by the extent of the transformation. "You sort of always pictured [Ted] with green eyeshade, dashing from scoop to scoop—just a tough, tough newspaperman," one staffer at the *Free Press* recalled after Ted had departed. "He was the big name, the front-page byline guy, all flash and beat-the-opposition. Most of us were absolutely flabbergasted when this hard-nosed character suddenly revealed himself as a religious person who wanted to dedicate himself to working with youth."[15]

"We saw our lives stretching out in front of us," Ted wrote later. "For me, the *Free Press*; for Ginger, years of diapers. Or was there something more central to life? If the Christian story was true, then nothing else in life mattered."[16]

— CHAPTER FOUR —

THE ST. JOHN'S CATHEDRAL BOYS' SCHOOL

We offer no fame, fortune, security or comfort—
only life, and that abundantly.

—St. John's recruiting pamphlet

The St. John's Cathedral Boys' School began with the friendship between Ted and schoolteacher Frank Wiens. They met at St. John's Cathedral in 1956 during the time when laymen were meeting for discussions in cell groups across the city in living rooms and beer parlours. Frank Wiens was the son of German Mennonite immigrants who had grown up on a Manitoba farm during the Great Depression. He had worked his way through university as a miner and railroad worker before starting as a teacher at Sargent Park School three years prior. Like Ted, he had also been strongly influenced by Anglican clergy—in his case, a priest named Harry Cartlidge who'd run boys' camps and served as a missionary in northern Canada.

Ted was drawn to Wiens immediately, spotting him on his first day in the choir, a man who had "a pixie-like face with twinkling eyes."[1] The two men walked home together that night, and their synergy was instantaneous. A pub between their homes and the Cathedral became a laboratory for the ideas that would launch them on an unexpected trajectory.

According to Mike Maunder, a teacher at St. John's and one of the authors of *Today My Sail I Lift: Memories of the St. John's Schools 1956-2008*, the two constantly sparred and spurred each other on. Ted was a nonstop font of ideas, logic, questions; Frank was "passion and drama and often talked of what he called 'heart.'"[2] Over frothing pints and Winnipeg's famous Ukrainian Kolbassa sausages, they often ended arguments by poking one another in the chest as the argument crested: "Well, what are you going to *do* about it?"[3]

In addition to G.K. Chesterton and C.S. Lewis, the men of the cell group also read the works of Dorothy L. Sayers. This triggered more discussion, and Ted developed a theory. The generations leading up to the War had acquired their values from four places: Home, especially mother and father; church, which reinforced what

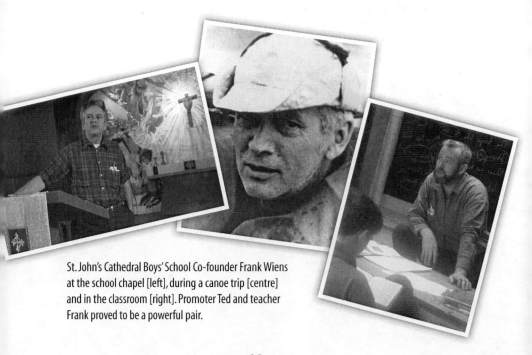

St. John's Cathedral Boys' School Co-founder Frank Wiens at the school chapel [left], during a canoe trip [centre] and in the classroom [right]. Promoter Ted and teacher Frank proved to be a powerful pair.

was taught at home; school, which bolstered what was learned at home and at church; and the media in its news, entertainment, and literary forms. It was clear to Ted and the men of the Cathedral that the fundamental roles of the family and the church were being usurped by the public education system and the media.

The solution, to Ted, seemed obvious (a characteristic of his that detractors and allies alike frequently found infuriating). The churches needed to run schools, as they had previously, and Christians needed to be far more involved in the media. These conclusions, reached around tables crowded with pints and loaded with food, would drive the entirety of Ted's life's work.

"In that cell," Ted said, sixty years later, "we knew what was going on and what needed to be changed. I was persuaded then, and am still persuaded now, that the goal of public schools is to break the hold of religion on the individual and to break the hold of the parent on the child because the state wants domination. That might not be the way a kindergarten teacher thinks, but that's the way the bureaucrats think." The evidence for Ted's thesis has accumulated at an alarming rate over the past several decades.

Ted and Frank helped run Sunday school for those who were part of the choir, but they wanted more for their sons. Ted remembered his Lakefield days and the thrill of the wilderness. Frank thought of the character-building hard work of the prairie farm. Ted's transformative encounters with strong Christian men drove his conviction that boys needed to be shaped by men, and that encountering strong Christians could produce strong Christians. And where could a boy get *that* these days?

In the spring of 1957, they purchased an old rowing cutter from the Navy League and began to repair it with the help of volunteers. Ted's connections came in handy. Mayor Steve Juba once gave him a large bottle of whisky for Christmas. When Dick Malone discovered this, he demanded that Ted give it back.

"I drank it," said Ted. "Buy him a new one," said Malone. The *Free Press* bought a bottle of whisky and gave it to Juba who, as a natural politician, now felt that the favour was still outstanding.

When Juba heard about the boating program, he promptly offered to help. He was a carpenter, and he had a car. Ted didn't have a vehicle and he needed to get around Winnipeg to buy hardware and supplies to outfit the boat.

"I can drive you around and you can pick it up," Juba told him. "But I want you to get rid of one word you just used."

"What's that?" asked Ted.

"*Buy*," said Juba. "Don't think 'buy.' Think *scrounge*."

"What do you mean?" asked Ted.

"I'll show you what I mean," said the mayor.

Juba headed into the hardware store, found the owner, and unleashed his pitch. There were these men, he explained, who were building boats for kids up in the North End...such *selflessness*, such a *worthy* cause. In no time flat, he'd wrangled several hundred dollars worth of supplies for free. Before he finished, the mayor had managed to scrape together everything Ted needed, including life preservers for all the boys. These were donated by Jewish businessmen and came with greatly discounted sleeping bags, a particularly generous gesture considering the fact that this was a Christian project.

"Let this be a lesson to you," Juba informed Ted. "Scrounge. Never pay for anything if you can get it for free." According to Ted, Juba was so adept at this that he once scrounged an entire bridge, persuading the feds and the province to pay every last dime. Juba would remain a strong supporter in the years ahead.

The maiden voyage of the cutter was launched shortly thereafter with eight choirboys aboard. As Maunder described it: "Lake Winnipeg was an hourglass-shaped lake whose small southern basin was dotted with dozens of summer cottage communities. Ted had already fallen in love with the lake, encountering the vibrant Icelandic communities around Hecla." The trip lasted two weeks and three hundred miles, with campouts along the way. Frank Wiens would later say that he learned more about boys in those two weeks than he had in a decade in the classroom.[4] Ever the promoter, Ted took photos of the boys rowing and wrote glowing blurbs for the newspapers.

That first trip also inaugurated one of St. John's most controversial traditions. Mike Byfield, a seven-year-old rower, recalled that one of the boys, who was dragging his oar through the water and not pulling his weight, got a good whack across the seat of his pants from Ted.[5] Ted had experienced this form of punishment at Lakefield and was of the opinion that it had done him much good. Not everyone was as assured of the virtues of corporal punishment as he was. Ted's view was maddeningly simple: "If it hurts, we won't do it. Nobody has ever improved on that." Ted didn't, anyhow.

The cell group began to expand their ambitions, implementing Dorothy Sayers' educational ideas in weekend and night classes and planning longer canoe trips while Frank recruited boys from Sargent Park School, where he taught.

In the summer of 1958, one of these trips almost went horribly wrong. The senior boys and their leaders rowed 100 miles to the isolated community of Berens River, but the wind kicked up waves so high that they were stopped cold several times. The crew lost all contact with shore for several days. Parents became stressed, then upset. Journalist Ann Henry, who had allowed her son Tim to go on what she was now convinced was a suicide mission, wrote an article for the *Winnipeg Tribune* condemning the reckless endeavour with the ominous headline: "Choir boys lost on lake."

A plane was hired to track the missing boys, who had made it thirty miles from Berens River by dark and then rowed through the night, searching for the lighthouse that could guide them into the river's mouth. Ted finally let the boys sleep just before dawn, rowing the cutter close to shore and pulling a tarp across them to sleep.

101

When they awoke, Ted "stiffened everyone with a swig of scotch whisky" and the light of morning guided them on their way. At Berens River, the wobbly boys pulled themselves out of the cutter and staggered onto the dock, the first time they'd made landfall for over 24 hours.[6] "The nuns at the hospital swept the boys up and put them to bed. They slept the clock around. [One boy] remembers the clean sheets and awakening to the smell of fresh baked bread."[7] At this point, the *Tribune's* plane found them—"We weren't actually lost," Ted insisted—and Tim Henry was airlifted home. Ted phoned in a story on their adventure to the *Free Press* to outflank the *Tribune*, which was determined to expose the criminal negligence of the voyage.

When a reporter and photographer from the *Tribune* arrived to document the tragedy, they attempted to persuade the boys to lie down on the dock in poses of exhausted dejection. Ted, however, was not about to lose a media war, and the group posed instead with their fists thrust in their air, bellowing manly defiance and flexing their muscles. No needless airlifts for this crew—they would finish what they had started.

The defiant crew of St. John's first cutter trip for boys in 1958 from Winnipeg to Berens River and back. [From left] Keith Bennett, Roger Caves, and [from right] Ted Byfield, Art Marsh, Ken Einarson and Terry Hatton.

"As they came down the southern lake," Mike Maunder record-ed, "cottagers and boaters came out to greet them. By the time the choirboys rowed up the Red River towards Winnipeg, people were lining the riverbank cheering."[8] The trip took two weeks, but the fatigued and muscle-sore boys reached home to a press reception and applause. Even the *Tribune* was won over. "CHOIRBOYS TRIUMPH OVER LAKE," was the following day's headline. "St. John's Cathedral Boys' School had been born."[9]

• • •

The school began as a part-time project and, much to the alarm of some churchmen, rapidly expanded, resulting in "heated meetings at the Cathedral as factions in the church wondered what was happening with this runaway program and its engineer, Ted Byfield."[10] Ted had allies, and in November of 1958, the Cathedral passed a motion creating the school. The Archbishop of Rupert's Land duly consented. The school would not be part of the choir but would fall under the jurisdiction of the Cathedral and the diocese.

The part-time school was staffed by six or seven men who taught a range of subjects including German, public speaking, composition, rhetoric, and Greek. All of the men held other jobs, which jostled uneasily with their new duties. Many were recruited by Ted; some were working journalists. Ted served as principal while continuing his work at the *Free Press*.

The first boys came from Winnipeg, and by 1959 there were forty of them. The junior boys, ages 8 to 11, arrived on Tuesdays; Friday nights and Saturday afternoons they had choir practice in the parish hall as well as classes in German, Latin, and poetry. Friday night they slept at 66 St. Cross Street, which was owned by the Cathedral and leased to the school. Saturdays were also spent working, mostly on the new forty-foot sloop the *St. Peter*, which

Men Wanted

UOSPMOHL QIAYQ

A Recruiting Booklet
For
THE COMPANY OF THE CROSS

"We promise you no rewards as this world understands rewards, no fame, no fortune, no security, no comfort. Only life and that abundantly."

was being constructed in the stable of a brewery on Redwood Avenue. It proved to be so enormous that the stable roof had to be taken off so the vessel could be extracted by a crane. The brewery no longer used horses and the stable was due to be demolished anyhow. A swarm of local politicians attended the official launch.

The senior boys arrived on Friday nights and returned home on Sunday evenings after church. Saturdays brought snowshoe runs around the city in winter, and cutter or canoe runs up and down the Red River after the ice broke up in spring. By the summer of 1959, the juniors were rowing up the Red River while the seniors attempted to paddle the entire length of Lake Winnipeg. By this time, Ted was covering the legislature for the *Free Press*. "It's the most boring thing in the world," he recalled. "You have to sit there while these guys ramble on and on. It's just awful. Occasionally they might get into a fight and you might get a story out of it, but mostly it was just boring."

While the politicians babbled, Ted took to reading *The Nor'Westers* by Marjorie Campbell, a history of the band of independent fur traders who launched an empire in 1779 stretching across the continent, reaching the Arctic, and trading wares around the Horn of Africa to China. Ted was captivated by all of it, and soon the boys were bellowing ancient paddling songs as their canoes skimmed the surface of Lake Winnipeg's gleaming waters.

• • •

Launching a school required money, and Ted turned out to be an extraordinarily talented fundraiser—a skill he would utilize many times over the ensuing decades. "I didn't know anything about administering schools," he said. "But I could do two things: Raise money and people."

In Winnipeg, the fast way to raise cash was to host a tea. Sufficiently wealthy members of society would be invited and treated to tea and refreshments, after which they would leave well irrigated and slightly poorer. Ted suggested that Ginger organize one, and she worked hard to select well-heeled prospects and send out invitations. She invited two women from the Cathedral to look over her preparations. As it turned out, there was a specific formula to these events that the Byfields, who were whatever the opposite of upper crust was, were unaware of. "This is a shambles," the women told the devastated Ginger.

Ted asked a local politician what he should do. "Call Ruby Locke!" came the reply.

Ruby Locke was the closest thing Winnipeg had to a grande dame, active in St. Luke's Anglican Church, the Women's Canadian Club, the Winnipeg Poetry Society, the Antique Art Society, and the Imperial Order Daughters of the Empire. She was also heavily involved in Conservative politics in Manitoba. In her seventies she was, Ted remembered, "a tiny little thing, sweet-natured, endlessly charming, but the velvet glove hid an iron hand." Ted called her, and she responded immediately. "I'll go talk to Virginia!" She promised to visit that very night at 8 PM.

At 7:15, Ted was sprawled out on the couch drinking a beer when the doorbell rang. It was Mrs. Ruby Locke. A brief scramble ensued, the bottle was stashed out of sight, and Ted invited her in and offered her tea. "You know," she replied thoughtfully. "There *is* something I would like."

"What's that?" asked Ted.

"A bottle of beer," she replied. There was a pause, and both erupted into gales of laughter.

Ruby reassured Ginger, gave her some suggestions, and Mrs. Byfield's morale shot back up. Locke, who earned the moniker "mother" of the St. John's Cathedral Boys' School, became a close friend of the family. "Whenever we went to her house, she would always have whisky ready. 'Now, what's happening at the school? Keep me informed!' she'd say. You'd always leave feeling like a million dollars. She was one of God's great creatures."*

Victor Sifton, the owner of the *Winnipeg Free Press*, could not support the school itself—the paper would not endorse an alternative to the public school system—but became a significant personal supporter of Ted's. Sifton's father Sir Clifford had been Minister of the Interior under Wilfrid Laurier; Victor served in the First World War and was wounded, demobilizing with the rank of Major and receiving the Distinguished Service Order for actions at the Battle of Amiens.** He moved to Winnipeg in 1935, served as executive assistant to the defence minister in World War II, and was named a Commander of the Order of the British Empire for his services. He also served for a time as Chancellor of the University of Manitoba and was heavily involved in the newspaper business.

Ted did not meet Victor Sifton at the *Free Press*. Instead, a fellow parishioner at the Cathedral invited Ted and Ginger to his house, saying there was someone he'd like them to meet. Ted, ever the establisher of convenient connections, happily obliged. When

---

* Ruby Locke died in 1982 at the age of 97; in 1965, she was given a Manitoba Golden Boy Award in recognition of her community service.

* His citation from August 9, 1918, read as follows: "Owing to his initiative, and as the result of a personal reconnaissance, he was able to save his company from heavy casualties by taking his men to a new jumping-off place. During an advance of four kilometres under heavy fire he directed the attack of three companies, two company commanders having become casualties, and then organised the battalion outpost line. Throughout the entire action he sent back valuable information to his C.O., and by personal reconnaissance established communications with the flanking units. He set a splendid example to all ranks."

they arrived, Sifton was waiting. He'd wanted to meet Ted, but on neutral ground—preferably ground that he did not own. The Byfields and Sifton soon struck up a friendship. Sifton occasionally drove him about when he needed to pick up supplies or out to Selkirk once the fulltime school was established.

This did create one small initial complication for Ted. "By this time, we'd bought a dog and I named the dog Victor as a joke. And who but Victor Sifton, the emperor himself, came to the house. We had to put the dog in the basement and warn the kids not to call him. I told Sifton this story later and he killed himself laughing. He turned out to be a magnificent guy. He was a very devout Christian." They became so close that when Sifton heard Ted was sick sometime later, he ordered his employee to move into his mansion, stay in bed, and read. "He'd come home in the evenings, and we'd argue religion. I got to know him really well."

• • •

Ted and Frank were a frequently volatile pair, but their partnership was dynamic. Both boys and volunteers were drawn to the school; many of the boys were doing well and simply wanted a classical education while others were doing badly, and their parents believed they needed the structure. "For all of them," Maunder wrote, "the school offered discipline, winter and summer adventures in the outdoor program and enriched classes that stressed memory work, poetry, logic, public speaking, detailed discussions in religious studies, and the basic religious experiences of practicing and performing in a choir. It was always the hope that these activities would draw the boys to the greatest adventure of all—the Christian faith."[11]

The decision was made to make the leap and start a full-time school. This was not easy for Ted, who was the highest-paid reporter at the *Winnipeg Free Press* while also doing freelance work for the Canadian Broadcasting Corporation, which paid handsomely. (At one point, the managing editor of the *Free Press* asked him with acid solicitousness: "Byfield, do you find that your work for the *Free Press* interferes with your freelancing?") To work fulltime, Ted would have to quit journalism. He was finally financially stable; he had a career and a future doing what he loved. The school, on the other hand, was a risky venture.

The answer crystallized for him one beautiful evening out on the water, canoeing with a crew of boys. They were rowing into a river off of Lake Winnipeg. It was a night of perfect calm, and the sun was setting as the choirboys sang a hymn: Charles Wesley's "Lead Me, Lord."

"It covered my thoughts," Ted remembered. "That line: *Lead me, Lord, lead me in thy righteousness, make thy way plain before my face*—it struck me. He did make it plain. I went with the school."

About 140 boys had formed the part-time school, which ended in 1962. "A significant milestone came in 1961 on a rainy and cold Holy Saturday, the day between Good Friday and Easter Sunday. A group of about a dozen braved the elements to erect a six-foot white cross in front of an old set of buildings three miles north of Selkirk. Through the support of many friends...the school had acquired a nominal 20-year lease on the old Dynevor Indian hospital, a federal property that had lain derelict for years."[12]

The Anglican Church's promotional material for the school emphasized the historic location: "The stone centre block faces the Red River, once a highway of Canadian explorers and fur traders. The boys dock their boats where Alexander Henry landed when he came this way. Across the river from them stands old St. Peter's Church, burial place of Chief Pegius, the Indian who saved Lord Selkirk's settlement."

Fifty-five boys arrived at the new school 25 miles north of Winnipeg in September 1962. Twenty of them, including Mike and Link Byfield, had been students at the part-time school. Some parents dropping off their sons were alarmed to observe the condition of the buildings, which were dangerously dilapidated. The old Indian hospital had once been used for tuberculosis patients.

"Boys explored endless nooks and crannies in the huge central building, the barn and outbuilding, and had the run of 640 acres of prairie bush. The school's boats were moored on the Red River flowing past the front door. For the first time a farm program was possible. Boys, staff, and volunteers spent much of that spring burning off the fields, hauling out and burning the old mattresses and converting the rambling old buildings into classrooms and dormitories," Maunder wrote. "Over the next three years, all of these boys would experience St. John's in different ways. Some were gifted; some were bullies. Some would thrive on the experience ahead of them; some would detest it. Some would run away within a week; some would stick it through for six years."[13]

As Maunder described it:

At the centre was the original "Dynevor" stone building. At the time that Winnipeg was still a village, it had been built as a rectory to St. Peter's across the river. Now it was a century old, with stone walls three feet thick, tiny windows and a dim interior. The chapel and offices were on the ground floor; classes and dorms on the upper floors. The basement was a rabbits' warren of little rooms. Farm crew would raise baby chicks there. Or, when student John Robertson's dad shot a moose, he'd donate the hide and maintenance crew would soak it in the basement to bake babiche for snowshoes.

Leaning against the stone building at all kinds of drunken angles were the three ramshackle wooden wings containing kitchen, dining hall, more classrooms and dormitories. They never quite joined properly. Many boys recalled snowdrifts working their way into their dorms on a cold prairie night. But the school prided itself on this ramshackle austerity. 'It's true the roof leaked,' said one report. 'But it's also true the boys learned to fix leaky roofs.[14]

In addition to Ted and Ginger Byfield, who lived with their children (there would eventually be six of them) in the three-story staff house which adjoined the school via the laundry facility wing, there were initially five other staff: Frank and Nancy Wiens, army cook Charlie Race, Keith Bennett (a gifted musician), and Father Arthur Millward, who was both the school chaplain and a classics scholar. Just as their home had been open to all in Winnipeg, staff often gravitated to the Byfield residence, where Ginger would expand the burbling stew to accommodate drop-ins. Ginger was an essential member of the team, renowned for her blunt efficiency. The staff met daily, and these meetings began to drag on over the years. Ginger swiftly discerned when meetings became a waste of time and would indecorously lead them to a close.

The old cottage on the property was used as a dormitory for the seventh-grade boys, and the two-story northern wing "was the heart of the school. On the ground floor was Charlie's kitchen and the dining room; on the second floor were the main dormitories. Staff ate meals with the boys, with a master sitting at each table. The dining hall served as study hall at night."[15]

Many parents sent their boys to St. John's to toughen up—at least two dozen parents over the years told Ted that they had been "in the War" and that their sons needed a character-building experience. "The kids were soft," Ted said. "They weren't being asked to do much of anything that was unpleasant. Before the War, Western Canada was populated by farmers. Many of the men who'd gone to war had been children on farms with heavy responsibilities from the age of twelve." The school replicated the tough physical circumstances that they thought boys needed, including lacrosse, snowshoeing, canoe trips, repairing the school, constructing new buildings, and even assisting local farmers in the harvest.

Ted taught French and history. Teaching history was easy if you knew how to tell stories well, and as a journalist, Ted was an expert at this. "Journalism is history—it's the history of what happened yesterday, so I naturally drifted to that subject," he recalled. "In journalism, you're always casting about for ways to capture the readers' interest. I simply transferred this to the classroom."

Ted was constantly experimenting with ways to capture the boys' attention. According to Maunder, he even created "a course in French based on the voyageurs and the fur trade; introduced the grade eight boys to the works of Francis Parkman to study Canadian history; introduced extensive reading and essay writing to senior levels of History. Many former students trace their present-day love of history to Ted's history classes in this period, although [they] did not much appreciate at the time the daily 'test swats' that ensured they were getting the reading done."[16]

Parkman, incidentally, had a significant impact on Ted's later work producing history books on Alberta and Christianity. "They were magnificent histories," he said, "and I've been imitating him ever since. Really, it's about people. You get to know them very well through Parkman."

Steve Weatherbe, who responded to an ad to become a teacher at St. John's in 1969, also recalled Ted's teaching talents:

Ted developed a French language curriculum that relied on these explorations and conflicts for vocabulary, prose comprehension passages and sentences posed for translation. St. John's boys became proficient in the specialist vocabulary of the fur trade. They knew the word for a 90-lb compressed bale of beaver pelts, the leather tumpline one needed to hump it 15 miles across the Grande Portage, and the names for paddlers at different positions in a supersized "Montreal canoe" that carried trade goods outward from Montreal to the Grand Portage on Lake Superior and brought beaver pelts back.

Byfield revelled—and tried to teach the boys to revel—in this history, to take pride in reviving the experience, the courage and endurance of those early voyageurs. At the Height of Land between the Hudson's Bay watershed covering Western Canada to the Rockies and the St. Lawrence River watershed to the east, he put the boys and men who steered the school's 22-foot canvas and wood canoes through the same ceremony as the voyageurs did with neophytes 160 years earlier. After days of warning about the coming initiation and many miles of paddling punctuated by back-breaking portages (four teenage boys under a 200-lb canoe), the boys were lined up and doused with water from the Hudson's Bay watershed. Each received a tot of rum and were then required to swear the oath that would make them "un Homme du Nord" and a man of the North country: "I promise never to kiss the wife of another Homme du Nord without her permission."

The whole thing, with the tot of rum and mildly risqué vow, seems to me to sum up in some way Byfield's intoxicatingly romantic conception of a boy's school.

Ted even had World War II veterans come in to talk to the boys—including a German paratrooper who had immigrated to Canada. The boys were particularly impressed when he showed them how parachutists had to learn how to fall and dropped to the floor to illustrate it.

Frank Wiens became like a second father to many and mentored hundreds of boys. He noticed when they were having a tough time and took care to wave them into his office for a talk. There were fights, bullying, and pecking orders, and Frank taught them how to cope. "Stoic, tough, rebellious, clever, sense of justice," wrote Maunder. "That was the boy code. It exists everywhere boys are struggling to be men and searching desperately to belong—teams, military units, summer camps, workplaces. [Former student] Richard de Candole remembered being bullied mercilessly at the prestigious private school he attended before St. John's, but not at all at St. John's."[17] Others, it must be said, had a miserable experience.

The Outdoor Program remained a primary focus. The first newsletter in 1963 praised "the snowshoeing accomplishments of the fulltime boys, particularly 11 seniors who were the first to complete the school's 50-mile race in one day, a standard, the newsletter was proud to point out, that even U.S. Marines were having trouble meeting."[18] Outdoor activities were not only an essential part of St. John's philosophy, but they were also necessary to give troubled boys sent to the school a productive outlet for their energy.

Former student Richard Bird, who attended from 1962 to 1965, described his experience with the Outdoor Program this way:

> There was hardship, but there was also the beauty of the Shield, the romance of the historical fur trade routes of 'les hommes du nord,' and the excitement of running a big rapid [in a canoe]. I remember looking down on my first Grand Portage trip into that huge sucking whirlpool of the Milky Way as our canoe fought its way upstream in the middle of the night on my first fifty-mile Lagomodiere senior race.[19]

It was an experience the boys would never forget.

• • •

There were many canoe trips over the years, including two-week to one-month wilderness trips down the North Saskatchewan, Columbia, Missouri, Athabasca-Slave, and Richelieu waterways, following the path of the Montreal fur traders of the Northwest and Hudson's Bay Companies. The 18th expedition in particular was exceptional. Five men and sixteen teenage boys set off in the summer of 1964 on a journey of only 200 miles, a far cry from some of the thousand-mile treks in past years. But this time, the crews would be following trails largely abandoned for generations, using guides, maps, and even the old journals of long-dead explorers.

"To people familiar with the story of the Canadian fur trade the name 'Methye Portage' holds a strange fascination," Ted wrote in the school's magazine following the venture.

Ted at the stern on a 1973 trip. In just the two summers of 1966 and 1967 St. John's canoes reached the shores of all three of Canada's oceans and even south towards the Gulf of Mexico.

114

It is a name out of the past, calling like a voice from nearly two centuries back. It speaks of still black waters and summer nights and the rollicking songs of those men in bark canoes who first ventured forth into what was awesomely called "the Great North West." It is in fact the name of a northern Saskatchewan bush trail that connects the Hudson Bay watershed with the Arctic.

To the French it was "Portage Laloche," named for the catfish. The English term "Methye" came from an Indian word. Whatever its name, the significance of the portage was beyond dispute. Peter Pond of Connecticut, a Nor'Wester, found it in about 1778. It led him out of the headwaters of the Churchill River into the Athabasca basin where he found the richest beaver territory since Cartier discovered the St. Lawrence.[20]

The Methye Portage was a part of the fabled Northwest Passage across North America. Sir Alexander Mackenzie had traveled it. So had Sir George Simpson. It was fourteen miles long and broken in the middle by a small lake, making it the fur trade's longest portage. Athabasca beaver furs had poured over the portage, headed for Montreal and the Bay. It was virtually inaccessible—and still is—but Ted and his crew were determined to find it. Ted's imagination had been particularly fired by Alexander Mackenzie's recorded reminisces.

As Ted described it: "Methye remains precisely as it was when the moccasined feet of hundreds of voyageurs tracked its sandy miles between east-flowing Lac Laloche and the east-flowing Clearwater. Only local Indian traffic has kept it open. Crossing the famous trail is something few Canadians have ever done. And at its western extremity the trail winds down a 1,000-foot drop, offering a view so spectacular the fur traders commented on it."[21] A few Hudson's Bay folks told Ted that it was still passable; Major

General Elliot Rodger had made the trip some years ago. It was risky, though.

"We would have to climb up that beautiful height, dragging our 400-pound canoes," Ted wrote. "There were ominous tales in the fur trade of a sheer 200-foot drop at one point and of a ledge along which one must walk. How long had it been since that ledge had carried any weight?"[22]

The expedition was a savage grind. The boys fought the currents for miles, drenched with sweat and spray. The canoes were heavily loaded; one ran aground on a gravel bar. At one point, it took nine hours of backbreaking work to make it a mere five miles. It rained except on the days it snowed—in August. The boys camped on muskeg so soft it was like walking on jelly. The portages tested them to the peak of their physical endurance. At several points, they came across signs that First Nations folks still traversed the area: ancient cabins, a wigwam, rotting canoes, and the remains of a recently butchered bear. Then, the climb. Ted recounted it in vivid detail:

> The journals say it's a mile. It seems more like five. Yet in the end there is indeed a great reward. We walk; we rest; we walk again. But the moment comes, very near the top of the trail, when we suddenly emerge from the surrounding forest. The sun blazes around us. We are standing on a ledge that is posed, like a grand balcony, above the most splendid landscape I have ever seen. Sir Alexander did not let us down.
>
> We lower the canoe and slump against it. In panting silence, we gaze awestruck. The entire valley of the Clearwater lies outspread before us. Its distant peaks stand defiant against a sky that blazes sapphire amid cushions of scudding white clouds. Beneath this the hills themselves glitter with every colour of the spectrum, their roots rising from the Clearwater's emerald valley. Finally, serpentine

across this valley lies the blue ribbon of the river itself, the path we had in so many days ascended. Its rapids now dance in the afternoon sun. Far downstream we can make out the spray of White Mud Falls. And beyond that, we know, is Waterways, lost in the gloom of an infinity.

Here on this spot, no doubt, had Sir Alexander stood. Here Sir George had paused. Here too the violent Peter Pond, and the mighty David Thompson himself. Now we had joined them all.

Among the boys, none spoke. A half minute passed, perhaps a minute, as we drank in that which so few had ever tasted. Finally, one of them turned to me as we prepared to move on. His clothes were tattered. His hands were grimy. His face was streaked with sweat and dirt and scratched by an encounter with an overhanging branch. He stared straight into my eyes. "Mr. Byfield," he said in unabashed honesty, "that's the most beautiful thing I've ever seen."

Then I knew that the trip was right. I knew that the flat, simple remark cannot come from the stifled and stunted sterility called "modern living." There was an outbreak of virility here, devastating in its implications. To draw that kind of comment from that kind of boy was the express purpose and intention of much of the nations' educational empire. I knew that the entire phantasmagoria of departments, committees, boards, societies, superintendents, training colleges and their glass-walled palaces was failing almost completely to do it...

For the only reason he really saw the Clearwater Valley was that in those exhausting previous days he had fought and won the Clearwater Valley. And what he had won was beauty and the humility that comes of beholding it. It was his now. No one could ever cheat him of it again. He had tasted the real thing. He might soon say, like Chesterton's "Convert"—"My name is Lazarus and I live." We camped that night atop Methye Heights with a joy that comes only of hard-won victories.[23]

During the descent, they slogged through massive, hardened ruts on the path, which they soon discovered had been made, generations before, by the famous two-wheeled Red River carts used by Métis to haul their belongings and their wares, the greaseless wooden axles producing a shriek that could be heard for kilometres. On the west shore of Lac Laloche, they came in sight of a log cabin and were greeted by a wizened old man who told them that a storm was incoming, and that they were welcome to weather it with the Lafontaine household.

"As our crews prepared the camp, Mr. Lafontaine introduced us to his son, his daughter-in-law and their several children who lived together in the one-room house on the proceeds of trapping and fishing," Ted recalled. "Mrs. Lafontaine, the daughter-in-law, was dark-eyed and pretty, typical of the daughters of the Chipewayans whose fair-skinned beauty had won the heart of many a weary voyageur."

The incoming storm trapped the crew for a day with heavy snowfall, and they visited with the Lafontaines while they waited. Lafontaine's father had come north from St. Boniface in the 1840s with the Hudson's Bay Company, married a Chipewyan girl, and settled at West Laloche to raise a family. The son had never visited his father's hometown, and like most who lived in the area, had never strayed very far. But there was one time, 79 years before, when many had suddenly left. As Ted recalled it:

> He had never been farther away than Waterways to the west and Île-à-la-Crosse to the east. The same was true of most of the people around the lake, he said.

Of course, there was a time when he was a very little boy that all the people of the district had gone south to the prairie country to fight. And he could remember the big fuss when they had taken over the local Hudson's Bay store.

"To fight?" I asked. "To fight whom?"

He couldn't remember, said Mr. Lafontaine. But he did remember that the place they went to was called Batoche and the man who called them there was Louis Riel.

Sitting around a campfire on the shores of Lac Laloche, Ted and the boys came face to face once again with history, just out of reach but yet present in the living memory of an old man who recalled when adults had left home to fight the decisive battle of the North-West Rebellion, which had pitted the Canadian authorities against a defiant force of First Nations and Métis peoples in 1885. After the Battle of Batoche, Louis Riel surrendered and was hung in Regina on November 16 of that year. It was all so very long ago, but on that expedition in 1964 Ted and the boys realized that the events in Francis Parkman's history books were still close enough to reach out and touch.

• • •

In 1965, the Company of the Cross, a lay religious order, was formally created by a bill passed in the Manitoba Legislature. It was based on the Dynevor Society, which the St. John's staff had founded as a community during the first year of the fulltime school. Members of the Company were signing up for a stringent regimen. "They promised to work for room and board plus $1 a day; to say prayers together daily; and to practice a 'rule of candour'—in which they promised not to criticize another member until they made that criticism directly to the member. This 'Rule of Life' they would vow to keep for a year, and then renew each year to the Archbishop of Rupert's Land, H.H. Clark."[24] The low salary was both to ensure the pure motives of the staff and because it was the only way the school could afford to operate.

Money was a perennial problem, and fundraising was constant. A new school building was needed, as a health inspector had informed them that the slumping structures housing the boys wouldn't pass muster much longer. A new 12,000-foot building was erected—costs were reduced on construction projects by utilizing staff and students as free labour. Other fundraisers included selling ham, bacon, and sausage door to door in Winnipeg. Ted's creativity was taxed as they worked out ways to keep the doors open and the programs roaring. As Maunder put it in *Today My Sail I Lift*:

> Ted was an inexhaustible source of energy during those years, recruiting and organizing committees of construction and design people to make the dream real, but more fundamentally, promoting publicity that brought boys and staff to the school—local articles, a *Wall Street Journal* 1966 article "This Could Be The Toughest School In North America"; a 1968 CBC "This Land of Ours" documentary. In those years, there were so many baby boomers turning 12 and 14, and so many parents who shared the value system of the school, that any publicity brought an increasing number of boys. But as Ted knew, when you open yourself up to publicity, you don't have total control, and he was devastated by a 1968 *Weekend* magazine article that criticized the school also under the headline "Toughest School in Canada."[25]

The school would not be financially stable until 1970, due in large part to a financing campaign undertaken by Neil Wood, the father of two boys at St. John's.

The Christianity of St. John's and the Company of the Cross was distinctly Anglican. Sunday services were mandatory, as were the morning and evening prayers on canoe trips. "On lonely, wind-chilled points in the utter wilderness across Western Canada, men and boys would gather and send hymns and plainsong chant up into the night along with the sparks from their campfires," Steve Weatherbe remembered.

Every night at St. John's there would be an optional fifteen-minute service known as Compline (also referred to as Night Prayer or Prayers at the End of the Day). The staff always attended, and many boys were drawn to the chapel to join them in repeating the ancient words with modern relevance: *In Thee O Lord, do I put my trust... Be present, O merciful God, and protect us through the weary hours of this night, so that we who are worried by the changes and chances of this fleeting world, may repose upon Thy eternal changelessness...*

The services always closed with singing. As Maunder remembered it, Ted was drawn to the Irish hymn "Be Thou My Vision"; Frank Wiens loved the German "Fairest Lord Jesus"; Keith Bennett led with the Welsh "The Lord's My Shepherd." The Christianity championed by the Company of the Cross was a muscular one, and the men and boys gravitated towards the hymns of the Church Militant in the "Pilgrimage and Conflict" section of the blue hymnbooks, songs that opened with lines like:

> The Son of God goes forth to war...
> A safe stronghold our God is still...
> Guide me, O Thou great Jehovah...
> Faith of our fathers! Living still...
> He who would valiant be 'gainst all disaster...

And of course, there was the anthem of St. John's, "Today My Sail I Lift":

1965 student canoe brigade photo taken on the school's Red River banks just north of Selkirk, Manitoba after completing the 800-mile trek from Thunder Bay [Ted is on the far right]. This trip would become an annual event for Grade 9 students who, upon crossing the infamously-grueling nine-mile 'Grande Portage' portion, would receive a traditional swig of rum and be officially declared 'hommes du nord' or 'men of the north.'

> I feel the winds of God today;
> today my sail I lift,
> though heavy oft with drenching spray
> and torn with many a rift;
> if hope but light the water's crest,
> and Christ my bark will use,
> I'll seek the seas at his behest,
> and brave another cruise.

Robbie Tomkinson remembered the St. John's "favourite of favourites" being "Jerusalem the Golden," penned by Bernard of Cluny in 1145. "Sung regularly with other muscular hymns in Chapel by baritones Byfield and Neelands, and by tenors Bennett, Wiens and Salway with the rest of us struggling to keep purchase on our paddles," he recalled. "On the best days Nancy and Barbara Wiens added the touch of angels. Softly at first and growing to a great harmonic *shout* that would set off the huskies; *conquered* sung as though it meant something; and a finish that would have more than one tearful eye."

There is the throne of David;
And there, from care released,
The shout of them that triumph,
The song of them that feast,
And they, who with their Leader,
Have conquered in the fight,
Forever and forever,
Are clad in robes of white.

Frequently, boys secretly smoking their last cigarette in the woods before bedtime would be drawn in by the laughter, music, and manly voices. There were also voluntary Bible studies organized by the staff in their homes, where baked goods served to lure in hungry boys. As Maunder recalled it, on Sunday evenings Frank Wiens would deliver a homily "on topics that were of concern to the boys—theft in the dorms, bullying, the way we were treating one another. Behind Frank as he spoke, a cross hung at the centre of a gorgeous illuminated mural. Around it were scenes of boys snowshoeing, studying, canoeing—the immense and full life of the school."

"This was the St. John's Faith," Maunder wrote. "A strong work ethic, pilgrimage and conflict, a small band of brothers on a quest, strong-willed, strong arguments, strong singing, strong action, camaraderie, a community bound by a common philosophy and acting it out in a world that was rapidly losing its faith. And amidst all this strong singing and strong action, there was space for a still small voice, the chance for magic to break through. That ancient liturgy showed again and again its unique grace to allow ordinary, sensual men to approach God and be swept by a sense of sanctity and the divine."[26]

Staff began the day at 6 AM with communal prayer, followed by daily meetings which ran on the principle of unanimity—a single vote could defeat a proposal. Ted's legendary temper was frequently on display during these meetings. Maunder remembered one blowup which had Ted and teacher Frank Doolan crimson with rage as they shouted at one another. Finally, Ted pushed his face into Frank's: "Here, you want to hit me? Go ahead. Give it your best shot. Right here."[27]

Looking back at age ninety, some scenes of the St. John's days remained bright in Ted's memory. The most vivid of them, he told me, were from snowshoeing. "If you're in the middle of a prairie field at night and three miles to your west there's a light in a farmhouse; five miles to the north there's another light; nothing at all to the east—it's like being at sea. There's nothing remotely like it."

"We were in teams of six, moving at the speed of the slowest man. You'd be walking across the prairie, and it was as if you were on another planet. Everything was so strange. The whiteness. The prairie itself just dissolves into the night. It's a haunting kind of feeling. Most of the routes we took were on the opposite side of the river and we had to cross it at night, and you could see at a distance of maybe half a mile the school itself, brightly lit up with the teams coming in from all over the place. The bright school lights after you'd been in the darkness of the prairie for hours struck you as home in a way that I can't remember anything else doing."

• • •

Trouble was soon brewing with the Anglican Church, which Ted felt was moving steadily in a liberal direction—as indeed it was. Ted, as always, was not. During the first years of the school from 1956 to 1970, Ted was backed by clergymen who were strongly supportive of the mission. In 1965, Ted even found himself celebrated by the Anglican hierarchy, receiving an enthusiastic ovation at the synod of Rupert's Land. That same year, legendary Canadian historian Pierre Berton released a broadside against the Anglican Church titled *The Comfortable Pew: A Critical Look at Christianity and the Religious Establishment in the New Age.*

Berton, then a forty-five-year-old journalist, broadcaster, and author, had been commissioned by the Religious Education Department of the Anglican Church to write a report on the state of the Church from the perspective of someone who had abandoned it. Unsurprisingly, Berton excoriated the Church as irrelevant to contemporary society and trapped by the burden of its outdated theology. The Church, Berton wrote, should challenge people to live Christian lives and thus serve as the nation's social conscience. Berton's idea of social justice, however, constituted causes such as the legalization of abortion, and he eventually served as an honourary director for the Canadian Association for the Repeal of Abortion Laws.

It soon became apparent that there was little appetite in the Church to defend traditional Christianity. Worse, many senior clergy agreed with Berton, and so Ted stepped into the gap, penning a small, 149-page book titled *Just Think, Mr. Berton (A Little Harder)*. Published by the Company of the Cross and sold for $1.50, the Company sent salesmen across the country to bookstores to sell the stock. For three months it was a non-fiction bestseller.

The book was classic Byfield—straightforward, savage, and very funny. Ted ruthlessly mocked Berton's objections to Christian values and introduced readers to many of the best arguments for

Christianity by recounting the story of his own conversion to the faith and describing many of the conversations that had so radically changed the course of his life. Ted's hilariously sarcastic recounting of the Church's identity crisis was the perfect way to puncture atheist sanctimoniousness:

> The clergy and laity are constantly being encouraged to make what are technically called "agonizing reappraisals." We have had nearly twenty agonizing reappraisals in the Anglican Diocese of Rupert's Land in the past twelve months, some of them more agonizing than others. I know this because they wanted a layman to lead them. Being a layman, and apparently regarded as sufficiently agonizing, I was called about to lead about ten of these conferences.
>
> The trend started with the Anglican Congress in Toronto in 1963. Our diocese, like others, later held what was quaintly called a "Little Anglican Congress" where the results of the international congress were explained to local church leaders. Naturally the keynote speech was to be called: "What's Wrong With the Church: An Agonizing Reappraisal." I was asked to deliver it.
>
> The Little Congress was so successful (i.e.—we discovered so much wrong with the Church) that even littler Anglican congresses were held in each parish.
>
> At each of the ten which I attended the routine was the same. I would make my speech on what was wrong with the Church; the people would be divided into groups; then each of the groups would reply with what they thought was wrong with the Church.
>
> The results were astounding and the wrongs were rampant. I watched Boy Scout leaders vehemently condemn everything that was wrong with the Boy Scout movement.

I saw vestrymen bitterly denounce both themselves and their vestries. I saw one gentle old lady suddenly become a flaming Jeremiah and savagely pitch into the complacencies of her Ladies Aid, of which she herself was the president.

As critics however all these people suffered from the same handicaps. They belonged to the Church. They were corrupted by presuppositions. They lacked the invaluable objectivity of the outsider...They kept dragging God into it. They could not begin to appreciate the really important matters of our time, like medicare and Playboy magazine. In other words, they conformed.[28]

The book easily constituted the most effective response to both liberalization within the Church and those urging liberalization from outside it.

Ted met Pierre Berton in person only once. The CBC asked Ted if he'd come on and defend the Church against Berton. Ted suggested they might get an actual clergyman. "No, we want you," he was told. Ted had found Berton's book riddled with errors, but the most significant of them was Berton's claim that Jesus was a social reformer who'd been put to death for disturbing the peace. Ted was incredulous when he read this, certain that Berton would correct the error at some point during the book. Jesus had been put to death for blasphemy because He had called Himself God—anyone who had read the New Testament knew this. Berton, it seemed, did not. In his book critiquing Christianity, he had gotten one of the fundamental facts of the Christian story wrong.

Ted brought this up on TV. "Mr. Berton, it says in all four Gospels that He was charged with blasphemy because He called himself God. It doesn't say anything about these troublemaking charges you're mentioning. How come?" Berton stumbled, muttered, and didn't answer. Later, Ted kicked himself—if he'd pressed harder in the moment, he said, "I could've killed him."

Berton was livid. As they were taking off their makeup after the show, Ted heard him muttering under his breath, cursing unnamed "stupid bastards" with premium profanity. As Ted looked at him quizzically, Berton shot him a look. "I didn't mean you," he said. "You did exactly what you should have done. I mean *them*."

"Who's them?" Ted inquired.

"I showed the text of that book to four people in the Anglican church head office, and not one mentioned [that mistake]," Berton replied. "*That's* what I mean."

"That's a better story than the book," Ted laughed later. "He realized that these guys were a bunch of phonies. No properly trained theologian would have missed that. Berton later said it was his worst book. It really was."

Despite that, Berton never held it against Ted—and Ted often credited Berton with rescuing Canadian history from the academics, telling magnificent stories in the tradition of Francis Parkman in the many volumes that followed in the years ahead. "Setting that one book aside, we owe him Canadian history."

• • •

The Company of the Cross soon expanded into Alberta. As usual, the second school was also Ted's initiative. During his trips fundraising for the Manitoba school, he discovered a demand for a similar institution in Alberta, which subsequently opened in 1968. In 1967, Ted launched a publicity stunt to raise funds and volunteers for the new school, rowing from Edmonton to Selkirk with his Grade 8 crew. Property was procured on the banks of the North Saskatchewan River at Genesee and teacher David Thompson was hired as headmaster. The school was created in under two years by Thompson, who organized contractors, architects, and financiers, with construction beginning and carrying on through the winter of 1968. When it opened in the fall, the school was not quite finished, and so the term kicked off with a canoe trip and snowshoe expedition while construction was completed.

Starting a second school soon proved to be more difficult than it seemed. The community that existed in Selkirk was not easily transferable, and with Ted and Thompson busy launching the Alberta school, an entire Grade 12 class in Manitoba failed. Frank Wiens had to deal with two of the best teachers being gone, and tensions rose. "Opening Alberta had been a great step forward, but there had been costs, and many of these deepest costs were in the whole fabric of the Company of the Cross, an understaffed organization still getting used to the intricacies of two distinct operations. Matters came to a head in the winter of 1969 when Ted Byfield was working on the Alberta campus on a fundraising program to help pay for some of Alberta's construction costs."[29] There was a blowup, and things were said. Thompson left, and Keith Bennett took over as headmaster in the fall of 1970.*

From 1970 to 1977, the Company of the Cross experienced explosive growth, much of it driven by Ted. Raising publicity for the schools had been a massive effort, and from 1968 to 1971 Ted had created annual magazines—the *St. John's Report*—booklets, and other pamphlets and publications to draw students and staff to the venture. Inevitably, demand rose for an Ontario school, which took more fundraising and recruiting. The Company of the Cross was even granted "missionary status," which allowed British teachers to show up—the Brits understood the values of such schools better than North Americans.

Not all publicity was good. In 1971, a boy named Markus

---

* Things were later patched up with David Thompson, who eventually sent his son to the school for three years.

In 1965 Ted and Virginia got back into the family game with Vincent [right] and later Thomas [left], an adopted Ojibwe child.

Over the years many Company of the Cross members tied the knot, the first being Ted's lifelong friend Keith Bennett to Clare de Candole.

Janisch collapsed and died during the Interschool Snowshoe Race. The school was not at fault—he was immediately attended by doctors and an autopsy report indicated that he had died from a brain aneurysm, which was undetectable by the medical technology of the time. "This raises the question of how dangerous the Outdoor Program devised largely by Ted was or was not," Steve Weatherbe reflected later, recalling "hairy" canoe trips he took with students. "The truth, in my view, was that Ted was prepared to take risks and trust God, and that the results of this approach sometimes risked boys' lives."* Others strongly disagreed. At every stage, Ted's career provoked strong supporters and detractors.

The press division of the St. John's schools was started in 1971, and the canoe trip that year on Lake Winnipeg was Ted's last major expedition with the school. With the creation of a press division at the Alberta school, Ted's attention was diverted from the schools to what soon became a newsmagazine. Ted, many of

---

* On a canoe trip from the Ontario school on June 11, 1978, 12 students and one staff member died on Lake Temiskaming from hypothermia and drowning. An inquest determined that the expedition could have been better planned, but that the school was not negligent. This occurred years after Ted's involvement with the schools ended.

those who knew him later said, had a pattern: He'd start an enormous project, persuade others to join and backers to materialize, and then be on to the next thing, leaving his previous brainchild in the care of others. As his son Link recalled: "My dad, as most egocentric geniuses do, has the habit of going off course in new and dangerous directions, while my mom ends up doing most of the work. He was the wind in the sails and she was the rudder."[30]

Steve Weatherbe, who was both a teacher and later a journalist with *Alberta Report*, concurred. "Byfield spent a lot of time on fundraising," he said. "He took advice from experts easily and one expert told us to go through the list of previous donors. Ted took many staff into Edmonton to somebody's borrowed office, assigned us each a phone, and off we went. Mostly a wasted effort, yielding me one possibility. My drive to Edmonton yielded me a grudging $10 donation from a man who disagreed with teaching French. This didn't pay for the gas. There is something typical about this in the lack of monitoring or supervision—and the optimism. Ted just assumed things would work out as hoped and moved on to something else." Ted was convicted and self-motivated—and he simply assumed others would be, too.

Another good description of Ted from this period comes from Pat Annesley, a Canadian journalist writing for *Impetus* magazine. In a profile published on September 29, 1973, titled "Ted Byfield: running a revolution on $1 a day," Annesley describes meeting with Byfield to discuss the schools:

> The only thing worse than a born do-gooder is a convert to the field—a blackguard who saw the light, changed his ways and turned into a walking testimonial to the evil of your ways and mine.
>
> But once in awhile, there's one like Ted Byfield. Sixteen years into his do-gooder career, and still coming on like

one of *us*. It's a long time since I've met a 45-year-old man—with or without a cause—who exhibits so little need to prove anything...

Ted, as a married man with six children, earns the standard St. John's salary: $1 a day plus $10 a month clothing allowance, monthly insurance premium ($25 for a married man) and $150 per person vacation pay for a two-week vacation. He looks embarrassed when he talks about it, as he does about pretty well anything even vaguely noble-sounding, as we sit talking in an Edmonton all-night restaurant.

He's wearing gray cotton pants, shirt and windbreaker. His hair is shorter than the current fashion dictates. All of which seems supremely irrelevant. He's a man with a good, strong face, a quiet but occasionally fierce manner. If you're a several-generations Canadian he's bound to remind you of your pioneer forbears. Contained strength might be the right expression. He laughs a lot, embarrassed but not embarrassingly, as he talks about his convictions, his so-called sacrifice of a promising future in journalism.

Of his earnings he says: "Well, that's not exactly prosperity. But you're sure not doing without anything. I've never once heard of anyone having a feeling of deprivation. There's a greater sacrifice in the limitations on your freedom of movement. That's what you notice. There's a certain amount of example-setting involved in this business, you know. But the conviction that you're doing the right thing...well, that's a gratification you just can't match."

His whole demeanour says he will forever see himself as an imperfect man. And that doesn't mean self-effacing. But his standards are high. He even minimizes his original transition from the would-be journalist star to the practising Christian, depicting it in terms of the directional crisis of today's average man.

"You come to a point where you realize you're not going to do all the things you thought you were going to do. You begin to question your judgement in wanting them in the first place. And eventually you begin to look around for more permanent values. You think: I'm going to be going from this earth in 50 or 60 years, and nobody's going to know it. Nobody will remember it. So...you look around and see what you can do for today."

"Your rejection of these things—status, future—is never successful really. You're always lured back to the glitter of this world."

Example? "Sure. Good example. When a lady calls up and says we're going to do a story on you in *IMPETUS*, I get all excited. And that's wrong. It's wrong to feel that success and failure depend on how much attention is paid to you in this world." Again the self-conscious laugh. As though he's all too aware that the values and concepts we've been discussing don't seriously fit into the world from which he surely thinks I've come: Toronto sophisticate. Bay Street. Profit above all.

Actually, of course, we were all figuratively born on a farm in Saskatchewan. We look upon the Ted Byfields of the world not with ridicule but, far more than we would admit, with envy.[31]

Little did Annesley—or Ted—know that he was about to embark on the second act of his life as a public Christian. This time, he would return to journalism—and transform Canada's political landscape in the decades ahead.

CHAPTER FIVE

A CHRISTIAN VOICE ENTERS THE MEDIA ARENA

The only people in Canada doing anything
worthwhile are those Byfields out West.

—George Grant, philosopher and
author of *Lament for a Nation*

I t was characteristic of Ted Byfield to launch a massive new
endeavour while his current mission was just taking off. Many
of his friends and former colleagues suspect that his frenetic
character and tendency to grow bored the moment routine
set in ensured that he leapt from one thing to the next, leaving
others—including Ginger and his children—struggling to keep up.
Just as his launch of the schools with Frank Wiens had overlapped
with his career at the *Winnipeg Free Press*, his second act as a newspaperman began while he was still managing the schools.

Although it seemed for a time that Ted had permanently departed the news business for a career as a teacher, it was the Company
of the Cross that provided him a path back into journalism. The
printing division set up at the Alberta school was initially intended
to be a meat processing plant producing money for St. John's,

but that scheme was derailed when it turned out that municipal regulations in Edmonton and Calgary forbade it. Ted decided to set up a printing division instead, and throughout 1971-72, they began doing small jobs. As usual, the workload was alleviated by a crew of students. As always, Ted soon began to envision something much larger.

The Company of the Cross had been formed to counter society's rapid departure from its Christian roots. The St. John's schools were an alternative to the public system. Ted felt that a newsmagazine produced by the Company's printing division could serve those fed up with the increasingly secular establishment media. He had long believed that secular culture was usurping two of society's four key institutions, education and the media (the others being the church and the family). With the schools, he and his partners had sought to address the first. With that underway, Ted set out to fill the media vacuum.

Staff were rapidly recruited: Gord Dewar, Gord Salway, Robbie Tomkinson, Rod Coates, Clint Kelly, Steve Weatherbe, Edwin Callaway, Aleta Schaedel, Dan Post, Doug Hoover. There were Byfields, too—Ginger, their daughter Philippa, and sons Mike, Vincent, and later Link would all eventually join the team—and Ted's father Vernon also reappeared "just in time to handle Alberta's Cosmopolitan Life Assurance scandal, one of the magazine's first major financial stories."* By 1973-74, there were over 25 staffers inhabiting trailers on the property of the Alberta school to man the growing press division. Things were getting crowded, and larger presses and more staff were soon necessary.

---

* Son Mike and daughter Philippa were all cranking out copy early on. Eight-year-old Vincent was cleaning the press for a princely sum of 60 cents an hour (a king's ransom compared to his parents' dollar-a-day salaries). Link signed on later to cover agriculture and youngest son Thomas bicycled down every street in Edmonton to verify maps for the *Atlas of Alberta*.

Cover of the 1973 pilot edition of *St. John's Edmonton Report* [inset] and some of its crew [left to right]: Robbie Tomkinson, Gord Salway, Mike Maunder, Ted Byfield, Gordon Dewar, Djeloul Marbrook, Eldon Milnes, Aleta Shadel (later Voss), and Mike Byfield.

To attract more members for the Company of the Cross, Ted ran ads all over the continent, hoping to attract people insane enough to live on a dollar a day. Many came; most stayed only a few months. Some stayed for years. Ralph Hedlin described the hilarity that ensued in *Alberta Report's* 1983 commemorative decennial edition:

> There was, for instance, an itinerant priest who was named 'sales manager.' He would return from Edmonton daily, either proclaiming himself 'slain in the spirit' and demanding prayers of thanksgiving from all, or else drunk, which was less taxing spiritually though not reassuring from a business point of view. There was a former hospital orderly who came as a truck driver. On one of his first trips to Edmonton he drove away from an A&W stand dragging away most of its canopy with him because he forgot he

136

was in a truck. There was a self-proclaimed southern lady who spent her first week closeted in her room, then mysteriously left so that practically no one learned her name, and a retired regimental sergeant major who tried so hard to be a lithographer that he became, he said, 'tense.' This condition he relieved by getting permanently and incoherently drunk so that he had to be hospitalized. Later there was to be a reporter who found covering the Edmonton city council so unnerving that he retreated to his bedroom and sat for hours on the floor rocking back and forth in agonizing rhythm.

Not all recruits, however, were losers. From New Orleans came one Richard Salmonson, experienced machinist, who took pity upon Mr. Byfield's efforts with the presses, persuaded him that he could be better occupied elsewhere, learned the machine rapidly and mastered it. From rural Manitoba came a towering ex-Royal Roads cadet named Gordon Salway who began driving the truck (the hospital orderly having altogether given up on it) and stayed to learn accountancy and steer the enterprise through the gruesome financial storms that lay ahead of it.[2]

There were also recruits like Saskatchewan-born illustrator Milton Fredlund, who set up the art department and began producing the first quality magazine covers, and Keith Bennett, who left his job as headmaster of the St. John's School of Alberta to run the press division's recruiting centre with his wife Clare. Many talented staffers switched from the school to the magazine. This caused tension between the two ventures, which were increasingly working at cross-purposes by dipping into the same pool of people and funds.

The press division was initially funded by a major printing contract set up by Trev Caithness, a parent of one of the schoolboys.

The Multiple Listings Service (MLS) contract consisted of printing a roughly 500-page directory of properties for the Edmonton Real Estate Board. It was an enormous task, with school staff joining the press division (and local hired help) at 4 AM every Monday to get it underway. The cash from this endeavour, which was worth some $7,000 a week, provided the capital necessary to launch the *St. John's Edmonton Report*. The difficulty, of course, was that the press division and the school staff increasingly inhabited entirely different spheres. "'Like ships passing in the night,' Ted commented to one teacher as they passed in the halls that year. The teacher's mind was filled with today's marking and tomorrow's classes; Ted's was filled with printing contracts and laying out schedules for the newsmagazines, reporters, and the real estate book."[3]

Despite the MLS contract, the slender budget demanded frugality. Thus, the cheap—or more accurately, affordable—press equipment Ted purchased was almost constantly breaking down, triggering similar malfunctions in stressed-out staff members. The affordable machinery would rapidly become unaffordable as it succumbed under the strain of utility, throwing the printing schedule into disarray and ensuring that new, more expensive replacements needed to be purchased in addition to the initial money-saving junk that had already been acquired. Pricey lessons were learned and relearned.

By the fall of 1973, the press was bringing in revenue but there was no evidence that a market existed for a newsmagazine. In December, the subscriber list numbered a mere 800 (schoolboys had tried to sell subscriptions door to door with limited success). With bills mounting and reporters commuting at least thirty miles into Edmonton each day to cover stories through record snowfalls. The reasonable thing to do would have been to cut losses and close down. Instead, Ted decided to expand. In 1974, the growing team of more than forty press staff moved into Edmonton after only six editions of the magazine, renting three suites in the Palisades

Apartments for the editorial staff with tables, chairs, cooking utensils, and bedding tossed in. Offices were found in the Tegler Building, with the team trooping back to the school each weekend to help the school staff set type and catch sleep.

The move was financed by a dramatic spike in subscriptions—and more assistance from Trev Caithness, who had helped land the real estate contract. The subscriptions came as a result of an American recruit, a former office manager of Bell & Howell in San Francisco named Calvin Demmon with aspirations of becoming a writer. He told Ted that he'd recently paid for university tuition as a telemarketer, and Ted told him that if he sold 10,000 subscriptions, he'd make Demmon a reporter. According to Ralph Hedlin, Demmon and a team of telemarketers pulled off this feat in six months.[4] By 1976, subscriptions had surpassed 20,000 and the press team—with recruits from all over the world—had grown to over sixty.

The team soon moved again, decamping from the Palisades to a building secured by Caithness. Ralph Hedlin described the move in *Alberta Report*, which included six married couples with children:

> In a transaction that has remained something of a mystery, [Trev Caithness] arranged for a company to acquire a 20-suite apartment building on 149 Street in west Edmonton for a down payment of $1. (When the time came to pay the $1, it transpired that purchaser Byfield was carrying no money whatsoever. Mr. Caithness wound up advancing the dollar as well.) At the same time, the printing equipment was moved to an office-warehouse plant on 142 Street.[5]

The low-rise apartment on 149 Street and 91st Avenue was called Waverly Place, and Ted remembered it as "like a monastery in some ways. There was a fleet of four or five cars, and you could sign out a car and take it wherever you needed to go. We couldn't afford

journalists at first, so we made journalists. We got a few people with experience, but first they'd join the Company of the Cross and live in the apartment block and learn how to write. We were running the best journalism school in Canada because everything was real."*
One of the basement apartments was turned into a chapel and distribution centre for groceries. Sixty-to-seventy-hour work weeks were the norm, and staff turnover was high—during a postal strike in 1975, staff even delivered the magazines all over the snowy city.

"The whole lifestyle was surreal," Vince Byfield remembered. People lived more or less on top of each other. The communal cars had to be signed out, but many people absconded without bothering to use the required sheet, causing fierce altercations with those left behind. The children were often left in the hands of some truly oddball characters. An Indigenous fellow named Wild Bill who frequently worked up north, allegedly pulling up fenceposts with his bare hands, was occasionally left to babysit. It was difficult to put both the magazine and the kids to bed at the same time, and thus the offspring of the staff were often left to fend for themselves.

The Byfield apartment featured a twelve-foot-long table with benches on both sides so that the many bachelor reporters who couldn't be bothered to cook for themselves could join for supper. Ginger was renowned for quite literally throwing meals together— as Keith Bennett remembered it, she'd chop up various foodstuffs, toss them into a pot, cook them for a few minutes, and then onto the table it went.

There were squabbles, including the 1976 "Great Liquor Ad War" during which several staffers vociferously objected to running any ads from booze companies. Ted, as a patron of such companies, was keenly aware of the hypocrisy that would accompany

---

* Ted generally preferred "reporter" to "journalist," which, he would often note derisively, was just a reporter with a beret and an umbrella.

any formal refusal and just as vociferously disagreed. Six staffers ended up quitting over the fiasco, including a young typesetter who announced that she was returning to her previous job, which turned out to be waitressing at a bar in San Francisco. Ted was encouraged enough by this discord to launch the *St. John's Calgary Report* the following year, "literally in the shadow of the Crowchild and Bow Trails, under a confusion of ramps and concrete pylons."[6] When at one point the discount office space hosted a fire, investigators speculated that the blaze might have been set to cover up a possible robbery evidenced by the shamble of papers, type-writers, books, and other equipment strewn about. Staff told them it always looked like that.

[Left photo] Supper at the Byfield apartment on Edmonton's 149 Street typically included a half-dozen single men. [Clockwise from bottom right] Vincent, Thomas, Virginia and Ted, Ed Calloway, and Joe Slay. [Photo below] Two services were held daily at the apartment chapel. [Left to right] Ed Vornholt, Don Dowd, Ted, Virginia, Sally Cleary, Suzy Schadel, Aleta Schadel (later Voss), and Father Sargeant.

Running two magazines in two different cities, however, was brutal for Ted and editors Joe Slay and Steve Hopkins, who had to edit more or less around the clock. By 1979—the year *Alberta Report* was formally born—it became untenable for Ted's media venture to remain with the Company. The dollar-a-day and communal living system had allowed the magazine to get off the ground in record time, but it proved unsustainable. Despite Ted's second-to-none recruiting abilities, he needed to offer sizeable salaries to attract staff with specific skills—not only reporters, whom he trained himself, but printers, machinists, and accountants. The Company had been founded to offer alternatives to secular culture, but it had been designed for schools, not magazines.

The switch to hiring had helped to onboard badly needed staff, but it had also offloaded badly needed money. Bills were frequently 120 days past due—even the Toronto-Dominion Bank's loan of $300,000 (with part of the school's property as security) promptly vanished. Ted desperately hunted for money wherever it could be found, soliciting loans from St. John's supporters that benefactors knew could likely never be repaid, with the two magazines losing around $10,000 weekly. Staffers handled creditor calls constantly, and each new edition of the magazine became a near-miraculous event. A key problem was an inability to afford paper, the necessary ingredient of both the magazines and the Edmonton real estate catalogue.

"What continued to keep them afloat at all, of course, were the weekly cheques from the real estate board and the daily flow of subscriber renewal cheques," Hedlin recorded. "But with the bank increasingly restive and the paper companies unwilling to release stocks without certified cheques, converting the deposits into cash for the paper became a hazardous business. The Byfield-invented solution for this was to have several bank accounts, one of them always healthy enough to put the cheques in and get the cash out."[7]

When the mail with the cheques arrived, staffers would race to the bank with the healthy account, obtain a certified cheque, and then speed to the warehouse. After the payment was suspiciously examined, the paper would be hastily loaded onto the truck and ferried back to feed into the waiting presses. This was the status quo for months.

The crisis grew even more pronounced when the financial committee of the St. John's schools decided to cut their losses, passing a resolution that publication of the magazines be halted. Ted begged for one more week, fundraised twenty $6,500 cheques from twenty foolhardy Albertans, and providentially met Al Hardy of Saxon International (providentially for Ted, anyway). Hardy was an entrepreneur working from the 14th floor of the Cambridge Building on Edmonton's Jasper Avenue, and he was fascinated by the publishing business. He cut Ted a cheque for $6,500, looked over his financial statements, and told him to double the price of the magazine or he'd go broke. If people wanted the product, Hardy informed the reluctant publisher, they'd pay more for it.

This was not so much the turning point as the moment the magazines went from an ongoing financial disaster to a publication with a potential future—and one that would go on to shape the titular province. Hardy transformed the magazine not only with desperately needed infusions of cash, but the equally necessary business advice. Hardy told Ted that all staff needed to be salaried—no two-tiered system with some getting paid a dollar a day through the Company and others getting full wages. He also advised them to merge the two magazines into one—the *Alberta Report*. He head-hunted staff, lent Ted his accounting and financial advisors to staunch the bleed (it was, after all, his blood), and lent the magazine $300,000 without a written agreement. In the winter of 1979-80, it was privately agreed that the magazine was his, a sale formalized in May 1980, with Ted maintaining editorial control.[8]

Ted's growing detachment from the schools was a major blow to the St. John's team, and there were misunderstandings and fierce debates as he shifted from involvement with the schools' operations to full-time with the growing newsmagazine, although for a time he maintained his role as director of the Company of the Cross and remained connected in an advisory role. His presence, however, was badly missed, as his energy and focus had been a key driver of the schools' vision.

Mike Maunder described the breaking point, which came in 1979:

> Ted and the press division were under extreme financial pressure (as they had been from the beginning, and as they would be for almost their entire history). One possible source of relief would be to take a mortgage on the Alberta school's property, but the financial committee of the three schools was not keen. At a broader Company meeting, the mortgage was declined and Ted had to set out to find other financing. Shortly after, the strains of running a press, running a magazine, seeking financing and attempting to run a national Company of the Cross just became too much; Ted and the press division made the decision to pull out of the Company of the Cross.[9]

At 51 years old, Ted Byfield was starting over once again.

• • •

Ted's newsroom, former staffer Paula Simons would remember fondly, was an explosive place, one which would "erupt frequently in loud, passionate political quarrels—not to mention personal ones. People shouted. They threw things. They stomped out in fits of pique. They rushed to the bank with their paycheques to make sure they didn't bounce. It was mad. It was wicked. It was heaven."[10] Or as another writer described the staff of *Alberta Report*: "In a country that prizes consensus, they were pranksters, merry hecklers, the nail that wears the hammer out, refusing to yield."[11]

The *St. John's Edmonton Report* launched in 1973, *St. John's Calgary Report* in 1977, and the two merged into *Alberta Report* in 1979. Along with other offshoot publications including *Western Report* (1983) and *BC Report* (1989), the tiny press division of the Edmonton school grew into a conservative media empire spanning Western Canada. The magazines were not explicitly Christian publications but, as Ted liked to say, they reported the news "as if Christianity were true." Every publication had a worldview, and Ted made no apologies for writing from his. He intended to counter the secular press, and the only difference was that he was honest about his perspective.

To launch a magazine, one needed a vision. Characteristically, Ted had one. Like many of his generation, he was an admirer of *Time*. In an era of print dailies, *Time*'s editors had launched a phenomenally successful weekly newsmagazine. Not incidentally, *Time*'s co-founder Henry Luce was a staunch anti-communist, giving the magazine a distinctly conservative flavour (which would vanish entirely in later years). *Time* had also perfected the art of following up on news stories to give details that initial reporting from the dailies had left out.*

"I thought this could be done on a local basis because so many of the towns and cities only had one newspaper," Ted recalled. "Calgary had two and Edmonton had one, but one had folded.

---

* Ted even adopted *Time*'s iconic, red-framed cover, and *Time* sent him a legal letter informing him that this broke trademark law. Ted declined to change his cover and instead launched a publicity campaign to inform other publications about the developing story. Begrudgingly, *Time* dropped the case. "We're terribly gratified," Byfield told *Maclean's* in 1983, "that [*Time*] would look down from New York and consider us a problem."

This monopoly resulted in dull reporting." There was the radio, of course, which meant little—and TV, which at the time meant even less. Most newspapers reported on a story and moved on. "If a story broke on Thursday, there were events that happened on Friday and Saturday that never got covered because they were no longer 'news.' By completing those stories, you got a new, breaking story. By doing this, we developed the technique of a newsmagazine on a local basis. It worked." Not only did it work, but *Alberta Report* also had a distinct advantage, as they could build on the initial reporting of the newspapers and the radio reporters as a starting point.

Alberta Report was a general newsmagazine, which meant it covered fires, accidents, crimes—the works. Unlike publications such as *Christianity Today*, *AR* was not overtly Christian. But if there was an applicable Christian position to take, Ted noted, "we would exercise the opportunity to point out the moral implications not often mentioned by the daily papers." By reporting from an implicitly Christian perspective rather than an explicit one, Ted soon began to garner a large audience. This made the *Report* magazines unique. Few other Christian publications since have picked up on what Ted pioneered.

As Ted put it in an address to the Company of the Cross in 1976: "Effective propaganda in the print media must be subtle. It's the implied lifestyle, the inferable values, the unsubstantiated moral assumption, that gets through. That's how the media works in any cause, Christian or anti-Christian. No, we do not have a cross on the cover. What we put on the cover is designed to entice people into the magazine. What matters is not that we look Christian, but that we are Christian."[12]

In most instances, Byfield and his staff could find a better, more comprehensive story than had been initially reported. Byfield would comb through newspapers from the *Toronto Star* and *Globe and Mail* to the prairie papers and, just as Vernon had taught him

146

back in Washington, D.C., pinpoint stories he felt had been poorly covered. When a big story broke, the *Report* would simply wait for more details to emerge, and then publish the "big picture." Predictably, this strategy made them few friends in the media world.

"This angered the dailies because they saw that we were using them as a tip sheet," Ted chortled later. "A lot of fights broke out. The most awful one was between me and the publisher of the *Edmonton Journal* (later of the *Calgary Herald*), Pat O'Callaghan. He was an Irishman, but a product of the British newspaper business. He wrote an article for a Saturday night magazine on me and *Alberta Report* years after the fight began, and it was apparently so libellous that they couldn't think about running it. I never did find out what was in it. He just loathed us."

Ted, for his part, was a gleeful participant in stoking the animosity. J. "Pat" O'Callaghan never went by his first name, so Ted launched a search to find out what it was and discovered, to his delight, that it was Jeremiah. Thereafter, to O'Callaghan's fury, Ted and his staff referred to him exclusively as Jeremiah P. O'Callaghan. O'Callaghan's irritation increased as Ted's children joined the family media business. "One Byfield was enough," he purportedly growled. "Now there's all these *little* Byfields, too."

• • •

Ted's recruiting efforts were unorthodox, constant, and frequently hilarious. "Gin and I must have gone on twenty recruiting trips, including to England two or three times," he recalled. "We'd pay their way over, they'd have a place to live, money for food. It wasn't a bad thing as long as they worked a five-day week." Most of the hires were Christian. Many of them said they were but weren't. Some of them said they weren't, and Ted hired them anyway because he thought they were good people. Several staffers told Ted later that they'd been nominal Christians, but that being surrounded by sincere Christians—there were mandatory chapel services at the magazine every morning and evening—brought them back to church. Later in life, he never tired of recounting these stories, and considered them among *AR's* greatest accomplishments.

It would take volumes to describe the eccentric and sometimes crazy characters who answered Ted's call to work in the magazine business. Ted's habit of "helping strays" and his Christian belief that everyone was entitled to multiple chances had some interesting results. One fellow from Ontario, for example, hung an axe behind his press with a sign reading: "For settling arguments." Most of his arguments were with production manager Robbie Tomkinson, who could not help but take this personally. Ted assured him that he was overreacting, and it was not until a week after the man quit that they discovered his impressive criminal record, which included assault with an assortment of deadly weapons.

In another instance, a psychiatrist friend of Ted's asked him for help rehabilitating a murderer who had been declared not guilty by reason of insanity and locked up in a mental hospital for ten years. The man had just been deemed fit for part-time release and was hankering to write. Ted agreed, as he needed a second-shift proofreader. When the fellow arrived, Steve Hopkins recalled, he "actually looked like he might be diabolically insane, projecting an eerie calmness due, I suspected, to some medication." Ted assured his editors that this person was no longer dangerous, while neglecting to mention the matter of the murder. He was let go after his creepiness led at least one woman to quit, unreasonably reject- ing the reassurance that a psychiatrist had approved the twitchy patient for part-time work.

"Then there was the folder operator who insisted on reading the Bible on the job while his machine sped on until it jammed, a typesetter who developed the habit of setting her own opinions in the midst of stories, and a former Playboy bunny who eloped with another recruit, a hippy-style photographer," Ralph Hedlin recalled in 1983. "She married him, only to discover that the man was married already. 'What can I do about that?' Mr. Byfield asked a friend who was a crown prosecutor. 'When you've told me, you've already done it,' the prosecutor replied. The man was arrested, charged, and served three months—practically the only bigamy case prosecuted in Alberta in the latter half of the 20th century."[13]

An applicant named Joanne Hatton from Sarnia, Ontario replying to an ad for a proofreader, on the other hand, ended up as a reporter, married Link Byfield in 1981, and stuck around.

Ted's recruiting trips frequently resulted in unlikely success. Steve Hopkins, for example, served at the *Alberta Report* for fourteen years as a reporter, editor, and editor-in-chief—but when Ted called him, he initially forgot he'd even applied for a job. It was 1976, he'd recently quit his job as a schoolteacher, was living in his parent's basement in New York State, and had responded to an ad in *The Buffalo News* advertising "An Adventure in Western Canada." Ted told him in a letter that the quickest way to figure out what journalism entailed was to watch *All the President's Men*, on the *Washington Post* reporters who had uncovered Watergate and brought down Richard Nixon.

Hopkins watched it, liked it, and heard nothing. Then he woke up to a phone call one morning at 7:15 AM. Ted and Ginger had already driven past his driveway once and were wondering if he could be ready for the interview in say, two minutes? Hopkins gulped coffee, pulled some clothes on, requested a half hour, and got twenty minutes. The interview was somewhat unpromising, with Ginger muttering to Ted that families had a hard time with the constraints of the Company of the Cross.

A week later, Ted called Hopkins and told him that the magazine was flying him to Edmonton for a five-day trial to see if he'd cut it. As Hopkins described it:

> During my initial trial at the magazine, Ted gave me a valuable reporting lesson by taking me to a regular meeting of the Edmonton Public School Board. An audience of 40 or so were in attendance along with a few reporters. Ted positioned the two of us so he could quietly explain things to me. As each new topic came up, he told me whether or not it might be a story—and why. (Was there a controversy? A principle at stake? A conflict of authority? An odour of malfeasance or sheer incompetence?) As the evening wore on, he grouped together each set of new notes identified by topic. At the end of the meeting, he held notes for six potential stories.
>
> At one point Ted brashly stood up with his camera, walked in front of everybody in the audience temporarily blocking views, and then proceeded around the participant's table and started taking pictures. He seemed visibly delighted with the occasional scowls of board members as he snapped various close-ups. Mid-way through the meeting, a 15-minute recess was called. Ted gestured toward a coffee pot where all the reporters (radio, TV, and newspaper) were gathered: "See what those guys are doing, talking to each other? Don't do that!" Instead, he explained, start asking questions to a trustee or administrator to follow up story possibilities. And that's just what he did as I tagged along. We followed up with more quick interviews after the meeting.
>
> On our way back to the apartment house, Ted reiterated his points: usually reporters from all other local media

outlets simply restated what was said in these meetings. They talked to one another way too much. I would need to tell our readers more—preferably with more insight. Similarly, I should always be taking fresh photos. All of our reporters had to use cameras because our one full-time photographer couldn't be everywhere. For his magazine, Ted said, I would always have to dig for additional information. I must never shy away from asking any question—no matter how simplistic or "stupid" it seemed.

Ted's informal, on-the-job journalism school became famous across the country. He loved explaining the mechanics of news stories (just as his father had for him) and would often submit his staff to exercises such as: "Rewrite this paragraph using half as many words without losing one fact." He would take apart stories the way a mechanic deconstructed engines to illustrate how they worked and why, and was obsessive about logic, clarity, and consistency. He also enjoyed providing formal instruction "by talking so loud on the phone that everybody else could hear how he conducted interviews, the kinds of questions he asked and how he came at questions from a variety of angles," Hopkins recalled. "He also liked to reframe people's answers and often read back for approval new quotations that made them sound witty and insightful."

Steve Weatherbe, who was recruited to the *Report* from the staff of the school in 1975, remembers staff coming from as far away as Switzerland. He shared an apartment in the complex with two other single guys—families ate together, and singles ate communally. As Weatherbe recalled it:

> Ted recruited Christians, along with older experienced journalists who had been sacked, usually for alcoholism. Ted believed in second and third chances. The training was

on-the-job—as usual, Ted flung himself into the project entirely. He staged a couple of memorable seminars on how to write a newsmagazine, but not too much on how to report. We were on our own and the results were often amateurish because Ted and the few pros on staff couldn't catch everything. I certainly was at a loss in several jobs— for example, in Edmonton I was assigned to the legislature with no idea how to do it. Nonetheless, *St. John's Edmonton Report* soon became well-known and controversial; a success, if underfinanced by its subscription stream.

It was Christian, with explicit coverage of religion and editorials by Ted every week, which were often Christian in theme or topic (about events in the Anglican or other Christian communities.) I quickly got handed the job of reviewing live theatre, because I had been active in theatre and because I was downtown anyway covering the courts. This provided another opportunity to moralize or theologize as only an arrogant and inexperienced twenty-something can do. As the only glossy and sometimes colour publication publishing soon after a play's opening to affect the box office, our opinion was regarded as important, though mildly deranged. I got whimsical recognition for the Christian stance I often took in theatre reviews when the theatre community staged a fundraiser for some cause and enlisted the city's reviewers to provide the entertainment. Each reviewer got a rubber duck award, appropriately adorned. Mine had a tinfoil lance and helmet and was called "the medieval crusader award." Bang on.

The holes in Ted's training, Hopkins recalled, were often derived from the fact that "Ted was so incredibly smart that even the big star journalists that came out of the magazine couldn't match him—there was nobody like him. He expected everybody to be smarter and couldn't understand why we weren't as brilliant as he was. He didn't see himself that way, but he was."

Hopkins gave one example of this. Ted was working on a tricky, complicated story at his desk that was due imminently—the magazine needed to go out, and Hopkins was waiting on him. Ted didn't appear to be typing anything. At 11:30 AM, Ted stood and announced that he was going to lunch, which he never missed. Hopkins was annoyed and a little worried. Ted strolled back into the office an hour and a half later,

Ted Byfield tackled by Nader Ghermezian during a stakeout of the back entrance of Edmonton's Law Courts building. Nader successfully destroyed Ted's camera, but a CBC news cameraman got the entire event on film.

and Hopkins headed to his desk. "How's that story coming?"

"It's great," Ted replied. "Don't worry. I wrote it over lunch." There was nothing in front of him. Then he said: "All I have to do is type it out." He'd written the full article in his head, and over the next hour, he banged out a few thousand words in his loud, two-fingered typing style. He submitted it on time.

• • •

Writing for *Alberta Report* in the early days was like entering the Wild West of journalism or, as one veteran put it, "like going through the war with your buddies." The magazine not only covered news—*AR* delivered dispatches from the front lines of the culture wars. Ted often relished the brawls that resulted. "[T] he combative, aggressive journalism he practiced and promoted had more than a whiff of brimstone about it, and that was an intoxicating lure," another *AR* alumni recalled.[14]

Everyone worked like dogs, frequently from 6:30 AM until early the next morning. "Times without number we sat up all night to get the magazine to the printer early in the morning," Ted recalled. "We'd work all night. Sometimes we assisted that process, late at night when people were almost done. I'd slip over to the liquor store before it closed at 11 and bring back a bottle. We'd get out the paper at 1 AM, have a small party, and head off to bed. It was a joyous thing. We worked very hard." There were weeks where Ted put in at least eighty hours— "my wife was only working 75," he said with a chuckle. It was common to see staffers catching a few minutes of sleep at their desks.

At one point during the early years, Ted and another editor fell asleep in an Edmonton tavern after working a 72-hour shift, their half-drunk pints resting next to them. The waiter woke the men up and asked them to leave lest they give the establishment a bad name.

"In almost any social setting—and certainly in his newsroom— Ted was an electrifying presence," Steve Hopkins remembered. "He projected energy that affected (and usually stressed) everyone around him. His very presence pumped up the adrenaline throughout the staff. Seeing him at his desk was a perpetual reminder that your reporting and writing absolutely had to meet his high standards. All reporters and editors had to be willing to devote an extraordinary amount of time to the job week after week—and to suspend their personal lives and plans on a moment's notice for the sake of a story."

Ted's tantrums as he tried to cajole good writing out of his staff were legendary, although he insisted that he never fired anyone while he was mad. "I probably looked preposterous," he said later. "All kinds of stories started circulating, about how I put my fist through a wall one time. That was wrong. I actually put a telephone through a wall, which my fist was holding."

Another legend had it that Ted got so angry after a story was screwed up that he thundered into one of the bathrooms and wrenched a sink off the wall. Others remembered him flinging coffee cups across the room. Turning in bad photographs for a story was almost guaranteed to be extremely provoking, and half-serious threats of violence could result. Considering the debilitating hours he worked and the constant financial pressure he was under, Ted's hair-trigger temper during the early years was unsurprising.

As Hopkins would recall it:

> Ted could be accurately labeled charismatic, charming, extremely intelligent, ambitious, energetic, imaginative, and optimistic. He was also strong-willed, demanding, and relentless in pursuit of a goal and defiantly independent and passionate about his beliefs and views. He was very witty with an appreciation of irony and a ready sense of humour (which was often self-deprecating). On the other hand, he was known to be manipulative, stubborn, obsessive, and capable of flamboyant temper tantrums. He was given to sudden bursts of outrage and capable of becoming a bully who might belittle subordinates and humiliate them with harsh criticism in front of their newsroom peers.

Which is not to say that Ted did not enjoy the fights. As he noted in his description of an office argument over a review of an Alberta photo exposition: "It provoked one of those uninhibited discussions. That is to say, people were yelling at each other, fingers were waving, and there was much jeering, taunting, absurd wagering, crude gesturing to underline telling points, and occasional desk-pounding orders to shut up and listen. In short it had all the essentials of meaningful philosophic and religious discourse, which resolves everything except the points at issue because eventually nobody can remember what they were. I myself felt especially gratified by this extravaganza because I was the one who started it."[15]

A profile of Ted published by the CBC in 2020 described him during those years as a cross between Humphrey Bogart and *60 Minutes* newsman Mike Wallace:

> The ramshackle Report office saw editors working at desks pushed together to resemble a table for six, firing away on typewriters loaded with eight-by-eleven-inch paper. When stories were completed, editors would staple them together and place them in a basket.
>
> "And Ted would come whirling in from a meeting and the copy would pile up," said former *Maclean's* senior writer D'Arcy Jenish, the Report's first Ottawa bureau chief. "He'd sit at the head of the table and start fishing out the stories in the copy basket...he'd get to yours, and you'd be on pins and needles hoping you got things right. Because if you didn't, the whole newsroom would hear about it."[16]

Ted's staff usually forgave him because he was a strict but extraordinary teacher, just as his father had been. It is true that bad copy could trigger outbursts. "But his appreciation of quality work was just as enthusiastic, and the writers who could handle the pressure blossomed beneath it," Carey Toane wrote in the *Ryerson Review of Journalism*. "His search for raw, malleable talent developed into a habit of rescuing strays, and the stories of transforming cab drivers, dropouts and barflies into competent reporters have graduated into legend. Like many editors, Byfield looked not for credentials or degrees, but instead for 'an infatuation for language...to be able to joyously tell a story is one of the essentials of a reporter, who is essentially a storyteller.'"[17]

Steve Hopkins recalled one moment when Ted was being particularly pigheaded about something especially unreasonable, a trait of his that could drive his colleagues mad. Hopkins let him have it loudly, and when Ted appeared impervious to his rebukes, turned to Ginger. "And you're *married* to him," Hopkins declaimed in disbelief. Ginger nodded. "And it's no better." And then, a moment later with a little smile: "But it's no worse, either."

As Gord Salway, who worked for the magazines for ten years, put it: "I've never loved and hated somebody so much in my life."

• • •

No history of *Alberta Report* is complete without a recognition of the fundamental role played by Ginger Byfield. Ted would have been lost without her. Her wit, editorial skills, and constant presence sustained both him and his many endeavours, including the newsmagazines. He never published a single word, he once said, without having Ginger look it over first.* While Ted was often rushing about fundraising and promoting *Alberta Report*, his wife took a direct role in overseeing the magazine.

Ginger was a lethal editor, and reporters trembled under her withering gaze as her pen swiftly slashed up their work. Mark Stevenson, who later served as an editor at *Maclean's*, remembered that "when she edited your copy, she would go right to the point. If there was a hole in your story, she would zero in on it—and look at you like you were an idiot."[18] Her grandson Colman Byfield put it more bluntly: "She could take a scalp with the flick of her tongue or the stroke of her pen. She was a fine writer and reporter, a voracious reader and razor-sharp editor, feared by old hands across the

---

* Indeed, when Ted wrote the foreword to my book *The Culture War*, he returned it to me late, with an apology. His wife had passed away in 2014, and without her editorial input, he said, he simply wasn't sure that what he'd written was any good.

country, who fondly conjure a chain-smoking matron tearing their copy apart while swilling rye from the bottle."[19]

Like Ted, she also reprised her former role as a reporter, covering law and later politics for the magazines. At one point, she caused a car accident after working 48 hours straight.

In addition to her editorial role, Ginger acted as a counterbalance to her occasionally volcanic husband. When Ted's ideas were, in her view, too extreme, she reigned him in like nobody else could—although that is not to say that the couple were not in lockstep on moral issues. As her *Globe and Mail* obituary put it: "In her own writing, Mrs. Byfield was uncompromising in her critiques of modern Christianity, sexuality, and education policy, such as a 1986 *Alberta Report* cover story declaiming 'The Seeming Suicide of the United Church,' referring to its acceptance of homosexuality."[20]

She was also an unorthodox morale booster. Once, when Ted was feeling sorry for himself and sought comfort from his wife, Ginger suggested he get over it. "I'd feel sorry for you," she told him, "But neither I nor anybody else could suggest any form of pity to extend to you that you're not already extending to yourself." Decades later, Ted never tired of relating this anecdote with delighted laughter. For their entire marriage, he revered her, and he chuckled when talking about their courtship as if he still couldn't quite believe he'd suckered her into marrying him. Ted sometimes clashed with his equally strong-willed wife in loud, legendary shouting matches, in which Ginger frequently put him in his place, leaving observers chuffed by the sight of Ted getting some of his own medicine.

Just as she had served as a hostess for the cell groups back in Winnipeg, Ginger also presided over the never-ending stream of people who trooped through the Byfield's Edmonton home, where writers, judges, politicians, clergy, and folks who had fallen on hard times regularly appeared for a bed or a beer. On Boxing Day, the house was packed for their legendary Boar's Head potluck dinners, and the house trembled to the rafters with laughter and song—including the many voyageur tunes Ted had learned on the lakes and rivers of Manitoba, accompanied by magnificent medleys of Christmas carols. These annual dinners formed a tradition that lasted thirty years.

The Byfield tradition of lending a hand to the underprivileged continued, as well. "We ran a pretty open household," Ted recalled. "Whenever any of us saw someone with a genuine need, we'd bring them home. I don't mean a drunk stumbling along the street, but people who were really in trouble. At the apartment building, we had people living there who had nowhere else to go. Often, they'd join us. We felt like it was something we were supposed to do. How my wife put up with it all those years I don't know." Vince Byfield once posed her the question. "Why Dad?" he asked. "Others talk about things," she replied. "Your father actually *does* things."

He tried to capture what Ginger meant to him in a poem he penned in March of 1989 titled "To A Wife," which hung on his office wall until he died:

Beyond the years that none would count
Beyond time's paceless flight,
Beyond a thousand crises gone
When black clouds met the night.

Beyond the times of children come
And on their own seas toss'd
Beyond a dozen battles won
Another thousand lost.

I see a woman tall with grace
Fashioned in God's design,
Whose mind is flint, whose smile is sun,
And I have made her mine.

"Listen, wife, the guns go off,
The sky has turned to black.
The cause is lost, there is no bread,
Where can we go but back?"

"Push you on," the woman said.
And said it times untold.
"For if we fall in God's good fight,
It's better than dying old."

Beyond the clock, beyond the stars,
When all the storms are stilled,
I see her stand in heaven's light
With every cause fulfilled.

And I wonder why, and I ask again
That which I cannot see
Of all the men that have filled the world
This should have come to me.

• • •

Despite not being explicitly Christian, the *Report* magazines swiftly became a staple in Christian homes across the Western prairies, in large part because Ted and his team covered Christian issues that were ignored by much of the mainstream media. It had once been common for the goings-on at churches and religious organizations to be a regular media beat, but as Christian values fell out of favour, this was increasingly left to religious circulars, newsletters, and church bulletins. *Alberta Report,* however, covered it all.

Ted reported on issues in a way that presupposed the truth of Christianity. He detailed the progress and excesses of the growing gay rights movement and refused to surrender his principles in the face of backlash. Maddeningly for many, he declined to get with the times like so many of his media counterparts. Like his American counterpart William F. Buckley of *National Review*, Ted "stood athwart history yelling Stop, at a time when few were inclined to do so, or to have much patience with those who urged it."

He summed up his position on sexual morality, for example, in a column on April 4, 1980: "If adultery or homosexuality is wrong in the sight of God, then all the task forces in Christendom aren't going to make it right. If God is timeless and changeless, then human conduct considered wrong in the eighth century is just as wrong in the twentieth."[21] This logical sentiment, of course, has since been rendered radical by the sexual revolution and the religious quislings who joined it.

"As the gay movement gained pace, our opposition to it gained likewise," Ted explained decades later. "It soon became evident that what the gay movement wanted was not tolerance, but something considerably beyond that—to be admired for what they were." All this, of course, has since come to pass.

Even some who despise Ted admit that he predicted much of what was to come. In a column that would produce panicked seizures in any editor today, he noted that the elimination of sexual boundaries would not stop once it had begun, and that there was much more in the proverbial closet than the revolutionaries cared to admit: "What will come next? In San Francisco, I'm told, the big question at high school is which boy will take which other boy to the spring prom. 'Consenting adults' very soon lead to consenting children. Child pornography is already on sale. Incest is widely advocated. The gaining popularity of sado-masochism filled four columns of *Time* magazine."[22]

His final paragraph summarized the Christian view of sexual restraint—and why society would continue to decline once it had thrown Scripture to the wind: "For where the closet exists, of course, is in the mind, in all our minds. What we close up in it is the ruthless, the insane, the diabolical. To open it therefore is to open the gates of the city to the wolf, to the marauder, to the powers of night."[23]

To progressives then and now, Ted posed a damning question that demanded a response: *What is progress?*

Ted wrote on abortion, too, calling it "barbarism" and reporting favourably on the pro-life movement. He once penned a column (published on August 21, 1989) summing up his thoughts on his nation's abortion regime titled "O Canada, where we celebrate freedom by ripping up a baby." He concluded with a dire warning: "Allowing people to be killed because some party in power has deemed them 'subhuman' is surely something this century has seen all it wants of."[24]

The pro-life issue was frequently a cover story. One account of rising abortion rates featured a baby (the newborn son of reporter Robbie Tomkinson) with a hypodermic needle hovering over him on the cover. It was hard to miss the point, and that was Ted's intention. Subtlety was never Ted's strong suit, but truth, after all, was not a subtle thing. It was the *truth*, regardless of the newly minted dictates of political correctness.

Ted even confronted celebrated abortion pioneer Henry Morgentaler on national TV. He related the story in one of his columns:

> Here is a problem in "values" of the type that modern social studies teachers are encouraged to pose. Several men are out in the woods hunting. Suddenly one of them sees something move in the bush. At last, he rejoices, a deer. Then a warning flashes through his mind. That might not be a deer. That might be one of the other hunters. Question for the class: should the hunter fire at the thing if there's a chance it's another human being? The approved answer is no.
>
> I encountered serious trouble once by asking this question on a CBC television program. In fact, the tape was killed, the program was never run, and I was never invited back. For the man I asked the question of was the celebrated Dr. Henry Morgentaler, who at the time was making his appeal from a conviction for performing abortions. He was one of the current heroes of the CBC and I was supposed to know that you did not ask him questions that were "hypothetical" or "unfair."[25]

He concluded this column by noting that abortionists surely knew the answer to that hypothetical question: "The abortionist trains himself, no doubt, not to observe that human eye staring at him as it is scraped off into the garbage bag. If the mere mention of these things is reprehensible, then what of the deed itself?"[26]

To the mainstream press, pro-life activists were reactionaries. To Ted, they were allies. It showed. Their enemies, after all, were *his* enemies, and Ted was a pro-lifer, too. "We were up against the furious thrust of the feminist movement," he recalled with a laugh. As Michael Wagner put it in his 2012 history *Standing on Guard for Thee: The Past, Present, and Future of Canada's Christian Right*, "The *Alberta Report*, and in later years its sister publications, *Western Report* and *BC Report*, was the closest thing the Christian Right in Canada ever had to a full-fledged magazine."[27]

But perhaps more fundamentally than all of that, Ted Byfield covered Christians with respect. "Even in the cities we were very popular with certain subsets of the population, such as Catholics," Steve Weatherbe remembered. "Ted was very respectful of small 'o' orthodoxy in areas such as sexual morality. We also even-handedly covered the Evangelicals in an uncritical, taking-at-face-value way that endeared us to them. Occasionally we mocked liberal churches in the way newsmagazines can do with the artful use of modifiers. I remember one of Ted's lessons about how newsmagazines can use adverbs and adjectives while newspaper stories cannot."

"That was the key," Weatherbe said. "Year-round, under Ted's leadership, we presented as a secular newsmagazine, speaking with the authoritative voice that is the newsmagazine's forte, but one which treated religious affairs as very important and treated Evangelicals as seriously as any other kind of Christian, endearing us to them. We often did cover stories on religious matters, especially at Christmas and Easter, rounding up leaders and treating their opinions as important."

As the sexual revolution progressed and colonized much of the media, Ted's magazines were one of the few print publications that told the other side of the story.

Finally, Ted—for obvious reasons—was a staunch defender of Christian schools. Michael Wagner makes the case in *Standing on Guard for Thee* that *Alberta Report* had a strong influence on the provincial government on this issue, as the Christian school movement was controversial throughout the 1980s. In 1988, when the Progressive Conservative government passed a School Act seen as highly favourable to private education, a number of progressive MLAs named-dropped Ted in the Legislature during their condemnations of the move. Calgary Liberal MLA Sheldon Chumir, for example, warned ominously that Christian schools would spring up like mushrooms after rain if the Act passed: "Mr. Byfield, who is a great and untiring advocate of private religious schools, has expressed ecstasy with respect to the changes in the Act."[28]

Ecstasy may have been a slight overstatement, but Ted certainly approved. Evidence of *AR's* effectiveness in driving both the public conversation and public policy was abundant.

• • •

Despite Ted's legendary temper, the defining characteristic of his journalistic career was how much he enjoyed it. Ted's Christian convictions were sincere, and he was playing for keeps in the cultural battles he engaged in. But that didn't mean he wasn't having fun.

As anger on the progressive Left grew and tolerance for the traditionalist views of the self-described "unrepentant redneck" shrank, Ted never considered backing down. "Unfortunately, I enjoy a good fight," he once told publisher Peter Stockland with a chuckle. "I enjoy a fight so much that the temptation is all in the other direction. My joy in life has been saying, 'If I were to write this, so-and-so would get so mad he'd go right through the clouds.'"[29]

The fact that so many of Ted's enemies found him impossible to hate is a testament to Ted's maddening warrior *joie de vivre*. In his golden years, when his gravelly baritone chuckle grew raspier but his views on abortion, feminism, homosexuality, and traditional Christianity stubbornly refused to change, many who wanted to despise him as a bigot could not help but either love him or be begrudgingly charmed by him.

A profile on Ted in the *Ryerson Review of Journalism* by Carey Toane summed it up in the title: "Sympathy for the Old Devil." Toane, like so many before her, discovered that Ted's well-earned reputation didn't do him justice. "The founder of the Christian conservative newsweekly formerly known as *Alberta Report* is surprisingly mellow," she wrote. "He isn't the fire-and-brimstone, holier-than-thou tight-ass I was expecting, yet everything he says and does is infused with the sort of energy that only visionaries and missionaries possess. He argues like a lawyer. He pontificates like a preacher. He waves his arms and pounds his fists like a politician."[30]

To accommodate the unwelcome discovery that they liked Ted Byfield, his ideological opponents frequently attempted to describe him as a Dr. Jekyll and Mr. Hyde figure. "At his best, Byfield is a seasoned journalist with a Rabelaisian spirit and an appetite for debate, a staunch supporter of the family, the church and, of course, the West," Toane wrote. "At his worst, he is an antigay, antiabortion, anti-feminist, anti-government, small c-conservative with a narrow mind and a big mouth...It is easy to hate Ted Byfield, but it's not that hard to like him, either. The relaxed indifference in his voice tells me that he doesn't [care] whether this young, impressionable journalist student, or anyone else for that matter, likes him or not."[31]

Fay Orr, communications director for Alberta Premier Ralph Klein and a former reporter for *AR*, echoed the sentiment. "There are two of them: the public, magazine Ted that is unyielding, one-dimensional, pigheaded, redneck and…proud of it. Then there is the private Ted, who counts communists, feminists, atheists, and homosexuals among some of his dearest colleagues and friends. The private Ted is far more balanced, understanding and open to ideas and discussion. The private Ted is brilliant, provocative, insightful, and charismatic. I love the private Ted."[32]

Even prominent abortion activist and CBC host Judy Rebick, former president of the National Action Committee on the Status of Women, ended up charmed by Ted despite despising *Alberta Report*. He came up to her at an event and introduced himself: "Hello Judy, I'm Ted Byfield. I'm your enemy."[33] The two laughed, struck up a conversation, and discovered that they had common ground: both deplored political correctness and the narrowing of debate they saw unfolding around them as younger, humourless progressives entered the political fray. It was these dogmatists who found it easy to hate Ted Byfield and anyone else who shared his views. In the minds of ideologues, there is rarely room for humanity—there are only enemies and comrades. Ted, many discovered, could somehow be both.

As Steve Hopkins described it, Ted's charm and skill as a journalist was due to the fact that he was genuinely interested in people. "When travelling or in informal public settings, he would strike up casual conversations with almost anyone he met—such as cab drivers or clerks in a checkout line—if there was not a rush," he wrote. "He was interested in their personal stories and family histories, even though he was unlikely ever to see them again."

Gord Salway recalled that when Ted met one of his neighbours, a man he'd known and been friends with for years, Ted had him discussing his experiences as a Holocaust survivor in no time—a background Salway had been totally unaware of. His liberal friends, Salway said, invariably thought Ted was a horrible person—but if they could be persuaded to come to dinner with him, found themselves hopelessly charmed within minutes.

"Working at *AR* didn't just make me a better reporter and editor," Paula Simons, a pro-choice agnostic wrote later. "It made me a better person, I think. It taught me that you could like, respect, and even love people whose values and beliefs were different from yours—that you could understand and tolerate different worldviews, without sharing or endorsing them."[34]

In the dozens of articles in which Ted's ideological foes and former colleagues attempted to work out why he was so likeable, few actually reached the correct and obvious conclusion. How could someone be loved as a person while simultaneously despised for his politics? For precisely the same reason that Ted could love the Marxists, feminists, and gays who were his friends: He loved the sinner and hated the sin. This, to Ted, was simply Christianity, and to the eternal frustration of those who wanted to hate him and found that they couldn't, he never compromised on either. Those who saw Ted as a bigot but loved him nonetheless were living out their own version of the Christian principle of loving the sinner but hating the sin. The irony was lost on most of them.

As evidenced by his own hiring practices, Ted was firmly opposed to what would now be called "cancel culture." Long-time *Report* staffer Paul Bunner, for example, had gotten his first media exposure in Cold Lake, Alberta, protesting American cruise missile activity and hosting professional peaceniks. His fashionably left-wing press releases and letters to the editor landed him a job in Meadow Lake, Saskatchewan—and then *Alberta Report* in 1986. An anonymous reader soon dug up some of Bunner's past work and sent Ted a scathing letter: "What's a pro-conservative, pro-family, pro-life and decency magazine doing with a hot dog 'LEFTIST' with a radical, ultra-feminist wife writing and reporting for the *Western Report*?"

The letter went on to advise Ted to do a "background check

on Comrade Paul Bunner" before "the egg on your face turns to something more unpleasant." Bunner discovered this when he found the letter sitting on his desk. Ted had scrawled a handwritten note across the top:

Paul: For whatever it's worth, stuff like this makes me ashamed to call myself a conservative—Byfield

• • •

Throughout all this, Ted struggled to keep the magazines afloat. Temporary financial stability arrived in the strangest way. On June 30, 1981, the Canadian Union of Postal Workers went on strike and mail carriers and sorters walked off the job. It was the culmination of an acrimonious debate over a range of issues including paid maternity leave and compensation for shift work, and it left newsmagazines like *Alberta Report* in a nasty position. As always, *AR* was in a financially precarious position and could not afford to lose the revenue. *AR* counted on Canada Post to deliver the magazines and subscription cheques from readers, the key source of income. A long strike threatened the continued existence of the magazine.

Alberta Report's business manager was resigned to the fact that the magazine would have to shut down, but Ted abruptly returned from vacation to deal with the emergency. In a burst of desperate creativity, Ted founded the Alberta Report Emergency Postal Service and assigned *AR's* art director, Alain Godbout, to design a faux postage stamp. The mock stamp included a disclaimer in tiny letters reading "This is not a postage stamp" to dodge legal issues, and if folks peered at it through a magnifying glass, they could discern a series of tiny hands offering the Trudeau salute. These, of course, were directed right at the federal government, and sold for $1 apiece.

169

"We recruited delivery boys easily through the Catholic schools," Steve Weatherbe recalled. "I cannot imagine this happening today, but back then we were accepted as a pro-Catholic, pro-Christian publication that would reliably support the church in any dispute. We set up our own delivery system, with Edmonton being split up among the staff, and with another staffer I drove around my district hitting up subscribers for cheques. I remember an old couple inviting me and a fellow reporter/collector in for peanut butter sandwiches. They were poor, but happy to support us."

The *Alberta Report* Emergency Postal Service actually attempted to deliver mail for everyone, or at least those willing to place their mail in the drop-box set up at *AR's* offices. Within weeks, circulation manager Keith Bennett had pickup locations in 28 places across Alberta.

The union threatened to sue but decided not to. It was a magnificent stunt, as the public was furious at the strikers—import and export orders were backlogged an estimated six months to a year for small businesses—and loved Ted's refusal to back down. Ted's temporary service ended up shipping mail all over Alberta, garnering province-wide goodwill. At one point during the strike, scab mailmen and *AR* staffers were running their own mail routes. "The idea was that we would charge a dollar, and deliver any package anywhere in Alberta," Ted recalled. "The *Globe and Mail* gave it an eight-column line above the fold on Page 1." It was also a top story on CBC national news.

Each of *Alberta Report's* infamous non-postage stamps delivered dozens of tiny red one-fingered salutes in its background, all pointed at Ottawa.

The strike lasted 42 days. Over 80% of CUPW's 23,000 members voted to accept the terms of a contract offered in August, and when it was over, Ted found himself in an unusual position: Money poured in as ten weeks worth of circulation revenue arrived at once. It ended up amounting to several hundred thousand dollars.

This windfall came at a particularly fortuitous time, as *AR's* previous owner, Al Hardy, had passed away from a heart attack in 1980 and the Hardy family had decided to unload the controversial magazine.* Hardy's executor had also been enormously distressed that he was in possession of a magazine that not only hemorrhaged money, but was running what was in all likelihood an illegal mail service.

"They didn't particularly want it as part of their portfolio," Ted chuckled later. "However, if it shut down, the assets—which included an apartment block—were substantial. The trouble was that everyone agreed that the greatest asset *Alberta Report* had was me. In effect, they were not selling the magazine—they were selling me. Our lawyer found this very amusing and asked if we could find anyone willing to pay $125,000 on our behalf."

Ted called his brother John, who was then a radiologist living in California. John mortgaged his San Diego home to produce the funds, and Ted bought the magazine from Hardy's widow. Now, only a short time later, Ted found himself in a position to buy his brother out (according to Mike Byfield, John was a passive partner holding 20% of the equity.) "I bought the magazine, paid my brother, and paid myself out of the circulation money," Ted recalled.

---

* Ted and Hardy had gone to the *Financial Post* conference on energy in New York together. On the second morning Hardy did not emerge for breakfast, and Ted was called urgently to the hotel desk. Al Hardy had passed away in his room.

For the first time in its history, *Alberta Report* was in excellent financial shape. Ted Byfield was now owner of the magazine—but this, he said later, was a double-edged sword. "I was a bad publisher," he said. "I've never been much of a businessman. I've always ended up trying to run businesses and not doing a very good job. Ideally, I could start them up and if somebody could take them over, that was a good idea. I was always able to raise money, but I didn't have the proper brain to spend it. This was the curse of my life. Everybody has something they can't do."

Nonetheless, the media ecosystem pioneered by the Byfields between 1973 and 2003 would revitalize Canadian conservatism, give voice to Western alienation, drive support for the new Reform Party, and provide a powerful right-wing counterbalance to the prevailing progressive media establishment. Their influence ensured that they were both loved and loathed, but their newsrooms became a thing of legend. You could hate Ted Byfield, but you could not ignore him. Most eventually gave up trying.

However, the socially conservative newsmagazine with a Christian foundation did not become a paradigm-shifting political phenomenon until, due to unpredictable historical circumstances, Ted Byfield became the spokesman for Western alienation. He already spoke for many Christians. When the *Report* joined the fray on behalf of Western Canada against the Laurentian elites, he spoke with the voice of millions of angry western conservatives and especially Albertans.

— CHAPTER SIX —

A STANDARD RAISED
IN THE WEST

*If you ask political observers who it was that elected Stephen
Harper prime minister, the answers would be of a sort. Guys
with bow ties would say Michael Ignatieff, Stephane Dion, Paul
Martin, or Jack Layton. A few especially trenchant thinkers
would say Preston Manning. One in 100 of these insightful types,
a coffee shop philosopher or a barstool PhD, would pull a straw
from his hair, chew it for a second, and say: "the Byfields."*

—Monte Solberg, *Toronto Sun*, September 28, 2014

During his time as a columnist and publisher, Ted was
famous for fulminating against anyone he perceived
as attacking Christianity or Western Canada, and
not necessarily in that order. The *Report* magazines
became known as championing two primary causes: Christian
values and the Canadian West. The primary enemy of both could
be found in the personage of Prime Minister Pierre Elliot Trudeau,
the man responsible for decriminalizing abortion, ushering in the
sexual revolution, and—at least as Ted and legions of likeminded
Canadians saw it—declaring war on the West.

"People say he is indifferent to Western Canada, and this may
once have been true," Ted wrote furiously in 1980. "I think it is

true no longer. He now hates us, and passionately. It is the hatred of the socialist for the individualist, the cold fear of the highborn for the self-made, the aversion of the theorist for the pragmatist, the derision of the urbanist for the peasant, the disdain of the intellectual for the uncouth, the contempt of the Gaul for the Slav. All these hatreds have helped to dictate the posture of the Trudeau government towards the West, and on Tuesday, the 28th of October, they were paraded before the nation in the form of public policy."

"History will one day record that it was on Tuesday, October 28, 1980, that a government of Canada by act of deliberate policy tried to destroy the prosperity of the one section of the country that had escaped the recession and offered the best hope for the whole nation's future. At the same time it indentured the country to the Middle East's oil producers and brought its own oil industry to a cat-astrophic halt. Historians will be hard pressed to find anywhere an act of government so irrespon-sible, so vindictive and so insane as that which was produced last week by Mr. Trudeau and his thugs at Ottawa."[1]

October 31, 1980 $1.25
ALBERTA REPORT
The Weekly Newsmagazine
BLOCKING THE GRAB
Peter Lougheed
defender of Alberta

The occasion of Ted's fury was the intro-duction of the National Energy Policy (NEP) in the Trudeau govern-ment's 1980 federal bud-get, a policy that would, for a time, make *Alberta*

Report the most-read magazine in the province. Trudeaumania hadn't lasted long in Western Canada, where the Liberals lost every federal race from 1972 to 1988. Trudeau's tenures were interrupted only briefly by the premiership of Joe Clark in 1979, with his government rising and falling nearly without a trace. But resentment turned to rage in Alberta when it became clear that Eastern Canada was determined to treat Western Canada as a collection of colonies for resource extraction rather than equal partners in Confederation—thus the title of Ted's first book of columns from this period: *The Deplorable Unrest in the Colonies*.

Pierre Trudeau and the Laurentian elites held the view that they were responsible for a Confederation that was primarily predicated on the French-English compact between Upper and Lower Canada, with the West's role being to keep raw materials flowing to the East. Western well-being and jobs played second fiddle—Ted once described this duality as "Upper Canada and Outer Canada." Quebec was staying in purely out of self-interest (and later at the behest of a razor-thin majority), and thus needed to be frequently bought off, usually with largesse provided by the West. This, at least, was the version of events held by many Westerners and amplified by the *Report* magazines.

This view appeared to be confirmed when a 1970s spike in oil prices brought about by the Middle Eastern oil cartel OPEC (Organization of the Petroleum Exporting Countries) resulted in a windfall for oil-rich Alberta. Ottawa was determined to claw this wealth eastward with special taxes—and even divert some of this boom in energy exploration to the Northwest Territories with corresponding tax breaks. Theoretically, provinces were supposed to control their own resources and the resulting revenues—but with the majority of the Canadian population and thus the majority of parliamentarians hailing from the East, the political deck was stacked against the West. As Ted summarized it:

First [there was] an export tax on oil—Canada had never before charged an export tax on anything—neatly siphoning off the added revenue to the federal treasury, and using the revenues to reduce the price of oil in Toronto and Montreal.

Then in 1980 the Trudeau government won election, with the full support of the Conservative government of Ontario, by promising to impose federal taxes directly on Alberta resources. This, of course, was against the law. But how do you "arrest" the federal government? The tax men entered the oil company offices and applied the taxes. Were these companies supposed to bar the doors? They had no option but to pay.

So the rules of the Canadian game were to be changed. They were sacrosanct only so long as Ontario and Quebec won by them. If the game started to go badly, you changed the rules. Alberta must learn to "share" with the rest of Canada, said Trudeau's energy minister, Marc Lalonde. Well, therefore, would a federal tax be levied on Quebec Hydro exports? Would Quebec be required to "share" its electric power with Nova Scotia, which depended on oil-fuelled thermal generators? Well no, that was a very different matter.

More and more it began to look as though Canada was a mere con game, being played out by Ontario and Quebec at the expense of the West. And the numbers proved it. Between 1969 and 1984, Alberta transferred more than $95 billion to the rest of Canada, most of it to Quebec, which gained $80 billion out of tax transfers and energy benefits during the same period. This money, had it remained in Alberta, would have financed industrial diversification in the bust that followed. But by then the money was gone.[2]

It was perhaps inevitable that the loudmouthed publisher who articulated his views with such certainty would become the spokesman for Western alienation. As a veteran of the *Winnipeg Free Press*, he understood the necessity of regional loyalties. "I was always aware," he told the *Ryerson Review of Journalism*, "that in the great western newspaper tradition, proper western papers represented the West before they represented Canada. If we don't speak up for the West, no one will."[3] The polarization of East and West provided the perfect opportunity for an able ideologue with both a keen sense of justice and a platform to make a difference, and Ted was the man for the moment.

He threw himself into opposing Trudeau and the NEP with a vengeance. "I was being interviewed every day by somebody down East," he remembered. "I was saying provocative things, which they wanted. We were talking about whether a province could vote itself out of Confederation. Quebec had talked about it, but they didn't have any money. *We* had money." So, for that matter, did *Alberta Report*. Being the voice of the West resulted in skyrocketing subscriptions, and for the first time in its history, the magazine was flush. Some staff remember getting hefty (and unprecedented) bonuses during this period. Western grievance was both genuine and, for a brief time, lucrative. At one point, the combined readership of the *Report* magazines was 400,000—and that was a conservative estimate.[4]

Ted was not committed to Alberta separatism but remained convinced that if a valid threat was not made, the province simply wouldn't be taken seriously by the Ottawa elites. Invoking the spectre of secession was a necessary evil not to leave the country, but to get a fair shake within Confederation—one that was being denied to the West by Trudeau. Most Albertans weren't separatists, but many were angry enough to consider it. In many rural communities, meeting at a coffee shop or restaurant to read *Alberta Report* became a weekly tradition.

As Ted summarized it: "We [were] presented with a paradox. The only way we could change Canada was to develop ways of getting out of Canada."[5]

Trudeau had scoffed at the idea of Western separatism during the 1980 election (calling the chances "nil") but the number of Albertans flirting with the idea doubled after he tabled his budget—with Ted's encouragement. The *Alberta Report* covered separatist leaders, meetings, and speeches with gusto, and Ted fuelled the fire in his own columns, announcing in 1981: "For me, I have long since made up my mind. If they take the resources, we should separate. I like Canada. But I like freedom a whole lot more. I have no intention to become a Lalonde sharecropper."[6]

Those were heady days, Ted recalled, and he spent much of his time brawling with Toronto talking heads who simply could not understand why Westerners were so angry. "Who was representing Alberta in the media?" he asked. "The *Edmonton Journal*? Head office—in Toronto! The *Calgary Herald*? Same thing! The CBC was run from Toronto. There was no Alberta-owned media. The local TV station, CFRN, took the Alberta position, but it was practically the only one. We became the lone voice for the province."

Unsurprisingly, Ted's media appearances frequently turned acrimonious. He was on CBC's *As It Happens* opposite a fellow from the *Edmonton Journal*, who advocated calm while Ted fulminated about the feds. Ted also regularly appeared on *Morningside* with legendary CBC radio interviewer Peter Gzowski. One morning, the question to be discussed was: "Why should Alberta leave Canada?" During a chat in their kitchen, Ginger suggested that Ted turn it around. As Ted remembered it, he posed his version of the question just after the introduction: "Why should Alberta *stay* in Canada?" The fellow opposite him, Geoffrey Stevens of the *Globe and Mail*, snapped back: "It's obvious."

Ted was enjoying himself. "State the obvious, then."

"I regard the question as absurd," said Stevens.

"That may be, but absurd or not, you're not answering it."

Gzowski was getting upset at this point, and Ted pounced. "We've got the managing editor of what calls itself the national newspaper, and he can't tell us why Alberta should stay in!"

The phone was ringing when he got home. His regular appearances on the CBC show had been cancelled. "I made the *Globe and Mail* look ridiculous," he chuckled. "You mustn't do that."

As Keith Watt, a producer on *Morningside*, remembered it: "Ted didn't play fair, rejecting Peter's 'we're all in this together' approach to looking at Canada. Instead, Ted took a distinctly 'the West has been screwed' point of view, and, week after week, he mopped the floor with his eastern counterparts. Finally, the word came down from Toronto: Byfield had to go, not because his cogent arguments about Western alienation were winning the rhetorical battle, but because his approach was 'too confrontational.' I thought it made great radio, but it did not correspond with St. Peter's view of Canada. After an extensive search for a replacement, we landed on a relative unknown at the time. But not for long—Ted's replacement on the national affairs panel was Preston Manning."[7]

Ted did not only engage in verbal combat—he also produced powerful, evocative columns that compellingly captured the milieu of the moment as the impact of the NEP began to be felt across the province:

> The phenomenon of widespread political anger is a strange thing to Canada. I can remember it clearly only once before—in the Legion halls and schoolhouses of small prairie towns in the year 1957, when angry farmers with mountains of unsold grain met and viciously razzed Liberal candidates in the election that doomed that party

thenceforward in the West. Again I can remember it, but only barely, in my boyhood during the "conscription issue" when mothers and wives were being told by Liberal candidates why replacements would not be sent overseas for their wounded sons and husbands, because it would distress the unity of Canada. Now I see it again. It is deep; it is bitter; it is dangerous, and it is everywhere.

I saw it repeatedly last week. I saw it in the eyes of the young lady I met in a Calgary restaurant whose father, a machinist in the oil industry, had worked a lifetime in order to start his own business and lost it within months… Later, at the airport, I met an old friend. Her husband, she said, isn't the jovial fellow he used to be. Yesterday he persuaded his Edmonton staff to take reduced hours so he wouldn't have to lay anybody off yet…That afternoon, back in Edmonton, I sensed it in another friend, this time in the voice. Cash just wasn't there to meet payments and payrolls in his vehicle rental company, he said. The competition was slashing prices to ruinous levels. He wasn't sure, he concluded, the palm of his hand evenly patting the arm of his chair, exactly what he would do…

All these stories are not merely narrated. They are always unfolded in one of two tones—either anger, or despair. But the despair is not of the kind that implies acceptance of the inevitable. Rather, it is the despair of rooted resentment. It seethes and it boils beneath the surface, waiting for the moment when it can burst forward and embrace any half plausible cause that promises to give it vent. Therein, of course, lies the danger.[8]

Ted's back-page column "Letter from the Publisher" became a clearinghouse for such stories—and the reason many people subscribed. Like the best of journalists, he listened and reported on what he heard, spurred on by his curiosity and genuine interest in other people. Steve Weatherbe recalled that Ted's telephone interviews often involved more interested prodding than actual questions: "Is that right, eh? Is that right, eh?" His tone conveyed his sincerity, and people felt they could tell him their stories.

What distinguished the *Report* magazines from many others was that the readers always came first. Readership surveys were conducted constantly to ensure that people were actually reading the magazine and that it was covering the issues they cared about. Steve Hopkins' wife would call at least forty readers and ask questions: "Why do you subscribe? What do you like? What do you want to read?" People often said they wanted serious stories about economics and politics, but actually remembered human interest stories on crime, fires, etc. Hopkins recalled that it was a competition during staff meetings to see whose story had garnered the most interest from readers.

Ted also attributed their success during these years to the skill of his reporting staff. His son Mike was one example. Mike was getting quite a few scoops covering the energy sector in Calgary, and when Ted asked him how he'd gained their trust, he replied: "I don't let them screw themselves." Most people talking to the press, Ted noted, didn't realize how their quotes would sound in print. "You had to protect them from themselves to a certain extent," he said. The *Report* staff would often read quotes back to the interviewees to let them know how it would sound and give them the chance to clarify. This proved an effective way to garner trust.

Ted's two great causes were distinct from one another, but the sense of righteous indignation he felt about the attacks on Christianity and the West was so fervent that occasionally he could not help conflating the two with a view that tended towards propagandistic idealism. "We stand closer than any of the other regions to our pioneer roots," he wrote in 1985. "For most of us the farm is but one generation behind. We are therefore closer than they to the beliefs and traditions of the past, and we have the advantage of seeing what happens when those values are too hurriedly cast aside in favour of state-centred secularism of glittering promise and baleful result. It is a view not well represented in the contemporary media of the West, an omission we propose to correct."[9]

The fusion of righteous indignation and fun-filled self-righteousness made for a heady newsroom mix. "Ted's conviction that we were doing a good thing—almost the best kind of work anyone could do—propelled all of us continually and really defined the culture of the magazine well into and through the 1980s," Steve Hopkins recalled. "We were striking blows against Ottawa's oppression, so we were repeatedly reenergized by the villainous Trudeau and his Eastern cohorts and minions. To us he was more reprehensible than Nixon. We were spearheading a noble fight for political and cultural justice. There's no doubt Trudeau infused our staff with a sense of righteous purpose."

This sense of purpose, incidentally, was important for practical as well as political reasons. As Gord Salway recalled: "There was no way you were going to get people to do a *job* for a dollar a day. But to join a mission against evil? That was a different story." Moral fervourer and good fun kept many working at the magazines despite warnings from friends, families, and financial advisors urging them towards more boring employers who paid with cheques that didn't bounce.

It helped that the *Report* magazines were making a discernible impact. "We were taken very seriously in Ottawa by the Trudeau government," Steve Hopkins explained. At one point, Energy Minister Marc Lalonde's office reached out—they wanted to give *AR* an interview in Calgary following a luncheon speech Lalonde was giving to oil industry executives. There was no press conference after the speech, and a cluster of news reporters howled questions at the minister as he walked out—and watched as Lalonde's aide whisked the editor from the upstart publication past them into a limo, leaving everyone else on the sidewalk. Hopkins was the only one to get an interview that day.

When he pulled out his tape recorder, Lalonde told him: "I know your magazine well. We get it in our office every week." Consequently, he wanted to explain the Trudeau government's point of view on energy policy directly to the *Report's* readers. The *AR* staff was, predictably, dissatisfied with Lalonde's answers, but they ran a full question and answer interview. The Eastern view was simply too different from the Western view. As Ted recalled after taking part in press scrums with Pierre Trudeau: "His view of the country was so different that it was like talking to someone from Japan."

It wasn't just Trudeau Liberals that took *AR* seriously, either. Shortly after Joe Clark was defeated, his public relations manager asked for a meeting. Ted and Hopkins met with Clark privately. "He basically pleaded with us to get behind him and help reestablish his Tory leadership," Hopkins recalled. The same held true for Alberta politicians. "We always had access to Peter Lougheed. He returned phone calls right away. In the week following the announcement that he'd be returning as premier he gave *Alberta Report* the only interview—an exclusive full hour. No other magazines."

As Peter Lougheed himself put it on the 25th anniversary of *Alberta Report*: "Week after week the *Alberta Report* made it clear to Albertans, and also to Canadians, that the federal government was attempting to destroy the right of ownership of oil and gas by Albertans...we discovered many Ottawa politicians, bureaucrats, and journalists at the time were reading the magazine intensely, and collectively coming to the conclusion that Albertans were united in taking such a strong stand against this attack upon their resources."[10]

• • •

The *Alberta Report's* prominence made it an inviting target. As Ted wrote in 1988 after the CBC produced a play authored by a disgruntled former *AR* employee, Frank Moher:

> One of the penalties you pay as proprietor of the last domestically owned general news publication in western Canada is the necessity of being recurrently "explained" by the CBC. Twice in the last couple of years I have been featured on CBC programs. I was the subject of a half-hour television documentary (dangerous ideologue) and a lengthy "treatment" on the national radio show Sunday Morning (religious fanatic). Now I notice that the CBC is prominent among the sponsors, and plans a national review on television, of yet another explanation, this one a stage play about this magazine called *Prairie Report* where I am once again featured (peevishly pompous bore). Now, I have it from no less authority than my wife that I am actually a very sweet person and I do not deserve all this abuse from the Canadian Broadcasting Corporation, especially after all the nice things I've said about them.[11]

Moher had been a book reviewer with pro-Western tendencies for *AR* between 1983 and 1986, but after acquiring more liberal views decided to skewer his former employer. *The Prairie Report* caricatured Ted as the character Dick Bennington, with Otis Bennington standing in as Link. The plot involved an attempted takeover of the magazine by an Eastern businessman determined to change the pro-Western sentiments of the magazine. A chagrined Moher paid tribute to Ted in the play's introduction: "Ted has harvested his bounty; he has managed to accumulate enough power over the years to begin reshaping the political agenda, at least in Alberta, and to use his ubiquitous identification with all things western to place his very profile upon the land."

Ted attended and reviewed the play himself, and his response was both respectful of Moher's talents and a hilariously devastating takedown of *The Prairie Report*. "He is a fine writer," Ted wrote. "He has since moved to live among the retired millionaires and aging hippies on Gabriola Island in the Georgia Strait. (I was going to say 'retired hippies,' but that would be inaccurate, it being impossible to retire if you've never worked.)" The fundamental problem with the play, wrote Ted, was that it took itself too seriously. It wasn't funny, it was preachy. His review was arguably funnier than the play:

> I went there expecting to see something like Ben Hecht's *Front Page* [a 1938 Broadway comedy about the newspaper business]. What I saw instead was an attempt to use a dash of Neil Simon as a kind of jocular introduction to the book of the prophet Jeremiah. Somehow it doesn't seem to work.

• • •

The National Energy Policy had spawned the anger that led to the election of a separatist MLA in a 1982 Albertan by-election, but separatist sentiment abated with the 1984 election of Progressive Conservative Brian Mulroney. With Trudeau gone, Westerners dared to hope that things might get better. The Conservative caucus included a large number of MPs from the West, and thus the prairie provinces presumably had a seat at the decision-making table. Relief turned to suspicion as Mulroney dragged his feet on rolling back the polices of the NEP. Mulroney, after all, was a Quebecer.

The definitive betrayal came in 1986. Bristol Aerospace Ltd. of Winnipeg and Canadair Ltd. of Montreal had both bid on a billion-dollar contract for maintenance of Canada's CF-18 fighter jets. The Winnipeg firm had a technically superior bid. But in November, while making much of what a "painful" and "difficult" decision it had been, Mulroney awarded the contract to Canadair in his home province. As Quebec Liberal MP Jacques Guilbault jubilantly put it: "There was bound to be someone happy and someone unhappy, and my area is happy."

Manitoba Premier Howard Pawley, who dubbed the decision "cynical and callous," declared that Mulroney had shafted the West for political purposes: "Frankly, I cannot trust the man. I cannot trust the Conservative Party." His area was decidedly unhappy.

The CF-18 fiasco was the straw that broke the camel's back. No longer was the West simply being ignored—the system itself was rigged. Ted was livid. Trudeau was an enemy, but Mulroney was a turncoat—and that was worse. In the pages of the *Report* magazines, Ted began to speculate about what a new political party might look like and what it might do. He began to tell anyone who would listen—and there were plenty—that a new party was an inevitability.

In a column on September 15, 1986, for example, he wrote about five of the "conditions which a western party should meet," proposing a "moderate political party that was neither separatist nor radically left or right but dedicated to western objectives and the Triple-E senate," observing later that this proposal "seems to have achieved the remarkable feat of satisfying absolutely nobody."[12]*(He suggested, in the same column, that such a party be headed by a Jewish leader as that would "discourage the weirdo element that seems to so inevitably attach itself to such movements

---

* Ted coined the soon-to-be ubiquitous term "Triple-E Senate" (I learned the phrase in high school social studies class), which stood for a senate that would be equal, elected, and effective. Elected senators would be able to exercise effective powers in numbers equally representative of each province.

in Alberta.") Prescient-
ly, he noted that such
a party would not be
a permanent one but
would merely "change
the system"—that com-
pleted, "it should fade
into history, its work
done."[13]

On January 21,
1987, Ted joined the
Scottish-Canadian
radio and TV host Jack
Webster on the show
Webster! to explain
where he saw Western
alienation heading. "I
was talking to a guy by the name of Doug Campbell, who used to
be premier of Manitoba in the '50s," Ted told Webster. "He's 93,
sharp as a tack...He said: 'I've seen this before. I saw this [with] the
farm movement. I saw it when Social Credit started. What happens
is people get disillusioned with the whole system and some new
party comes along and picks them all up. That's his prophecy, and
he's just looking at the West from the point of view of Winnipeg
and Manitoba."

Webster pressed him on who the leader of such a party might
be, and Ted admitted that he didn't know yet. "What you'll find,"
he responded, "is the situation throws up a new leader."[14]

In the meantime, the son of former Alberta premier Ernest
Manning, Preston Manning, was also planning. From May 29 to
31, 1987, a conference called "A Western Assembly on Canada's
Economic and Political Future" was held in at the Hyatt Regency

Hotel in Vancouver, British Columbia. The *Report* magazines advertised for the conference, with Ted noting approvingly in an April column that "reputable business consultant and economist" Preston Manning would be there. He urged his readers to attend, to talk about it, to tell their neighbours.

Ted delivered the inaugural address, priming the crowd to the prospect of a new political party—one that would make the voice of the West thunder through the halls of Ottawa. "The West," Ted famously declared, "wants in."*

It was a receptive audience of about 800, Steve Weatherbe remembered, filled with "a lot of political neophytes, a lot of Christians, a lot of *Alberta Report* subscribers." Preston Manning recalled Ted's speech as a barn burner that ignited the appetite for a new political movement. Stephen Harper was there, too, with a paper on taxes that he handed to Manning, landing him the role of the Reform Party's chief policy advisor. The founding convention of the new party was held in Winnipeg on October 30, 1987, also heavily populated by *Alberta Report* readers. A leadership race swiftly established Preston Manning in the top slot over Stan Waters of British Columbia, with Ted Byfield as his champion.

The partnership had begun when Ted met with Manning several months earlier for dinner. Ted was already pitching a new party to his readers, and he wanted to back a leader, too. As one of his colleagues put it, Ted "went out for dinner one night with Preston Manning and he came back the next day convinced that Preston Manning was the answer and that he had the answers."[15] What he heard that night convinced him that Manning, an ideological centrist, was the man to make a new political movement happen, and he decided to marshal the influence of his magazines on Manning's behalf.

---

* This line is generally attributed to Ted, but he noted that it was originally coined by *AR* columnist Ralph Hedlin.

Like most popular movements, the idea was decidedly unpopular to many—at first. Mulroney, after all, had won a sweeping 211-seat majority only three years earlier. In the federal election of November 1988, the Reform Party fielded candidates from British Columbia, Alberta, Saskatchewan, and Manitoba. They won no seats, but several Alberta candidates placed second. When a Progressive Conservative MP passed away suddenly, a 1989 by-election sent Reform Party MP Deborah Grey to Ottawa. Stephen Harper accompanied her as an assistant. That same year, an Alberta senatorial election resulted in a victory for Reform candidate Stan Waters. The upstart party now had to be taken seriously.

Political scientist Michael Wagner notes in his 2009 book *Alberta Separatism: Then and Now* that the creation of the Reform Party drastically reduced support for separatism. The splintered separatist groups had no leadership or unifying voice to channel the simmering discontent, and the Reform Party channeled Western alienation into a viable political project.

In his memo "A Western Reform Movement: The Responsible Alternative to Western Separatism," Preston Manning had laid out the blueprint. His party would carry out the plan almost to a tee.

In 1991 the Reform Party went national, running candidates across the country—and two years later in 1993, they secured 52 parliamentary seats, a stunning political achievement for a six-year-old political party. Only one seat was in Ontario—the rest were in the West. One of them was occupied by Stephen Harper. The Progressive Conservatives were reduced from 156 seats to a mere 2 (three less, it was often noted, than a Honda Civic). This produced three Jean Chretien Liberal majorities while the Right struggled to reunite.

In 2000, a majority of Reform Party members voted to merge with the Canadian Alliance Party, and Stockwell Day defeated Manning for the leadership of the new party in the second round of voting. Ted threw himself into supporting Day. But on election day November 27, 2000, the Canadian Alliance won only 66 seats. Stephen Harper defeated Day for the leadership of Canadian Alliance in 2002, facilitated a merger with the federal Progressive Conservative Party in 2003, and in January 2006, the newly minted Conservative Party secured enough seats to form a minority government. In 2011, the Conservative Party won a majority government with a prime minister from Calgary. The West was in.

• • •

The alleged "pivot" of the Byfield media empire to a focus on socially conservative or culture war issues in the 1990s has been much discussed. Some have alleged that this coverage was an effort to pander to a Christian audience that was becoming a more entrenched minority as the culture shifted, but this ignores the fact that Christians had supported Ted all along—and that Christian values had been both a presupposition and a priority for the *Report* magazines from the beginning. From the outset, it was the Christian foundation of Ted's media enterprise that made his magazines unique from the others on offer.

Ted and his son Link—who actually ran the *Report* magazines as editor for far longer than Ted did—were in full agreement on moral issues, and Link was an able ideologue himself. Link had taken a more circuitous route into the family business than his parents might have hoped—in his late teens and early twenties he'd been a long-haired hippie who hitchhiked across Canada and ended up in Manitoba's Headingley Prison on pot charges. Ted claimed Link only cut his hair when someone who'd picked him up on the road told him it made him "look like that guy Trudeau." Link left all that behind, became both Christian

Although all of Ted and Virginia's offspring worked for the magazines at one point or another, two sons stayed on the longest: Link Byfield [above] became publisher of *Alberta Report* in 1985, and Vince Byfield [inset photo, working at the folder in 1974] who would go on to manage *BC Report* in 1990.

and conservative, and (as Ted liked to tell it) when someone asked Link's wife Joanne if he lived in the 19th century, she responded: "That's absurd. He's living in the 16th century."* The *Report* magazines, needless to say, reflected the values of the Byfield family.

It is true that the *Report* magazines struggled from financial difficulties—there were only a few brief moments when this was not the case. But the reason there appeared to be a shift in the *Report's* coverage was simply because cultural shifts were accelerating. The Byfields covered the LGBT movement, and it began to gain more traction in the '90s— gay rights activists even admitted that the *Report* magazines were among the few publications to recognize and report on what was happening, albeit from the increasingly despised Christian position. From Ted's perspective, there were more threats to Canada's moral fabric to report on, and so he and his team reported on them.

Indeed, as feminist researcher Gloria Filax put it in a review of *AR's* coverage from 1992 to 1998: "While in many ways a fiscally marginal magazine, *Alberta Report* had a significant impact on discourses about social values...As well as being a ubiquitous presence in Alberta, remarkably, *Alberta Report* has the most complete

---

* In 2007, a few years after the magazine folded, Link Byfield co-founded the Wildrose Party and ran for the provincial legislature twice. He was also voted a senator-in-waiting from Alberta but withdrew his name after Ottawa ignored the election for six years.

and comprehensive coverage of queer issues in the province during the 1990s. Unlike the mainstream media, *Alberta Report* took (the perceived threat of) sexual minority peoples seriously."[16]

As Ted put it: "As the gay movement gained pace, our opposition to it gained likewise."

It is undoubtedly true that by reporting on the pro-life movement, the gay rights movement, feminism, and a range of other social issues, the *Report* magazines became more marginal. This, however, was more a function of the success of Canada's cultural revolutionaries and the acceleration of secularization (or, more accurately, de-Christianization) than of any distinctive change in what the Byfields were offering. It is also true that they became more controversial, but that again was simply because moral stances once considered obvious by almost everyone had become, seemingly overnight, controversial. Progressive activists responded to this coverage by calling on mainstream advertisers to boycott, launching defamation lawsuits, and lodging human rights complaints. This hurt the already precarious finances of the magazines.

The *Report* magazines never stopped being a voice for Western Canada, but as the crises of the 1980s faded, some readers drifted away as their galvanizing issue lost its urgency. The *Report* magazines had been the voices of both regionalism and religion, and as Western alienation was sated by political representation and the culture wars heated, up, social issues considered to be religious by many Canadians frequently—or at least, most memorably—dominated the headlines. The *Report* magazines were simply no longer necessary as an urgent political outlet, a function they had served magnificently. Additionally, many loyal readers were simply becoming older.

In short, the Byfield media empire shrank to the margins not because of any shift, but because of consistency. Canada's moral Overton Window moved, and in many ways left them—and the millions of Canadians they still spoke for—behind. Ted Byfield remained true to his Christian convictions, but Canada was becoming a post-Christian nation. He and his colleagues were reporting from the losing side of the culture wars, and none of their schemes to keep the magazines afloat could counteract the tides of history.

There were other factors, of course. Ted's self-confessed lack of money management skills, staff turnover, changing markets, and run-of-the-mill mistakes all resulted in the eventual demise of the *Report* magazines. (As Ken Whyte put it: "He was a great entrepreneur, but a terrible businessman. He had this gift of being able to raise a lot of money, but his enthusiasm would always outrun his means."[17]) But the Byfields nonetheless accomplished what they set out to do. Ted always said that nothing he did was for money, and nobody who knew him questioned this assertion. His entire career confirmed it.

Ted was always up front about this. One former investor remembered Ted coming to Prince George, British Columbia to fundraise for the *Western Report*. "One of the stranger investment meetings I've ever been to," Gary Clarke told me. "He attracted a pretty sizeable crowd at the local hotel. 'Probably one of the worst financial investments you'll ever make,' he pitched us. 'You'll probably lose all your money.' He went on to explain how important it was for the West to have a voice, and why his journal was important to the conservative rebirth. Many of us agreed. I think I gave him $1,000, and never regretted the investment."

"You're left with a choice," Link Byfield once observed. "You either publish to make a profit or you make a profit so you can publish. Dad and I have always had this attitude that while we respect the necessity of a bottom line, that's not why we're here. What we try to do is preserve a discussion, an awareness, a sort of mutual knowledge between those who are religious and those who are not, those who are pro-life and those who are born-again Christian, those who are regional in their outlook and those who are national in their outlook. There are legitimate points to be made by all concerned in these areas and they should be made. They have to be made."[18]

In 1999, an attempt at public offering failed, forcing the three magazines to consolidate into a single national edition published fortnightly rather than weekly, with reporters being laid off and the survivors responsible for an enormous amount of copy. Editing got sparser due to frenetic schedules, provincial coverage waned, and the magazine shed 10,000 paying subscribers between 1999 and 2002, a death spiral from which it could not recover. The parent company, United Western Communications Ltd., sold off the *Report's* assets, including their photographs, in order to neutralize the debt. Link Byfield made one last-ditch attempt to keep the mission alive by founding the Citizens Centre for Freedom and Democracy, but to no avail. The *Report's* last edition came out in 2003, and a unique era in the history of Canadian publishing came to an end.

As always, Ted's perspective remained sanguine. Although he noted in the *National Post* that Canada's Christians were losing a powerful voice, his comment to the *Calgary Herald* summed up the motto of his career: "Nothing's permanent on this side of paradise."

• • •

What role did Ted Byfield and the *Report* magazines play in Canada's history during the last decades of the 20th century? The answer depends on who you ask. As CBC host and abortion activist Judy Rebick once ruefully ruminated: "At the time, it was considered to be very marginal. It turned out later to be basically in the vanguard of elite conservative thought."[19]

Ted always insisted that he was given too much credit. At a 2011 event celebrating both Prime Minister Stephen Harper's majority government and *Alberta Report* called "The West Is In" hosted at the Coast Edmonton Plaza Hotel, he sat and listened to the accolades showered on him by cabinet minister Jason Kenney and Preston Manning, who praised his pen and his publications for paving the way and making the moment possible. The dinner program called the event a "national gala to reunite the original authors of Harper's historic victory," and a jovial Kenney announced that it was "a real honour to be speaking here to this nostalgic reunion of the vast right-wing conspiracy."

Ted listened to a letter from the prime minister being read aloud. "Ted Byfield and Preston Manning have done so much to inspire, inform, and lead the Conservative movement in Canada," Harper wrote. The enthusiastic crowd agreed. Paul Wells of *Maclean's* noted drily that the crowd in the ballroom featured a lot of the same people that packed Harper's election night headquarters earlier that year. (I was there on election night 2011 as well, and along with Preston Manning, a lot of Byfield veterans were in attendance—a number of *AR* alumni made up Harper's speechwriting team.)

The contrarian columnist then stood up and voiced his objection. "The way this thing has been presented, which is very much appreciated, suggests that the Reform movement was a product of Ted Byfield and Preston Manning," he said. "This is nonsense. The Reform party was a product of Preston Manning. The rest of us helped a bit."[20]

That is an understatement. Ted's decision to throw in with Manning, Ken Whyte of *Maclean's* (and a former *Report* staffer) reflected later, was "a historic choice, [and] just one of the many reasons why Ted stands as one of the greatest journalists Canada has ever produced."[21] According to Whyte, Ted's speech at the Western Assembly and his backing of Manning were pivotal. "At the time, Manning was one of a dozen or more people wandering around Alberta complaining about the Mulroney government and looking to capitalize on the hatred towards Ottawa," Whyte noted. "Ted met with almost all of them, but he was really taken with Manning and his approach. It was crucially important to Manning's credibility that he had the approval of *Alberta Report*."[22]

But in many interviews in the years leading up to his death, when Ted was considering his legacy and discussing his career, he remained consistent on this point. "All I did was write about it," he told me. "I knew them and talked a lot to them."

Ted Byfield did for Canadian conservatism what William F. Buckley did for the American Right: He popularized it. A new conservative political party needed a voice, and they certainly weren't going to get it from the mainstream media. As the *Toronto Sun* observed: "It was the Byfields who popularized the arguments that would influence and activate the hundreds of thousands of westerners who would become the political army behind Preston Manning and the Reform Party. One of the lieutenants in that army was Stephen Harper."[23]

Preston Manning certainly sees *Alberta Report*—and Ted himself—as a key component of the Reform Party's success. "The ideas were floating around, the concerns were floating around, but he gave voice to it," Manning told the CBC years later. "He's a very good writer, very good speaker. He was giving voice to things that people were saying in the coffee shops." The ideas that appeared in *Alberta Report* would profoundly influence the new party's platform. "That statement of principles was virtually the same from Reform to the Canadian Alliance, and then of course Stephen Harper and Peter MacKay did one more round of coalition building...to create the Conservative Party of Canada. Ted's perspective, the statement of principles—even the Conservative Party of Canada today, over half the statement of principles are exactly the same ones that were written in those original Reform documents. Ted has a lot to do with that."[24]

In fact, at an event celebrating Link Byfield several years later, Manning would estimate that between 85 to 90% of those present at the Reform Party's founding meeting had some connection *to Alberta Report*.

Ken Whyte wrote several years after *AR* ceased publishing that the magazine "played a huge role in Alberta and regional life in the broadest sense. Ted has been the most important voice in journalistic Canada for half a century. He raised a generation or two of other journalists, and in the end this is a far greater accomplishment than that of many Canadian journalists who are much more celebrated."[25] Or as former MP Monte Solberg put it: "The Byfields almost single-handedly kept the flickering Canadian conservative flame alive when it was almost snuffed out, and then they used it to help set the fire that became the Reform Party."[26]

David Frum put it more bluntly, writing from Washington, D.C. in 1997: "Any future historian trying to understand Canada's troubles in the late twentieth century will want to look at Mr. Byfield's work. Unless you read Mr. Byfield, you won't ever properly understand the anger of the west at central Canada, the reasons for the destruction of the once-unbreakable Conservative grip on the west, and the birth of the Reform Party."[27]

Canadian journalist Peter Stockland agrees. "No Byfields, no *Alberta Report*. No *Alberta Report*, no Reform Party as it was formed. No Reform Party, no PC collapse. No PC collapse, no Harper government. It's shorthand history, but it's fair shorthand history."[28]

Additionally, Ted Byfield's informal journalism school supplied nearly every publication in the country. *Report* alumni include *Calgary Sun* columnist Rick Bell, *The Dorchester Review* editor Chris Champion, *Edmonton Sun* columnist Lorne Gunter, Rebel News founder Ezra Levant, *Globe and Mail* European Bureau chief Eric

Reguly, *Maclean's* and *National Post* editor Ken Whyte, *National Post* columnist Colby Cosh, and many others. Ted changed the landscape of Canadian media like no other journalist in the country—just not in the way he had necessarily intended.

• • •

But on many of the issues most dear to him, Ted did lose. Over nearly a decade in power, Stephen Harper did his best to marginalize nearly every moral issue Ted cared about. During the years of Harper's minority governments, Ted defended him. But after his 2011 majority and his subsequent muzzling of pro-life parliamentarians, the truth became impossible to ignore. Harper was some sort of conservative, but he certainly wasn't a Byfield conservative. In fact, the devastating Supreme Court decisions of Ted's final years—the legalization of assisted suicide, and the gutting of religious liberty—were largely decided by justices appointed by Harper.

It became clear that Canada's Conservative Party wanted socially conservative Christians like Ted in the tent, but off the platform—permanently. There was peace between libertarian fiscal conservatives and social conservatives for only a handful of the Harper years, after which the notion of a "progressive" Conservative reared its head once again.

In the end, Steve Weatherbe reflected later, both the Reform Party and *Alberta Report* faced the same challenge: finding a large enough market for its ideology. "Both went national in search of it. This worked for the Reform Party, but not for *AR*. Social conservatives are taken for granted today just as Western conservatives were in the mid-1980s." In the Conservative coalition, social conservatives got as raw of a deal as Alberta had gotten from Confederation—their interests could always be sacrificed.

As Weatherbe put it: "Ted made conservatism credible and kept it that way for longer than anywhere else in Canada. Unfortunately, the politicians who owed their careers to the Reform movement lacked his courage, conviction, or willingness to defend social conservative and Christian values against the spirit of the age on issues such as abortion, homosexuality, or the absurdity of transgenderism." In many cases, they simply lacked his beliefs.

People can say what they like about the *Report*—and most people do. But if you happen to be a Christian, and share Ted's worldview—if you think, for example, that the Canadian courts are now a law unto themselves; that the LGBT movement is radically redefining not only accepted morality and human relationships, but (with the transgender movement) the very nature of what it means to be human; if you think that the taxpayer-funded killing of babies in the womb up until nine months of pregnancy is horrifying, or even just that Western Canada often gets a raw deal from Confederation—if you believe these things, then reading through old issues of the *Report* might surprise you. Most of the predictions in its pages turned out to be prophecies, but because the progressives won, Ted's prescience is ignored.

Ted Byfield wasn't wrong. He was, from the perspective of the post-Christian Canadian elites, simply on the wrong side.

CHAPTER SEVEN

THE HISTORIAN

"Are you a dinosaur?" Susan Ormiston, host of CTV's W5 asked.
"I hope so," Ted Byfield solemnly replied.

As the '90s dawned, Ted Byfield was doing well for himself. He was the figurehead of a nationally recognized magazine with powerful political clout that his son Link was now successfully running. He had purchased a large house at 531 Lessard Drive Northwest in Edmonton in 1983 for the rock-bottom price of $175,000, where he and Ginger hosted a nonstop train of writers, relatives, and ne'er-do-wells in need of a place to stay. He had six grown children, including an adopted son (shortly after Vince was born, he and Ginger had adopted their youngest, an Indigenous boy, Thomas.) He'd purchased a small yacht and taken up sailing. Grandchildren were beginning to arrive at consistent intervals. It was clearly time, Ted thought, to begin another massive undertaking.

It is appropriate that aside from the three books to Ted's name—*Just Think, Mr. Berton (A Little Harder)* and two collections of columns, *The Deplorable Unrest in the Colonies* (1983) and *The Book of Ted: Epistles of an Unrepentant Redneck* (1998)—the two great book projects Ted would devote himself to were histories of his two great loves, Alberta and Christianity. A gargantuan history of his adopted home province—*Alberta in the Twentieth Century*—would come first and would prove by far the most financially successful, providing a valuable revenue stream for the magazines.

Ted was a fan of the many history books put out by *Time-Life*, which focused on stories, powerful photographs, and beautiful artwork. In both the magazines and books, visual quality was essential to Ted. Colby Cosh, who worked on the Alberta History series, recalled that Ted also liked the business model: "You could start selling the first book as soon as it was finished to raise money and provide a customer list for later volumes. When you were finished, you had a box set you could sell at a premium."

Paul Bunner describes the series as one of Ted's "greatest lifetime achievements." Emerging from the brutal East versus West brawls of the '80s, Ted's characteristically modest vision for the series was to crystallize Alberta's unique identity by telling her stories and celebrating her people the way Marjorie Campbell had for the Nor'westers and Pierre Berton had done for all of Canada. Ted's goal was to have the books completed by the Alberta Centennial in 2005. To accomplish this, the staff of the *Report* magazines and the other veteran writers and researchers Ted hired for the project would have to produce roughly a book each year.

To launch the project, Ted approached several writers and old-time journalists with long careers in the Canadian news business who might be looking for work. Reporters didn't get pensions, and many of them were still hacking away to make a living. Ted offered good money for good writing, and new hires did much of the heavy lifting as the project got underway. Many of them were well-known in Canadian journalism and had worked for publications such as *Reader's Digest* and were thus acceptable to the mainstream media in a way that Ted would never quite manage to be.

Ted was involved in every step of the venture. "He would read the existing histories of Alberta to develop the contextual framework for each volume, lay out the schematics for each chapter, generate original sidebar ideas, and assign the researchers to go and fill the holes," Bunner recalled. "That first year, Ted conceived a plan to reduce the frequency of publication of the magazine to every second week throughout the summer of 1991. On alternate weeks, the newsroom staff would produce the magazine one week, then chapters and sidebars in the history books the following week. It was discombobulating to go from

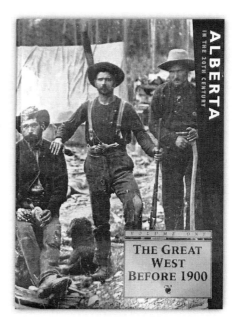

current events to century-old events from week to week. We had a very big, talented newsroom staff—some great writers who produced great chapters in volume one."

The first volume, with its soaring stories of settlements and frontier fights, was everyone's favourite. In later volumes, Bunner recalled, writers were recording events they'd lived through and opined on in the pages of the *Report* magazines, and "it was occasionally hard to remain as dispassionate and objective." The cultural revolution of the 1960s, for example, was the target of "some pretty feisty stuff," and Trudeau got treated "pretty much the way we did it at the magazine." All told, however, the books were well-written and well-received popular histories that sold hundreds of thousands of copies. Bunner, who managed the project for several later volumes, spent much time marketing the books.

Colby Cosh, who later went on to work for *Maclean's* and the *National Post*, was asked by Ted to sign on as editor for volume eight. As Cosh recalled it, Ted attempted to teach him layout, typography, and photo reproduction in a single afternoon. Cosh ended up reneging on the layout work and falling hopelessly behind. This had a deleterious effect on the production schedule, and Ted was displeased when he found out what was causing the delay—which could cause serious financial distress. As Cosh recollected:

> That's when I found out how Ted Byfield solves problems. His angry astonishment at my dereliction was genuine and hard to bear, but it did not last long. Ted had a temper (all Byfields do), but he practiced Christian virtues with great effectiveness—not that it is my place to judge him on that score, but over the years I saw him give room, board and jobs to dozens of hopeless misfits who couldn't have made it anywhere else. When it came my turn to be forgiven and helped, it happened immediately.
>
> He decided we would work together, at his house, on layout and editing, for as long as it took. Work would commence at 10 a.m. and go till 6 p.m. As Ted's people will know, he always insisted on putting down tools at the exact stroke of that hour, and he would wander over to the liquor cabinet to pour everyone in the room the Scotch whisky of their choice. (Blends, not single malts.)
>
> Over a period of weeks, I found myself working as hard as I ever have, trying to rebound from my cowardly error. Ted worked just as hard. It really did seem a lot easier when you could look forward to the guillotine-like 6 p.m. cut-off, and to a couple hours (or three, or four, or five) of arguing and theorizing with a piercingly intelligent gentleman. Having us move the work to the Byfield Manor was smart leadership, but he just liked to find excuses to keep writers around the place, too.[1]

Each of the volumes began with Ted's introductory take on that period in Alberta's history with, as Cosh put it, "all the theories and high points baked in, a narrative of struggle against the Laurentian centre. He didn't seem to need to do much extra research despite being something of an arriviste in Alberta." Which isn't to say Ted's research standards were not high—he would hire four to six researchers to read every edition of every major Albertan daily newspaper on microfilm for the relevant period. Useful facts or stories would be recorded on index cards for the writers. "The use of newspapers was, for him, the essence of the series," said Cosh. "Ted did think of the project as 'newspaper history.'"

Ted summarized the success of the series in a celebratory column in 1999. "There is developing in Alberta a very powerful provincial identity," he wrote. "Perhaps it's because we have so often been called 'redneck' by the rest of Canada, perhaps because we have so often resisted trends in the rest of Canada, perhaps because we live closer to our frontier origins, perhaps because from our very beginning almost everything we produce must be sold on a world market, not a protected local one. And finally, perhaps because our national identity has become so confused of late that it's hard to define what being a Canadian is supposed to mean. There's little doubt what being an Albertan means, and this has a deepening significance. That, we believe, is one of the chief reasons for the success of the history series."[2]

Ted paused only briefly before flinging himself into the next project. By the early 2000s, it was becoming clear that the Canada of Ted's youth had vanished, and that a new, post-Christian country was taking shape around him. Christians were fighting, he once wryly put it, "with our backs to the sea." For Ted this was not so much a historical fact as a challenge to be surmounted. As the second Christian millennium drew to an end, Ted and Ginger knelt in prayer to ask God what they should do next.

The solution, unsurprisingly, just happened to be uniquely suited to Ted's skills—and one he would call their "greatest adventure yet." Due to the liberalization of many churches and the progressive colonization of public education—subjects on which Ted had written acres of copy—Christians and citizens of the West more generally had forgotten the history of Christianity and of Western civilization, histories which were inextricably intertwined. These stories needed to be retold, and who better to tell them than journalists? If reporters could write history's first draft, they could certainly produce a more conclusive one. Ted had proof of concept with the Alberta history series, and simply needed to reapply it to a history of the past two thousand years.

In Ted's view, Christians needed to read more religious history. "The idea that Christianity itself was a story was not well-known," he recalled. "I thought: Before I die, I want to tell that story and tell it with power." Ever the optimist, he described his vision for The Christian History Project, which would eventually become the Society to Explore and Record Christian History (SEARCH) in 2007:

> [W]e realized that the liberal educators, front-runners of this disastrous [cultural] revolution, had left an opening. They quit teaching history, since their aim is to produce a human being wholly enslaved by the spirit of the age, totally captive to the current fashion in everything. History, by introducing people to other ages and eras, provides them with a platform from which to view their own. So the progressives taught sociology instead and said it was history.
>
> Yet human curiosity to know where we're from, and how we got here, is impossible to kill. The educators had thus left in their program of indoctrination an unintended

void—which could be our opportunity. If we could offer
something to fill it, to satisfy that curiosity, and could
do it with narrative, with stories, we could show a new
generation the way home.[3]

This ambitious plan—to produce a powerfully written and
beautifully illustrated popular history of the Christian faith—had
an even more ambitious goal. Ted wanted to marshal the power of
storytelling in the service of Christianity, and thus create a bridge-
head for re-Christianization. As always, his vision was a grand
one: to reintroduce the Christian story to Christians and pagans
alike, fan the flames of rekindled interest, bring the teaching of
history back into the schools, and then "set on foot a change in the
culture…popular being history is the tool which can bring such a
change about." Ted firmly believed that others would see in these
stories what he saw:

> Before any substantial return to our Christian origins
> can occur, there needs to be a restatement of what those
> origins are—that is, a presentation of the whole two-
> thousand-year Christian story, enticing to an educated
> reader, generally acceptable to Protestant, Catholic, and
> Orthodox, to the religious sceptical and the doctrinally
> polemical, always in sufficient detail for all the major events
> to be adequately described and all the foremost players
> to be seen in their historic roles. Upon that foundation,
> children's books can be produced, and the other media will
> be free to find subjects of wide popular interest.
>
> What am I suggesting? That the direction of society can
> be changed by a set of books? No. But as the old Jewish
> saying goes, it's better to light one candle than complain
> about the dark. This series, we believe, is such a candle.[4]

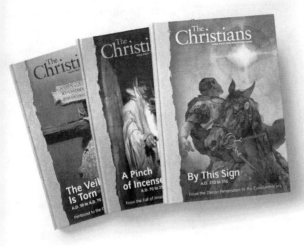

Additionally, the jihadist terrorist attacks of September 11, 2001, had created the sense that the centuries-old conflict between Christianity and Islam—detailed in powerful, imagery-laden prose in *The Christians*—was on the cusp of reigniting into a new era of conflict between the Christian West and Muslim world. (The difficulty with this narrative, of course, was that the Christian West had since become post-Christian, and the idea that reincarnations of the great struggles of Tours or Vienna were in the offing would eventually give way to the renewed realization that the Middle East is still the graveyard of empires.)

Like all of Ted's endeavours, the Christian History Project soon ballooned in size. News articles about the inauguration of the project estimated anywhere between 12 and 40 volumes. Ted envisioned gorgeous books with unique, commissioned art, beautiful pictures, and stunning sidebars. The price tag for all of this grew steadily, and the final cost amounted to over $6 million, with non-profit charities (SEARCH) founded in both Edmonton and Virginia to sell subscriptions of the series to over 10,000 donors. "The series is to our knowledge the only one of its kind ever produced," Ted pitched, "conveying in a lively, popular style the compelling story of Christian tribulations and triumphs throughout the world, epoch by epoch, to the present."

As Steve Weatherbe recalled it: "Ted recruited journalistic friends and current and former staff like me to each take a chapter of a volume of history. He hired researchers to dig up and photocopy history books and newspaper articles. He researched each topic himself and created a detailed outline which each writer received along with file cards based on the photocopied materials, which they were given as well. It was a big writing machine, and we were paid very well by freelance standards in Canada."

With dozens of veteran journalists who had once been on the payroll of the *Report* magazines, family members, and other Christian connections—even Bob Saunders came in from Winnipeg to help with editing on volume six—the greatest story Ted ever told took shape over nearly a decade and a half. The project survived bankruptcy after volume six and had to be bailed out by faithful donors, many of whom had funded Ted's career as a public Christian for years. He had spent much of his adult life speaking for Christians, and no matter what he turned his hand to, they supported him with their hard-earned money.

The final volume, covering 1914 to 2001, was completed in 2013. Colby Cosh's review in *Maclean's* summed it up best:

> It is worth remembering that same-sex marriage was still more or less pie in the sky in the spring of 2003, when *Alberta Report* closed its doors; in the blink of an eye, it became an untouchable part of the Canadian political order, indeed, a point of chauvinistic national pride. That reflects the precipitous pace of secularization in Canada, the speed with which our social order is shifting to a foundation of liberal pluralism. So, too, does the rapid redefinition of the "Conservative" party as a protector of abortion, not only unregulated but tax-funded, to boot. *The Christians: Their First Two Thousand Years* is Byfield's answer, his grand gesture of defiance and recrimination. You can hear both the hope and the despair in that word "First."[5]

The only part of Cosh's analysis I would quibble with is the insinuation that Ted experienced despair. Ted was an irrepressible optimist until the end, always certain that things were about to change, that a new generation was rising to turn the tide, that the truth that seemed so obvious to him was about prove its power once again. Several times he told me that he thought abortion would be illegal within 25 years; on his 93rd birthday (his last), he told the assembled guests that he could feel a change in the air once again, and that all those present were a part of it. His infectious enthusiasm, fused with an intimidating work ethic, always put those who shared his convictions to shame.

He remained convinced that the post-Christian era was merely a pre-Christian era, and that a new dawn might be just around the corner.

Despite the mainstream media's consensus opinion that *The Christians* was a "right-wing take" (*Toronto Star*, *National Post*) on the history of Christianity, the completion of this mammoth project was well-covered. The reviews were generally positive, with predictable tut-tutting over Ted's refusal to offer grovelling apologies for events such as the Crusades—although nobody who read the books could accuse Ted of being an apologist for the crimes of Christendom or her more sinister characters. The Bible presented the heroes of faith as the blemished, saved sinners that they were. Ted and his team did, too. Even at the age of 84, everything Ted Byfield did was newsworthy.

Over 185,000 individual books from *The Christians* have been distributed—although a third of those being the first volume, *The Veil Is Torn*. The series continues to find new readers and has recently been discovered by many American Christians. Ted was a great storyteller, and the story of Christianity is just one of the many he bequeathed to upcoming generations.

• • •

Throughout this period, Ted was also fulfilling his dream of becoming a yachtsman. In the late 1980s, he purchased a Maple Leaf 42 sailing yacht, with the intention, he said half-jokingly, of "living as a bohemian writer in the Mediterranean." He called his sloop *Credimus*, Latin for "We Believe." He soon discovered that a sailboat of this size required a lifeboat, which Ted felt undermined the spirit of *Credimus*. He named the lifeboat *Suspicamus*, or "We suspect." Ginger suggested an entirely different name. "Has it occurred to you that *Credimus* was misnamed?" she asked her enthusiastic husband. Characteristically, it had not. "It really should have been called *Volo*," she told him. Translated: "I want."

Ted and Ginger first practiced sailing on Wabamun Lake. "This boat was not going to be just an accessory," Vince Byfield recalled. "This was going to be Ted's new lifestyle."

Ted's vision was to sail around the world. He and Ginger would start from Vancouver Island, head to the Panama Canal, sail up to Nova Scotia, cross the Atlantic, navigate through the Red Sea, around India, and then up to Japan before crossing back over. As he recalled it, he also wanted to spend some time in the Mediterranean, docking *Credimus* and visiting the places they were writing about. When Vince asked him about the dangers involved, Ted said romantically: "I've always had this dream of dying at sea in a storm with Mom." The usual chuckle of endorsement from Ginger was not forthcoming, and the ominous silence indicated that for once, the Byfields had different dreams.

The odyssey of *Credimus* became another Byfield legend. Ted, with a rotating crew of friends and family members, sailed from Vancouver to San Francisco and then launched off on a long voyage to the Panama Canal and up to Florida. Docking somewhere in Mexico to eat, a solicitous taxi driver dropped the Christian crew of *Credimus* off at a brothel, which the ravenous sailors apparently did not notice until partway through the meal.

At another point, the U.S. Coast Guard stopped *Credimus* to inform Ted that pirates in the Caribbean had ceased their previous courtesy of stranding bereft boat owners in dinghies upon discovering that breathing boatsmen did, in fact, tell tales. The pirates were instead killing yachtsmen and feeding them to the fish. The Coast Guard patrolled for sunburned sportsmen, rounded them up, and accompanied them to Florida in a convoy of annoyed but alive potential targets of piracy. Ted was among them.

From Florida, Ted headed to Norfolk, Virginia. Despite Ted's faith, *Credimus* was in suspiciously bad shape, with constant engine problems causing great concern. Ted was no mechanic, and he

was beginning to run low on mechanically inclined friends he could press-gang into service. Vince was recruited to sail with his parents from Norfolk to Halifax. The journey didn't go as planned. "I was thrown off the boat in New Jersey, just shy of Manhattan," said Vince.

When Vince joined the voyage, he was a teenager, freshly dating, and miserably in love. "Rather than experience this trip with joy and gratitude, I spent most of it sulking at the front of the boat writing love letters," Vince recalled. "By

Ted at the wheel of *Credimus*, a 42-foot sloop they purchased with the intention to eventually circumnavigate the globe.

the time we got to Manhattan, Dad couldn't take it anymore. 'No woman is worth this,' he said." Vince, greatly aggrieved, replied: "Take that back or I'm going to have to punch your face in."

"He stopped, and he didn't say anything but there was about a five second pause. I'm pretty sure he was trying to decide whether or not I'd be able to take him. Finally, he said, 'You know Vince, I think this is your stop.'" They dropped anchor and Ginger rowed him to shore, inquiring with concern about the state of his mind and finances. Vince was beached on a military base, picked up by military police as he wandered about, and dropped off at a bus stop. It was a long commute back to Alberta.

By the time *Credimus* limped into Halifax, Ted realized that his plans to sail around the world were unrealistic. It was very unlikely that his vessel would make it across the ocean, and he perceived a distinct lack of enthusiasm when he pitched seafaring adventures to friends. He'd purchased a vessel built for the Pacific rather than the Atlantic, and so he had it towed across the country, docked it in a marina in downtown Vancouver, and worked with Ginger on the *BC Report* for the magazine's first year. He wrote his columns on *Credimus* and sent them in by satellite phone through modems.

But despite the end of Ted's globe-trotting dreams, *Credimus* became the source of a Byfield family tradition, with Ted taking his grandchildren for sailing trips when they turned eight years old. As Eli Byfield recalled:

In 1990 I boarded a plane in Edmonton for my first trip to Vancouver. For eight-year-old me it was exhilarating: soaring unaccompanied over the Rockies, meeting my grandfather at the airport, steering *Credimus* through the Strait of Georgia, hiking twenty-five miles through the mountains with Gramps. The novelty was exciting. Receiving the undivided attention of this great man was even more so.

I got a second trip with Gramps all to myself. By the third Luc and Cole had turned eight so they got invitations too. Before long Phil, Trinity and Silas were impressed also.

Our expeditions gradually evolved the attendant trappings of ritual. My siblings, cousins from various far-flung corners of North America (California, Mexico, etc.) and I would deplane at Vancouver airport within a few hours of each other. Grandpa (and Grandma for the first four or five trips) collected us all.

The journey to *Credimus'* eventual berth at Salt Spring Island involved a lengthy ferry ride. En route Gramps produced several large nautical maps, compasses, a marine ruler, pencils and a bag of loonies. *"Silas!"* Gramps would announce in his booming, big-city baritone, "If you correctly plot our position on *this map*, you will earn *one loonie.*" (He had developed his own mode of speech, placing great emphasis on particular words thus compelling one's interest in where the sentence was going. Old radio dramas or Christopher Walken have a somewhat similar cadence.) For a so-called 'fiscal hawk,' Ted dispersed his bounty liberally. Half an hour later his bag much lighter, we six grandkids were dismissed to explore the vessel and redistribute our newfound prosperity to the BC ferry vending machine service. (This teaching exercise likely inculcated a lifelong love of compasses which no doubt proved useful in my surveying career.)

Upon embarking at his ship, we unpacked our things. *Credimus* contained fore and aft sleeping berths. In a pinch the dining area in the galley could accommodate a pair of sleepers as well. (Gram and Gramps used it a few times.) I slept in the cockpit once or twice which was okay if it didn't rain. By the time Trinity and Silas joined our squadron,

Ted resting briefly while ascending Mount Tuam in 1993 with grandsons
[left to right] Colman and Elias Byfield, Philip and Luc Doucedame.

Grandpa had to rent a second boat and supplement the officer corps with relatives and old drinking buddies.

Before we got too comfortable, Gramps would review the duty roster. We enlisted sailors were each expected to cook dinner once. By prior instruction on the ferry, we each announced what meal we'd be preparing for our night. Armed with a menu, he'd depart for the grocery store and return amply stocked with provisions. We spent the first night in harbour playing a board game or some other pleasant diversion. We normally shoved off on the morning of day two.

Days under sail (or, depending on schedule, under motor) followed a regular pattern. Early morning prayers, then breakfast. We launched by 7am. Each crew consisted of at least three grandchildren and one or two adults. We had assigned turns at the helm, navigating and cooking/cleaning. As only steering demanded constant attention, this left us relatively free to do as we pleased about two thirds of the time. While we would anchor on occasion, (after one bitter experience) this was not our preferred way to spend the night. We docked at port usually by 4pm (depending how far away the next town was). While one enthusiastic chef from each boat remained with the officers to prepare supper, the rest of us were granted shore leave.

Then there were the walks. If memory serves, Grandpa never worked Sundays. Whether in Edmonton, Vancouver or Salt Spring Island, his 'day off' included a stroll of between fifteen and twenty-five miles (a regimen maintained into his seventies). Each sailing trip included one such hike. We kids accompanied Gramps who passed the time telling stories, teaching us songs and relating the history of railroads and rivers along the way.

A keen logistical mind complemented Ted's meticulous memory. When scheduling, he planned to the minute. "*Prayers* will begin at *4:06*! *Breakfast* will be at *4:13*." A tremendous capacity to focus reinforced both these gifts. Consequently, Grandpa had an uncommon ability to execute plans. He also had another weapon in his arsenal. When his common sense failed (as it sometimes might in the flood of his own ebullience), Grandma Byfield's allotment often redeemed the lapse. Hers was a very different (but no less impressive) character.

These journeys would always end with an expensive supper at a fancy restaurant for the entire crew, paid for by Ted. As a father, Ted had always been incessantly working—one of his sons joked that working with Ted was the best way to spend quality time with him. But Ted loved his family dearly and prized the time he spent with his grandchildren. His praise—which he doled out liberally—meant much. As Eli Byfield put it:

Ted often walked for hours from the family home in West Edmonton to the Beverly Crest Hotel in northeast Edmonton. In 1995 sons Vincent, Michael and Link accompanied him.

I will briefly comment on Ted's personal flaws (as I see them) now legendary in family lore. These had nothing to do with hate or bigotry. They were chiefly egotism and his afore-mentioned temper. He wasn't a particularly proud man. He could mock himself and possessed a kind of humility. It seemed to me that his ego and temper were outgrowths of his passion and drive. To him, his own mission took precedence over *all* other considerations. Thankfully his ambition was bridled at least somewhat beneath the yoke of a religious code. I shudder to imagine what a man of his talent and energy might have become had he not succumbed to church in young adulthood.

217

Which brings me to the most remarkable trait of a remarkable man: resolve. He had a species of courage evidently routed in faith. He could not only dream big dreams; he could act on them. He could throw away a thriving journalism career to start a private school with little backing. He could leave that successful venture to found a provincial magazine on little more than a prayer. He could make up his mind that he *should* do a thing, and then go out and do it. One of his favourite poets might say he 'could squarely push the logic of a fact to its ultimate conclusion in unmitigated act.' Perhaps it is easy for a brilliant man of invincible confidence to ignore his own misgivings, but I've never found it so of others.

To put it simply: For all his many and obvious flaws, Ted Byfield was a great man.

• • •

[Left to right] St. John's veteran headmasters Dave Neelands, Mike Maunder, Frank Wiens and Ted enjoying themselves prior to one of Byfield's infamous Boxing Day parties.

Ted's Christian journey eventually led him to reluctantly abandon the church of his youth. After nearly a lifetime in the Anglican Church, a book written in her defence, and the founding of an Anglican religious order, Ted and Virginia became Orthodox in 1996, joining Saint Herman of Alaska Church in Edmonton. After watching—and railing against—the gutting of their beloved Anglican Church and the resolute refusal of her own clergy to defend her, the Byfields sought a church that would not be swept along with the tides of the times. "How many Orthodox priests does it take to change a light bulb?" Ginger once joked. The answer: "Change—what's that?"

Despite his close friendship with many Catholics—indeed, his son Link converted to Catholicism—Ted couldn't make the leap. There were two doctrines he simply could not bring himself to accept: the veneration of the Virgin Mary and papal infallibility. Thus, it was to Orthodoxy that Ted and Ginger fled rather than the Church of Rome. They were joined by their daughter Philippa.

The Byfields were active participants in their parish, opening their home for church events, helping to sell garlic sausages before Easter, and participating in the church's charitable endeavours. Ted sang with the basses. Soon after joining, Ted pioneered the publishing of a booklet about Orthodoxy in general and Saint Herman's in particular and joined in distributing them door to door to 10,000 households across west Edmonton. In 2001, Ted participated in the Archdiocese of Canada Assembly, leading a workshop on the subject "Living Counter-Culture."

The completion of *The Christians* was a triumph made sweeter by how financially difficult it had been, but Ted's twilight years also brought many sorrows as loved ones took their leave before him—including two children. The first to go was Philippa, who had served as a reporter for *Alberta Report* and worked as general secretary for the Christian History Project. She died at the age of

The 2007 fire that claimed both the family home and daughter Philippa, who succumbed to her injuries a few days later.

53 on October 8, 2007 before the series was finished, succumbing to both lung cancer and extensive burns to the face and mouth.

Living as a palliative patient in a second-story bedroom of the Byfields' Edmonton home, she had lit a cigarette next to her oxygen tank, having started smoking again after being told her cancer was terminal. The tank exploded and set the house ablaze, levelling the 3,200 square-foot home and causing close to $1.5 million in damage—although firefighters managed to rescue one of Ted's computers from his office on the ground floor containing years' worth of research and writing for his books. It took nearly fifty firefighters to get the fire under control.

Philippa was laid to rest on October 12 in the Holy Cross Cemetery. The home at 531 Lessard Drive was rebuilt on the same site, and in 2011, Vince, his wife Grace, and their children moved in with Ted and Ginger.

Ginger was diagnosed with cancer several years later and died with Ted at her side on July 21, 2014. His devastation was total. He wanted to die, too—and his wife must have sensed it. Her last words to him, he said, were: "Don't. You. Quit." They were in love to the last, and until his death seven years later, he never tired of directing any conversation towards Ginger. After sixty-five years together, he was bereft without her. He would often wake up in the middle of the night to respond to a phone call or a disturbance and would reach out to her in bed to reassure her. When his hand struck the empty place where she had slept beside him for so long, the pain would suddenly be new again and grief would overwhelm him with breathtaking force.

Ginger had taken singing lessons for five years in order to participate in the liturgy at St. Herman's, her voice being one of the few things she felt insecure about. She once asked her husband in a worried tone if her singing was okay: "Am I putting them off?" Ted could not tell this story without tears: "No, no honey." There were tapes of her singing lessons, but he couldn't listen to them lest he "go all to pieces." After she died, he never listened to them again. Often, he told me, the lines of an old Barbara Streisand song from the 1970s would run through his mind as he remembered her face and their adventure-filled life together:

Mem'ries light the corners of my mind
Misty water-colored mem'ries of the way we were
Scattered pictures of the smiles we left behind
Smiles we gave to one another for the way we were
Can it be that it was all so simple then
Or has time rewritten every line
If we had the chance to do it all again, tell me,
would we, could we
Mem'ries may be beautiful and yet
What's too painful to remember
We simply choose to forget
So it's the laughter we will remember
Whenever we remember the way we were
The way we were.

Virginia Byfield was buried in the same plot as her daughter Philippa on Saturday, July 26, following a funeral service at St. Herman's. The funeral included no eulogies or speeches—nothing modern at all, in fact. Just, as some guests observed, as Ginger would have wanted.

Link was the last Byfield to predecease Ted, dying on January 24, 2015, at the young age of 63. He had been diagnosed with incurable stage IV cancer of the esophagus and liver on June 5, 2014, scarcely two months before his mother's passing. On September 24, 2014, Preston Manning hosted a tribute to Link and the *Alberta Report*. Ted Morton talked about *AR's* role in birthing the Canadian conservative movement during the 1990s, and Manning was effusive in his praise. "You integrated faith with things the world tries to keep separate," he told Link. "You are salt and light. You are a blessing."

Mike Byfield, too, paid tribute to his younger sibling. "I've never heard my brother lie. I've never heard my brother in any vicious way criticize anybody. I have never heard my brother be greedy, not once. I've never seen my brother cheat anyone and I've rarely heard him complain or get angry...I'm immensely proud of how well Link faces what he's facing."

Surveying the battles and losses of the decades behind him, Link summed it up simply: "Think how much worse it would be if we had not fought the fights we fought."

The following year, needing a way to cope with his grief, Ted set off across the country to visit the many places he and Ginger had lived out their lives. He made a pilgrimage to the places where they'd lived and worked, tracing their lives together across the country, heading eastward. If he had revisited their old haunts in Timmins, he would have found them unrecognizable. The Empire Hotel had become a homeless shelter. The past is a land no man can return to, no matter how deep his grief or desperate his desire.

• • •

On October 19, 2017, Senator Betty Unger announced that Ted would be one of only fourteen Albertans to receive the Canadian Senate's 150th Commemorative Medals. It was not the Order of Canada—an award rendered almost valueless by the inclusion of men such as abortion pioneer Henry Morgentaler and other cultural revolutionaries who had transformed the country—but it was, at least, a glimmer of the recognition Ted's life and achievements deserved. It is almost certain that if Ted had championed the progressive values that now make up Canada's national identity, the elites would have showered him with every honour at their disposal. Instead, he fought them to the last.

Ted heeded Ginger's final words—although one suspects that he would have been constitutionally incapable of quitting even if he wanted to. He never stopped seeking new projects. In his eighties, he worked with the Alberta Home Education Association, teaching students how to write so that they could enter journalism and be a Christian influence in a secular media environment. Despite the homogenous nature of Canadian media—staffed, in many places, by veterans of his own publications—Ted remained not only a believer in Christianity, but in the ability of Christians to change the country.

Following the publication of the books, Ted and SEARCH established a web journal to track Christianity's progress into the 21st century, launched an Editor Tutorial Program, and began blogging again. Ted was relentlessly on the lookout for ways to teach Christianity to the upcoming generation and to present it to the culture, and even while struggling to understand new technologies (and sometimes hilariously failing), he tenaciously kept at it. At one point, he produced the plans for an entire series of Dorothy Sayers-style plays based on *The Christians*, to be produced with the quality (but presumably not the budget) of the BBC. That project, like many others, was eventually forgotten.

I cannot count the number of calls I got from Ted during the last years of his life in which he wanted to pitch some new scheme. When he discovered podcasts, he wanted to know if he should launch one to promote *The Christians*; perhaps a radio show, with a young social conservative and himself; when he died, he was serving as the general editor on a new book project called *The Fruits of Christendom*, for which he was to write a chapter on education. His work was his passion, and he often noted, with a gleeful chuckle, that he'd never worked a day in his life. (Ted's grandson Eli Byfield wryly recalled his mother joking when he was a boy that when Link retired, his job would be "driving Grandpa to work.")

Ted never lost his sense of humour, and still cackled delightedly whenever reading a good line or hearing a good story. While many other conservative and Christian writers succumbed to doom and gloom, Ted did not. He wrote in a fashion reminiscent of G.K. Chesterton, who frequently wrote in a restaurant in Fleet Street. An anecdote included in the final volume of The Christians series recorded the observation of a Chinese waiter, who told a friend of Chesterton: "Your friend, that big man, he very intelligent. He eat and he laugh. Then he take up a pencil and he write. Then he laugh at what he write."

I asked him once how he stayed so cheerful. His answer came without hesitation. "It's from reading history. We Christians have been through some ghastly times. We don't see this world as anything. Being here is a very short experience. Whatever you go through here is almost irrelevant compared with what you might be going through, good or bad. Your focus has to stay not on this world, but the next world. If you lose that, you lose everything. When you see how Christians endured the first three centuries of the Christian era, you realize that bad news is simply part of it." The other aspect of it, he said, was prayer. To imagine living without praying, Ted noted, was like imagining living without breathing.

I grew up reading Ted's work but spoke with him for the first time in 2009, interviewing him while I wrote for Simon Fraser University's student newspaper. I was nervous calling him—Ted was a journalism legend, and I was a kid. But Ted put me at ease immediately, and at several points reversed the interview to ask me questions. He urged me to call him if I was ever in Edmonton. The next time I was, I didn't need to call him—I was attending the March for Life, and he was one of the keynote speakers. I spoke and met with him many times over the next few years about different projects, and we had lunch in Toronto while he was traversing the country on his pilgrimage of remembrance for Ginger.

I first approached Ted with the idea of a biography in early 2017, certain that somebody was already working on one. To my surprise, nobody was. I wanted to record his memories while it was still possible, and he enthusiastically agreed. I met with him to discuss the outline that April, and he insisted that we begin with a glass of wine and lunch at a little Italian café he frequented. With his button-up shirt, black suspenders, gravelly voice, and glinting eyes, he looked every bit the aging newspaperman. All he wanted to talk about was Ginger, resisting my attempts to channel his memories elsewhere.

When the waiter came over—an Italian fellow oddly named Walter—Ted waved his hand in my direction. "He's writing a book on a very important and prestigious subject." The waiter paused; Ted held the punchline in for less than second. "Me!" Walter, who obviously knew Ted well, broke into laughter on cue. "Haha! Wonderful to see you again, Mr. Byfield."

Back at his office, I wandered around while he poured a couple of whiskies. There was a photo of Ginger at the age he met her, young and vibrant and beautiful. The overflowing bookcases were shedding papers of all sorts, and an equally overflowing bar lined with bottles of Scotch and an assortment of other liquors he claimed he didn't like but people kept giving him. A wooden sign over the bookcase read *Illegitimi non carborundum*: "Don't let the bastards grind you down."

His love of the English apologists was obvious, too. The fireplace featured a plaque with a quote from G.K. Chesterton: "A queer fancy seems to be current that a fire exists to warm people. It exists to warm people, to light their darkness, to raise their spirits, to toast their muffins, to air their rooms, to cook their chestnuts, to tell stories to their children, to make chequered shadows on their walls, to boil their hurried kettles, and to be the red heart of a man's house and that hearth for which, as the great heathens said, a man should die."

As we talked and I took notes, fat white snowflakes started falling softly outside, hissing into piles on the deck. Staring out the window, Ted's train of thought shifted abruptly and he stopped in mid-sentence, paused, and began to quote Robert Frost, first quietly, then louder:

> Whose woods these are I think I know.
> His house is in the village though;
> He will not see me stopping here
> To watch his woods fill up with snow.
>
> My little horse must think it queer
> To stop without a farmhouse near
> Between the woods and frozen lake
> The darkest evening of the year.
>
> He gives his harness bells a shake
> To ask if there is some mistake.
> The only other sound's the sweep
> Of easy wind and downy flake.

The woods are lovely, dark and deep,
But I have promises to keep,
And miles to go before I sleep,
And miles to go before I sleep.

Thankfully, he did have more miles to go. During the years that followed, I spent dozens of hours interviewing Ted about his life, recording, transcribing, doubling back with more questions. He often disintegrated into gales of laughter while attempting to finish some hilarious story; he frequently managed to end completely unrelated stories with some compliment to Ginger. His lifetime as a journalist often kicked in, and if I wasn't careful I would find Ted interrogating me, always with great interest: "Is that right, eh? Is

Ted on a Sylvan Lake, Alberta hotel bed in 2012. He and Virginia would often hide out there as deadlines approached for his work on the history book series *The Christians: Their First Two Thousand Years.*

that right?" And always, at the end of the interview or discussion: "Just call me if you need anything at all."

In Winnipeg, Mike Maunder drove me around to the places where Ted and Ginger had begun their lives as Christians: The St John's Cathedral, their little house, the ancient, sagging Dynevor school building in Selkirk, held erect only by massive steel brackets bolted to the brick. The old dormitories were falling apart, and the white frame chapel with its magnificent mural was shuttered and piled with chairs, desks, and the refuse of years long past. Buildings that had once rung with the voices of boys and men were quiet but for the wind, and even the Red River, which had swept the crews on their way to adventure, was still, frozen nearly solid.

During the last year of his life, Ted's memory began to scatter and his sharpness dulled somewhat, although he was still a consummate storyteller. He could tell he was reaching for things he could no longer find, and it frustrated him. When I drove him to the barber for a haircut about six months before he died and waited for him in the car, I ended up getting a call forty-five minutes later from Vincent—Ted had just arrived home, looking dapper. He'd forgotten that I had driven him and had hitched a ride home with a friend.

I last saw Ted in July of 2021 on the weekend of his 93rd birthday. The first draft of the biography was nearly complete, and we spent several days together sitting in his office and outside on the sunny deck of his Edmonton home while I read the chapters aloud to him. He listened intently, riveted both by his own life and how fast it seemed to have gone. Frequently, he would interrupt with additional details, or break out into that wonderful, raspy chuckle his friends know so well. When I looked up after reading about his beloved Ginger, he had tears trailing down his face. He shed many, most of them happy, during those hours of reading. He was grateful, he said shaking his head, for the life he had been given.

On July 10, friends and family gathered at his home for

his birthday. Veterans of *Alberta Report* and journalists; MPs and MLAs; friends and family members toasted the prairie lion of Canadian conservatism and sang him their best wishes. Ezra Levant flew in; Stockwell Day arrived to wish him well. It was the last time many of the attendees would see him.

On December 16, 2021, Vince Byfield sent an email to Ted's family and friends.

Dad was admitted to Misericordia Hospital yesterday morning. He is in considerable pain and his lungs are very congested. I was able to stay by his bedside until about 7:45 last night. He is now in isolation pending COVID test results. The morphine seems to have had little effect. His memory is not great and he often is unaware of where he is or why.

The following day, Vince sent out an update:

I was able to talk to him last night. He was heavily drugged and very much not himself. In his deluded state and not recognizing me at all (I have literally been by his side most of every day for over a decade) he begged for bus fare so he could get home. He tried communicating multiple times in my allotted 30 minutes that he wanted out of his restraints and out of the hospital. When I was out of his eyesight talking to the nurse he continued to yell as much. Seeing Dad in this state still brings tears as I write this.

But even after 38 hours of such existence there remains much vigor in Dad. I find this remarkable. An elderly woman from Dad's church once told him: "Russian proverb: An old lion is still a lion."

Unfortunately under current lockdown policies only two designated visitors are able to visit with him and only for 30 minutes each. Those two are myself and my brother Mike. No substitutions are allowed for the duration of the hospital stay. Clergy are not exempted from this restriction so even Father Vincent cannot be with him unless Mike or I surrender our right to see our Dad in what might very well be his last days. Dad tested COVID negative by the way.

Thankfully, Ted was released from the hospital into the loving care of his son, who had lived with him since 2011 and worked by his side for years. Vince reported that Ted was back in "his favourite chair and enjoying Handel's *Messiah*." Many of us hoped he was on the mend, but it was not to be.

A bed was set up for him in his ground floor office, surrounded by his bookshelves and walls filled with mementoes of his life and loves. His children flew in to be with him—Mary Frances from California, Mike from Mexico. Vince slept at his side. Ted was unconscious during his final night, but Vince heard him mumbling scattered lines from the Psalms throughout that restless sleep.

At 9:16 PM on Thursday, December 23, 2021, Ted Byfield drew his last breath, and died.

Ted and Virginia's family legacy taken in 2009. [Back row left to right] Deborah, Thomas, Daniel and Tristan Byfield; [Second row from back] Vincent Byfield, Luc, Philip, and Link Doucedame, Link, Colman and Benjamin Byfield; [Third row from back] Mary Frances Doucedame (nee Byfield), Elise, Gunilla, Virginia, Ted, Michael and Silas Byfield; [Fourth row from back] Trinity, Joanne, Andria Byfield, [seated] Pippa Broadhurst and Sally Cleary (Virginia's sisters), Alma Byfield, Alison Maher (Sally's daughter); [Front row] Grace, Cordelia, Edward, Mercia, Johannes, Melanie, Liberty, Elias and Symphony Byfield.

EPILOGUE

Imagine yourself as a living house. God comes in to rebuild that house. At first, perhaps, you can understand what He is doing. He is getting the drains right and stopping the leaks in the roof and so on; you knew that those jobs needed doing and so you are not surprised. But presently He starts knocking the house about in a way that hurts abominably and does not seem to make any sense. What on earth is He up to? The explanation is that He is building quite a different house from the one you thought of—throwing out a new wing here, putting on an extra floor there, running up towers, making court-yards. You thought you were being made into a decent little cottage: but He is building a palace. He intends to come and live in it Himself.

—C.S. Lewis in *Mere Christianity*, printed on the back
of the program for Ted Byfield's burial service

E dward "Ted" Bartlett Byfield was laid to rest in Holy Cross Cemetery in Edmonton, Alberta on Thursday, December 30, 2021. It was white and bright in the snowy graveyard, and a small group of about fifty mourners, bundled up against temperatures of -30 degrees Celsius, attended his interment alongside his beloved Ginger and daughter Philippa. A bagpiper playing "Flowers of the Forest" led Ted's casket to the open grave, borne by his son and grandsons and draped in the Alberta flag. The piper played "Amazing Grace" and the crowd sang along for a few verses, muffled by scarves and hoods.

The funeral service itself, held at St. Herman of Alaska Ortho-dox Church, was limited primarily to family due to government COVID-19 restrictions, but old friends and young friends alike gathered at the graveside, joined by Premier Jason Kenney, former MLA Danielle Smith, and a smattering of activists and journalists. Father Vincent and choir members from St. Herman's sang, the casket was lowered into the ground, and the mourners decamped to 531 Lessard Drive, where they gathered once again in Ted's office to swap stories and remembrances and talk politics. It was almost as if he were there.

The tributes came pouring in—as did the hate. LGBT activists on Twitter celebrated his death with remarkable bile, condemning his alleged intolerance with fierce hatred and a distinct lack of self-awareness. (I chuckled at one point when I considered how chuffed Ted would have been to find himself getting smeared by a man with clarifying "he/him" pronouns in his Twitter bio.) Ken Whyte, a former colleague and editor of both *Maclean's* and the *National Post,* was one of the first to eulogize him: "RIP Ted Byfield. He was a great man and a true original, perhaps the only Canadian to sustain a politically important periodical outside Ont./Que. He was also my journalism school and a good friend. Sincere condolences to the Byfield family."

Premier Jason Kenney also offered public condolences: "A remarkable man and a great Albertan: old school journalist, educator, historian, publisher, entrepreneur. An irascible character with a heart of gold who had an enormous impact on Canadian journalism and politics. One of his enduring legacies will be the masterful 11 volume *Alberta in the 20th Century* series, a colourful, popular history." Former leader of the Conservative Party Andrew Scheer added his own tribute: "Sad to hear of Ted Byfield's death. Deepest sympathies to his family. I grew up reading my dad's copies of the *Alberta Report.* A champion for Western Canada and for principles like smaller govt and greater individual liberty."

The CBC called Ted an "iconic Alberta conservative publisher"; the *National Post* said he was the "catalyst for the rise of

Western conservatism"; and the *Globe and Mail* concurred with a long, largely laudatory obituary by Peter Shawn Taylor titled "Influential Alberta Report publisher Ted Byfield gave voice to a nascent Reform Party." Rick Bell penned a short, heartfelt piece for the *Sun* papers titled "Ted Byfield, he changed the course of my life," and Terry O'Neill offered his own memories in a *BC Catholic* column that celebrated the "rich legacy left by a crusading Christian journalist."

Preston Manning also sent a beautiful letter to Vince Byfield, noting that former Prime Minister Stephen Harper had greatly admired Ted and offering his own view of Ted's legacy. It read in part:

My personal involvement with Ted was of course mainly in the political field where he was a great champion of western and conservative interests and a key Founder of the Reform Party. He gave the best and most inspirational speech at Reform's founding meeting in Vancouver in 1987 which got the whole exercise launched - an exercise which eventually led to the election of a majority federal government under Stephen Harper.

You and your brothers and sisters should take immense pride in this achievement as there are very few families in Canada who can say their patriarch said and did things that profoundly affected their country's politics and government in this way.

But as you all also know, Ted was a great advocate and champion in several other spheres as well - on the educational front and the spiritual front - fronts of even more fundamental importance and value to Canada and society than the political front. His consistent adherence to the basic tenets of the Christian faith especially will insure [sic] that he has already heard the Saviour whom he served say - "Well done thou good and faithful servant."

While Ted's passing no doubt casts a shadow of sadness over your celebration of Christmas - the time of year when we celebrate

God's gift to us - perhaps that shadow may be lightened when you think that your family has just given back to God the gift of your father's presence in the heavenly kingdom.

Some public figures who knew and loved Ted kept silent for fear that their remembrances would draw the wrath of the progressive forces that the happy warrior had battled for a half-century, but Ted was mourned, remembered, and celebrated, nonetheless. "Ted and Link fought the zeitgeist valiantly and apparently lost," Steve Weatherbe reflected. "There are worse things."

Ted would have been more optimistic. Secular societies such as ours, he once wrote, are inevitably overpowered by societies with more self-discipline, or they regain faith through renewal and revival. "Out of the darkness comes a Gregory, or a Francis, or a Wesley, and we regain that which we have lost," he said. "The latter, when one beholds the squalid condition of the modern church, does not seem too probable. But then again, it never has."

ABOUT THE AUTHOR

J onathon Van Maren is a writer, public speaker, and activist. His work has appeared in *First Things*, *National Review*, *The American Conservative*, *Christianity Today*, the *National Post*, and he is a contributing editor at *The European Conservative*. He is the author of several books including *The Culture War*, *Patriots: The Untold Story of Ireland's Pro-Life Movement*, and co-author of *A Guide to Discussing Assisted Suicide*. He is the communications director for the Canadian Centre for Bio-Ethical Reform.

ENDNOTES

PREFACE

1   Michael Wagner, *True Right: Genuine Conservative Leaders of Western Canada* (St. Catharines, ON: Freedom Press Canada Inc., 2016), 88-89

2   Michael Wagner, *Alberta Separatism Then and Now* (St. Catharines, ON: Freedom Press Canada Inc., 2015), 52

CHAPTER ONE

1   Carey Toane, "Sympathy for the Old Devil," *Ryerson Review of Journalism*, March 1, 2000

2   Ted Byfield, *The Book of Ted: Epistles of an Unrepentant Redneck* (Edmonton: Keystone Press Inc., 1998), 258

3   Ted Byfield, *The Deplorable Unrest in the Colonies* (Edmonton: *Alberta Report*, 1983), 35

4   Ibid, 35

5   Ted Byfield, "Macho Males don't produce rednecks; it's macho females—like this one," *Alberta Report*, March 11, 1996, 44

6   Ibid

7   "A Provocative Public Voice," Christianity.ca, last accessed January 25, 2022, https://www.christianity.ca/page.aspx?pid=12742

8   Ernest Hemingway, "Sporting Mayor at Boxing Bouts," *Toronto Star Weekly*, first published March 13, 1920, https://ehto.thestar.com/marks/sporting-mayor-at-boxing-bouts

9   "1939 Royal Tour," *The Canadian Encyclopedia*, last accessed January 25, 2022, https://www.thecanadianencyclopedia.ca/en/article/1939-royal-tour

10 Ted Byfield, Ted Byfield Blog, "Why did the Humboldt hockey bus crash become a national tragedy?", first published April 23, 2018, last accessed January 25, 2022, https://ted-byfield.wordpress.com/2018/04/23/why-did-the-humboldt-hockey-bus-crash-become-a-national-tragedy/

11 Ted Byfield, "Macho Males don't produce rednecks; it's macho females—like this one," *Alberta Report*, March 11, 1996, 44

12 Ted Byfield, *The Deplorable Unrest in the Colonies* (Edmonton: *Alberta Report*, 1983), viii

13 Ted Byfield, *Just Think, Mr. Berton (a little harder)* (Winnipeg: The Company of the Cross, Wallingford Press, 1965), 32

14 Ibid

15 Ibid, 33

16 Ted Byfield, "Macho Males don't produce rednecks; it's macho females—like this one," *Alberta Report*, March 11, 1996, 44

17 Ibid

18 Ibid

19 Ibid

CHAPTER TWO

1   Ted Byfield, *The Deplorable Unrest in the Colonies* (Edmonton: *Alberta Report*, 1983), viii

2   Carey Toane, "Sympathy for the Old Devil," *Ryerson Review of Journalism*, March 1, 2000

3   Ted Byfield, *Just Think, Mr. Berton (a little harder)* (Winnipeg: The Company of the Cross, Wallingford Press, 1965), 38-39

4   Ibid, 41-42

CHAPTER THREE

1   Michael Wagner, *True Right: Genuine Conservative Leaders of Western Canada* (St. Catharines, ON: Freedom Press Canada Inc., 2016), 119

2   Ted Byfield, Ted Byfield Blog, "Farewell to the speechless man who made it all happen", first published March 27, 2019, last accessed January 25, 2022, https://tedbyfield.wordpress. com/2019/03/27/farewell-to-the-speechless-man-who-made-it-all-happen/

3   Ibid

4   Ibid

5   Carey Toane, "Sympathy for the Old Devil," *Ryerson Review of Journalism*, March 1, 2000

6   Boyce Richardson, *Memoirs of a Media Maverick* (Toronto: Between the Lines, 2003), 94-95

7   A Provocative Public Voice," Christianity.ca, last accessed January 25, 2022, https://www.christianity.ca/page.aspx?pid=12742

8   Ted Byfield, *Just Think, Mr. Berton (a little harder)* (Winnipeg: The Company of the Cross, Wallingford Press, 1965), 66

9   Ibid, 106-7

10 Ibid, 110-111

11 Ibid, 115

12 Ted Byfield, *The Deplorable Unrest in the Colonies* (Edmonton: *Alberta Report*, 1983), ix-x

13 Ibid, 139

14 Ted Byfield, *Just Think, Mr. Berton (a little harder)* (Winnipeg: The Company of the Cross, Wallingford Press, 1965), 142

15 Pat Annesley, "Ted Byfield: running a revolution on $1 a day," *Impetus Magazine*, September 29, 1973

16 Mike Maunder; Barbara McKay; Laura Botsford; Carolina Jakeway Roemmich, *Today My Sail I Lift: Memories of the St. John's Schools 1956-2008* (Stony Plain, Alberta: Company of the Cross, 2012), 12

CHAPTER FOUR

1   Ibid, 13
2   Ibid
3   Ibid
4   Ibid, 14
5   Ibid, 15
6   Ibid, 16
7   Ibid,17
8   Ibid
9   Ibid
10 Ibid, 18
11 Ibid, 22
12 Ibid, 22
13 Ibid, 22-34
14 Ibid, 26
15 Ibid, 28-9
16 Ibid, 31-2
17 Ibid, 34
18 Ibid, 32
19 Ibid, 37

20 Ted Byfield, "By Lakes and Rivers," *The Annual Report of St. John's Cathedral Boys' School*, 1966, 14

21 Ibid

22 Ibid, 15

23 Ibid, 16-17

24 Mike Maunder; Barbara McKay; Laura Botsford; Carolina Jakeway Roemmich, *Today My Sail I Lift: Memories of the St. John's Schools 1956-2008* (Stony Plain, Alberta: Company of the Cross, 2012), 46

25 Ibid, 40

26 Ibid, 49

27 Ibid, 50

28 Ted Byfield, *Just Think, Mr. Berton (a little harder)* (Winnipeg: The Company of the Cross, Wallingford Press, 1965), 17-18

29 Mike Maunder; Barbara McKay; Laura Botsford; Carolina Jakeway Roemmich, *Today My Sail I Lift: Memories of the St. John's Schools 1956-2008* (Stony Plain, Alberta: Company of the Cross, 2012), 58

30 Peter Shawn Taylor, "Formidable editor Ginger Byfield left an indelible mark," *Globe and Mail*, August 1, 2014

31 Pat Annesley, "Ted Byfield: running a revolution on $1 a day," *Impetus Magazine*, September 29, 1973, 5 7,18

CHAPTER FIVE

1 Hedlin, Ralph, "Ten Tumultuous Years: Alberta's weekly newsmagazine marks a full decade," *Alberta Report*, November 28, 1983

2 Ibid

3 Mike Maunder; Barbara McKay; Laura Botsford; Carolina Jakeway Roemmich, *Today My Sail I Lift:* *Memories of the St. John's Schools 1956-2008* (Stony Plain, Alberta: Company of the Cross, 2012), 68

4 Hedlin, Ralph, "Ten Tumultuous Years: Alberta's weekly newsmagazine marks a full decade," *Alberta Report*, November 28, 1983

5 Ibid

6 Ibid

7 Ibid

8 Ibid

9 Mike Maunder; Barbara McKay; Laura Botsford; Carolina Jakeway Roemmich, *Today My Sail I Lift: Memories of the St. John's Schools 1956-2008* (Stony Plain, Alberta: Company of the Cross, 2012), 139

10 Paula Simons, "An Alberta Report Girl," *Edmonton Journal*, September 15, 2011

11 Jeremy Lott, "Byfield Dreams," *Alberta Views*, May 1, 2004, https://albertaviews.ca/byfield-dreams/

12 Carole Paquin, "How the West was Won," *Ryerson Review of Journalism*, March 1, 1991

13 Hedlin, Ralph, "Ten Tumultuous Years: Alberta's weekly newsmagazine marks a full decade," *Alberta Report*, November 28, 1983

14 Paula Simons, "An Alberta Report Girl," *Edmonton Journal*, September 15, 2011

15 Ted Byfield, *The Deplorable Unrest in the Colonies* (Edmonton: *Alberta Report*, 1983), 179

16 Joel Dryden, "A Voice Echoes in the West," CBC, September 5, 2020, https://newsinteractives.cbc.ca/longform/alberta-report

17 Carey Toane, "Sympathy for the Old Devil," *Ryerson Review of Journalism*, March 1, 2000

18 Paula Simons, "Virginia Byfield was midwife of prairie conservatism," *Calgary Herald*, July 28, 2014

19 Colman Byfield, "She Could Take a Scalp with a Stroke of her Pen," *C2C Journal*, August 1, 2014, https://c2cjournal.ca/2014/08/she-could-take-a-scalp-with-a-stroke-of-her-pen/

20 Peter Shawn Taylor, "Formidable editor Ginger Byfield left an indelible mark," *Globe and Mail*, August 1, 2014

21 Brian Bergman, "The Ranting Redneck," *Maclean's*, January 25, 1999, https://archive.macleans.ca/article/1999/1/25/the-ranting-redneck

22 Ted Byfield, *The Deplorable Unrest in the Colonies* (Edmonton: *Alberta Report*, 1983), 215

23 Ibid

24 Ted Byfield, *The Book of Ted: Epistles of an Unrepentant Redneck* (Edmonton: Keystone Press Inc., 1998), 108

25 Ted Byfield, *The Deplorable Unrest in the Colonies* (Edmonton: *Alberta Report*, 1983), 204

26 Ibid, 205

27 Michael Wagner, *Standing on Guard for Thee: The Past, Present, and Future of Canada's Religious Right* (St. Catharines, ON: Freedom Press Inc., 2013), 53

28 Ibid, 56

29 Peter Stockland, "Unfortunately, I Enjoy a Good Fight," *Convivium Magazine*, December 1, 2014, convivium.ca/articles/unfortunately-i-enjoy-a-fight/

30 Carey Toane, "Sympathy for the Old Devil," *Ryerson Review of Journalism*, March 1, 2000

31 Ibid

32 Ibid

33 Ibid

34 Paula Simons, "An Alberta Report Girl," *Edmonton Journal*, September 15, 2011

CHAPTER SIX

1 Michael Wagner, *Alberta Separatism Then and Now* (St. Catharines, ON: Freedom Press Canada Inc., 2015), 41-42

2 Michael Wagner, *True Right: Genuine Conservative Leaders of Western Canada* (St. Catharines, ON: Freedom Press Canada Inc., 2016), 90-91

3 Carole Paquin, "How the West was Won," *Ryerson Review of Journalism*, March 1, 1991

4 Ted Byfield, *The Book of Ted: Epistles of an Unrepentant Redneck* (Edmonton: Keystone Press Inc., 1998), back cover

5 Michael Wagner, *True Right: Genuine Conservative Leaders of Western Canada* (St. Catharines, ON: Freedom Press Canada Inc., 2016), 95

6 Michael Wagner, *Alberta: Separatism Then and Now* (St. Catharines, ON: Freedom Press Canada Inc., 2009), 49

7 Keith Watt, letter to the editor, *National Post*, September 20, 2011, https://nationalpost.com/opinion/todays-letters-the-men-who-gave-western-canada-a-voice

8 Ted Byfield, *The Deplorable Unrest in the Colonies* (Edmonton: *Alberta Report*, 1983), 79-81

9   Michael Wagner, *True Right: Genuine Conservative Leaders of Western Canada* (St. Catharines, ON: Freedom Press Canada Inc., 2016), 92

10 Ibid, 70

11 Ted Byfield, *The Book of Ted: Epistles of an Unrepentant Redneck* (Edmonton: Keystone Press Inc., 1998), 158

12 Ibid, 3-4

13 Ibid, 241

14 "Webster! Full Episode January 21, 1987," Royal BC Museum, October 19, 2016, YouTube Video, 48:35, https://www.youtube.com/watch?v=_FzE9brA8fg&ab_channel=RoyalBCMuseum

15 Paul Wells, "Right place, right time, right party," *Maclean's*, September 23, 2011

16 Michael Wagner, *True Right: Genuine Conservative Leaders of Western Canada* (St. Catharines, ON: Freedom Press Canada Inc., 2016), 73

17 Peter Shawn Taylor, "Influential Alberta Report publisher Ted Byfield gave voice to a nascent Reform Party," *Globe and Mail*, January 11, 2022

18 Carey Toane, "Sympathy for the Old Devil," *Ryerson Review of Journalism*, March 1, 2000

19 Ibid

20 Kevin Libin, "How the West Won Ottawa," *National Post*, September 17, 2011

21 Paul Wells, "Right place, right time, right party," *Maclean's*, September 23, 2011

22 Peter Shawn Taylor, "The Passing of a Prairie Lion," *C2C Journal*, January 13, 2022, https://c2cjournal.ca/2022/01/the-passing-of-a-prairie-lion-ted-byfield-1928-2021/

23 Monte Solberg, "Byfields Kept Flickering Conservative Flame Alive," *Toronto Sun*, September 28, 2014, https://torontosun.com/2014/09/28/byfields-kept-conservative-flame-alive

24 https://newsinteractives.cbc.ca/longform/alberta-report

25 "A Provocative Public Voice," Christianity.ca, last accessed January 25, 2022, https://www.christianity.ca/page.aspx?pid=12742

26 Monte Solberg, "Byfields Kept Flickering Conservative Flame Alive," *Toronto Sun*, September 28, 2014, https://torontosun.com/2014/09/28/byfields-kept-conservative-flame-alive

27 David Frum, foreword to *The Book of Ted: Epistles of an Unrepentant Redneck*, by Ted Byfield (Edmonton: Keystone Press Inc., 1998), 3-4

28 Peter Stockland, "A Publisher Who Took A Stand," *Convivium Magazine*, September 26, 2014, https://www.convivium.ca/articles/a-publisher-who-took-a-stand/

CHAPTER SEVEN

1   Colby Cosh, "Saved from Drowning," *National Post Platformed*, 2022

2   Michael Wagner, *True Right: Genuine Conservative Leaders of Western Canada* (St. Catharines, ON: Freedom Press Canada Inc., 2016), 94

3   Ibid, 122-123

4   Byfield, Ted. *Why History Matters*. Edmonton: SEARCH, 2008. https://www.hslda.ca/wp-content/uploads/2017/01/NLC-2011-Why-History-Matters_ted-byfield.pdf

5   Colby Cosh, "The greatest story Ted Byfield ever told," *Maclean's*, April 12, 2013

INDEX

K

Kelly, Clint, 135

Kenney, Jason, 196, 232

Knowles, Bob, 34-35

L

Lafontaine family, 118-119

Lakefield Preparatory School, 30-33

Lalonde, Marc, 176, 182-183

Levant, Ezra, 198, 229

Lewis, C.S., 87-88, 93, 231

Locke, Ruby, 105-106

Lougheed, Peter, 183

Luce, Henry, 145

Lynch, Charlie, 49, 51-52, 53

Lyons, Frances, 55, 56

M

MacKay, Peter, 197

Mackenzie, Alexander, 115, 117

Malone, Richard S., 76-77

Mann, Donald, 3-4

Manning, Preston, 179, 187-189, 196-197, 222, 233

Maunder, Mike, 98, 103, 107, 109, 113, 120, 123, 144

Mazzone, Charlie, 80, 81

Methye Portage, 114-118

Millward, Arthur, 110

Moher, Frank, 184-185

Morgentaler, Henry, 163

Morton, Ted, 222

Mulroney, Brian, 185

N

National Energy Policy (1980), 174-176, 177, 185

Naval Cadet Corps, 31

Netherlands, emigrées to Canada, ix-x

*Nor'Westers, The,*104

Northumberland (ship), 28-29

Northwest Territories, 175

O

O'Callaghan, J. "Pat," 147

O'Neill, Terry, 233

OPEC oil cartel, 175

Ormiston, Susan, 201

Orr, Fay, 167

P

Parkman, Francis, 111

Pattison, Bill, 4-6

Pawley, Howard, 186

Philadelphia Story, The (movie), 43

Post, Dan, 135

Prairie Report, The (play), 184-185

press, ethics of, 51, 84-86

Manufactured by Amazon.ca
Acheson, AB